history
YEAR BY YEAR

SECOND EDITION

Editor Jessica Cawthra
Senior Art Editor Sheila Collins
Jacket Designer Surabhi Wadhwa
Jacket Editor Emma Dawson
Jacket Design Development Manager Sophia MTT
Senior Producer, Pre-production Andy Hilliard
Senior Producer Jude Crozier
Managing Editor Francesca Baines
Managing Art Editor Philip Letsu
Publisher Andrew Macintyre
Associate Publishing Director Liz Wheeler
Art Director Karen Self
Design Director Phil Ormerod
Publishing Director Jonathan Metcalf

FIRST EDITION
DK LONDON
Senior Editor Francesca Baines
Senior Art Editor Sheila Collins
Editors Steven Carton, Clare Hibbert, Andrea Mills
Designers David Ball, Jeongeun Park, Stefan Podhorodecki,
Mary Sandberg, Jane Thomas
Illustrator Jeongeun Park
Managing Editor Linda Esposito
Managing Art Editor Diane Peyton Jones
Category Publisher Andrew Macintyre
Producer Mary Slater
Senior Producer, Pre-production Ben Marcus
Producer, Pre-production Rachel Ng
Picture Researcher Nic Dean
DK Picture Librarian Romaine Werblow
Jacket Editor Manisha Majithia
Jacket Designer Mark Cavanagh
Jacket Design Development Manager Sophia MTT
Publishing Director Jonathan Metcalf
Associate Publishing Director Liz Wheeler
Art Director Phil Ormerod

DK INDIA
Editor Bharti Bedi
Art Editors Deep Shikha Walia, Shipra Jain, Pankaj Bhatia
DTP Designers Neeraj Bhatia, Tanveer Abbas Zaidi
Deputy Managing Editor Kingshuk Ghoshal
Deputy Managing Art Editor Govind Mittal
Pre-production Manager Balwant Singh
Production Manager Pankaj Sharma

This edition published in 2019
First published in Great Britain in 2013 by
Dorling Kindersley Limited,
80 Strand, London, WC2R 0RL

Copyright © 2013, 2019 Dorling Kindersley Limited
A Penguin Random House Company
10 9 8 7 6 5 4 3 2 1
001 – 314181 – July/2019

A CIP catalogue record for this book
is available from the British Library.

ISBN 978-0-2413-7976-9

Colour reproduction by Opus Multimedia Services, Delhi, India
Printed and bound in Malaysia

A WORLD OF IDEAS:
SEE ALL THERE IS TO KNOW
www.dk.com

DK SMITHSONIAN

history
YEAR BY YEAR

Written by
Peter Chrisp, Joe Fullman,
and Susan Kennedy

Consultant
Philip Parker

Contents

Traveling through time

The earliest events in this book took place a very long time ago.
Some dates may be followed by the letters MYA, short for "million
years ago." Other dates have BCE and CE after them. These are short for
"before the Common Era" and "Common Era." The Common Era
was originally based on the birth of Jesus. When the exact date of an
event is not used, the letter *c.* is used. This is short for the Latin word
circa, meaning "round," and indicates that the date is approximate.

6.5 MYA–3000 BCE
Before history began

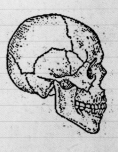

The human story began more than six million years ago, in Africa, when our apelike ancestors first began to walk upright. Over time they evolved, becoming bigger and more intelligent. One species, *Homo erectus*, learned how to use fire and to make stone tools. They were followed by more advanced species until, around 200,000 years ago, our own species, *Homo sapiens*, appeared. As hunter-gatherers, modern humans settled every inhabited part of the planet. Then, around 9500 BCE, humans began to farm, which led to a new way of life.

6.5 ▶ 0.2 MYA

The "cradle of humankind"

Humans belong to a family of upright walking apes, called hominins, which evolved in East and South Africa. We know about hominins thanks to their fossils. One of the most important sites is the Olduvai Gorge in Tanzania, where hominin fossils date from around 1.9 MYA. The gorge is known as "the cradle of humankind."

6.5 MYA

Two-legged apes

The first apes able to walk upright appeared in the forests of Africa. They combined walking with swinging from trees. The earliest evidence found so far is called *Sahelanthropus tchadensis* ("Human fossil from Sahel").

Fossil footprints reveal a species walking on two legs.

3.9 MYA

Human ancestors

A new group of hominins, called Australopithecines, spread across the dry grasslands of East and South Africa. They were small, with brains a third the size of those of modern humans, but their footprints were much like ours.

6 MYA   5 MYA   4 MYA

> ❝We hope to find more pieces of the puzzle, which will shed light on the connection between this upright, walking ape, our early ancestor, and modern man.❞
>
> Richard Leakey,
> Kenyan anthropologist

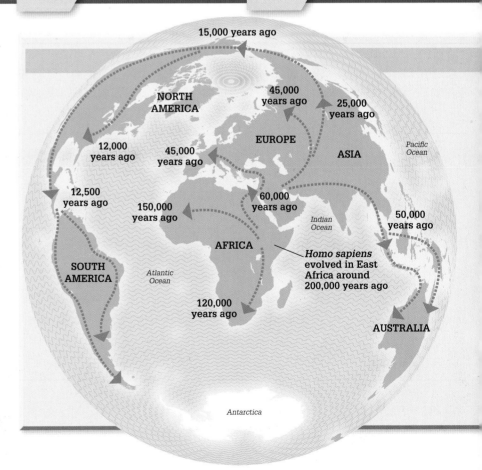

15,000 years ago

NORTH AMERICA

45,000 years ago

25,000 years ago

EUROPE

12,000 years ago

45,000 years ago

ASIA

Pacific Ocean

12,500 years ago

150,000 years ago

60,000 years ago

Indian Ocean

50,000 years ago

AFRICA

Homo sapiens evolved in East Africa around 200,000 years ago

SOUTH AMERICA

Atlantic Ocean

120,000 years ago

AUSTRALIA

Antarctica

A new tool
Homo erectus invented a new kind of stone tool, the leaf-shaped hand ax, in Africa around 1.9 MYA. This was the first tool to be made to a design, and it would remain the main hominin tool for over a million years.

3.3 MYA

Early toolmakers
An early hominin species, possibly *Australopithecus*, learned how to make stone tools by striking pebbles with other stones to create a cutting edge. They used their tools to dig up roots, open nuts, and smash open bones to get at edible marrow on the inside.

1.9 MYA

Human-sized
Homo erectus (upright man), a descendant of *Homo habilis*, evolved in East Africa. The discovery of an almost complete skeleton, called the Turkana Boy, showed that *Homo erectus* was the first hominin to grow as tall as modern humans.

Skull of Turkana Boy

0.5 MYA

First shelters
Descendants of *Homo erectus*, called *Homo heidelbergensis*, moved into Europe, where they hunted elephants and hippos with stone-tipped spears. They were the first hominins to build shelters out of wood.

3 MYA ▸   **2 MYA** ●   **1 MYA** ▸   ▸▸

0.2 MYA

Modern humans
The first modern humans, called *Homo sapiens* (thinking man), appeared in Africa 200,000 years ago. They were larger-brained descendants of *Homo heidelbergensis*. Our distinguishing features are a high forehead with slight brow ridges, a small face, and a projecting chin.

OUT OF AFRICA

Less than 100,000 years ago, our species, *Homo sapiens*, moved out of Africa to settle the world, as shown on this map. We were not the first hominins to leave Africa. Around 1.9 MYA *Homo erectus* moved out of Africa into Eurasia.

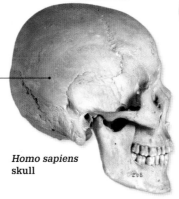

High skull case to hold large brain

Homo sapiens skull

Longest-standing hominin
Homo erectus was the longest-surviving hominin species. They lived across large areas of Africa, Southern Europe, Asia, and Indonesia for more than 1.5 million years.

Back-sloping forehead, low brain case, and thick brow ridges

Homo erectus skull from Kenya, East Africa

Making fire
Homo erectus learned how to make fire. This provided warmth, light, and protection from wild animals, and was used to cook meat. Fire allowed hominins to move into colder areas of the planet.

Carved antler spear-thrower in the shape of a mammoth

Hunter-gatherers

Until just 10,000 years ago, all humans survived by hunting animals and gathering plants for food. This can only support a small population, so hunter-gatherers usually lived in bands of fewer than fifty people, who often had to move on to find fresh food supplies. It was as hunter-gatherers, searching for new sources of food, that people settled in every continent of the world except Antarctica.

Spear-thrower

Hunting methods changed over time. One invention, before 21,000 BCE, was the spear-thrower, which adds length and leverage to a throwing arm. In Europe, people decorated their spear-throwers with carvings of the animals they hunted.

> **"The choice for hunters was brutal: starve or move."**
>
> Dr. Jacob Bronowski,
> *The Ascent of Man*, 1973

Hunting with dogs

At some point before 35,000 BCE, hunters domesticated dogs. Dogs were skilled trackers, with their acute senses of smell and hearing, and they provided speed and sharp teeth for the kill. Dogs also learned new skills, such as how to understand human emotions.

Cave painting of a hunter from Tassili-n-Ajjer, Algeria

After the Ice Age

From around 12,000 BCE, the world's climate warmed. As ice sheets melted, forests spread and rivers and lakes formed. During the new period, called the Mesolithic (Middle Stone) Age, people ate a wider variety of plant foods. The bow, ideal for woodlands, became their most important hunting weapon.

Key events

62,000 BCE

Arrowheads, found in a South African cave, provide the earliest evidence of the bow and arrow. The bow allowed hunters to kill their prey from a distance.

39,000 BCE

People in Asia and Europe began to make cave paintings of animals, such as babirusa (deer-pig) and aurochs (wild cattle).

35,000 BCE

Earliest evidence of domesticated dogs, from a cave in Belgium. Dogs were domesticated from wolves, by raising them from puppies.

21,000 BCE

People in Europe first used spear-throwers, tools that increased the speed and force of a spear through the air.

Bow

Choose your weapon

During the Mesolithic period, people invented many specialized tools for different purposes. Hunters made antler and bone harpoons, arrows with flint blades, and spears, traps, and nets for fishing.

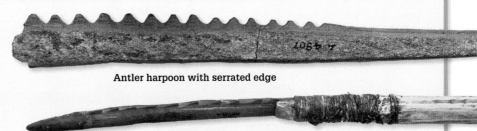

Antler harpoon with serrated edge

Fishing spear

Arrow with flint blade

Hunter-gatherers today

In a few areas of the world today, people still live as hunter-gatherers. Learning about these societies can help us understand how the first people might have lived. In most cases, hunting is left to men, while the gathering of plant foods is the work of women and children. People own few personal possessions, and share everything they have.

Tracking prey

The San Bushmen of South Africa are modern-day hunter-gatherers. Expert trackers and hunters, they use bows and arrows to kill deer, antelope, zebra, and other animals. They tip their arrows with poison, which they extract from beetle larvae.

Prehistoric menu

Mesolithic people learned to eat a highly varied diet. Here are some of the foods they would have eaten:

- Berries
- Nuts
- Seeds
- Leaves
- Grasses
- Roots
- Shellfish
- Snails
- Fish
- Meat
- Eggs

Cranberries

Hazelnuts

Blackberries

Snail

Flint arrowhead

13,000 BCE

Mammoth hunters in Ukraine built constructions from the bones of their prey. It is not known if these were simply shelters or had some ritual purpose.

12,000 BCE

Mesolithic hunter-gatherers in the Near East became so skilled at gathering wild foods that they were able to settle down in early villages.

12,000 BCE

As the climate in Northern Europe warmed up, many large mammals, including woolly rhinos and mammoths, became extinct.

200,000 ▶ 10,000 BCE

110,000 BCE

Ice sheets
This period marked the beginning of a 100,000-year-long cold phase in the Earth's climate, in which ice sheets periodically spread south from the Arctic and sea levels sank. In Eurasia, forests gave way to steppe and grassland, inhabited by animals adapted to the cold, such as the woolly mammoth and woolly rhinoceros.

Woolly mammoth

◆◆ 200,000 ● ● ● ● 150,000 ● ● ● 100,000

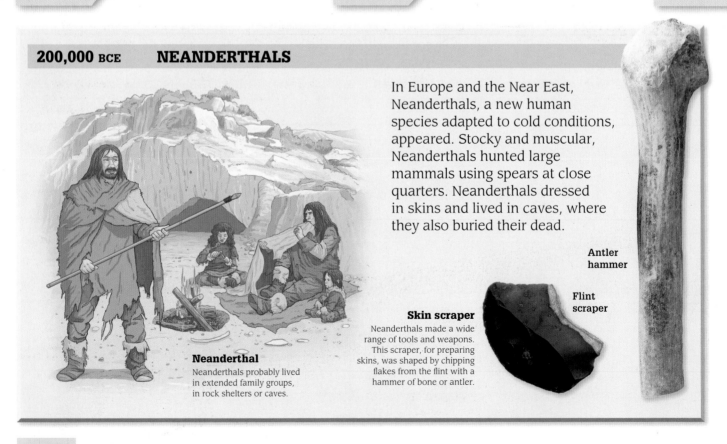

200,000 BCE **NEANDERTHALS**

In Europe and the Near East, Neanderthals, a new human species adapted to cold conditions, appeared. Stocky and muscular, Neanderthals hunted large mammals using spears at close quarters. Neanderthals dressed in skins and lived in caves, where they also buried their dead.

Antler hammer

Flint scraper

Skin scraper
Neanderthals made a wide range of tools and weapons. This scraper, for preparing skins, was shaped by chipping flakes from the flint with a hammer of bone or antler.

Neanderthal
Neanderthals probably lived in extended family groups, in rock shelters or caves.

Hand painting from a cave at Chauvet, France

> **"If we went back 100,000 years... there might have been as many as six different kinds of humans on the Earth. All those other kinds have disappeared, and left us as the sole survivors."**
>
> Dr. Chris Stringer of the Natural History Museum, London

85,000–70,000 BCE

Into Asia
Modern humans, *Homo sapiens*, moved out of Africa and into Asia. They then spread east across South Asia, keeping to the warmer southern regions. The previous human species in Asia, *Homo erectus*, had already become extinct.

39,000 BCE

First artists
Early humans created works of art—cave paintings of animals and carvings of animals and people. They also left images of their own hands on the cave walls, by spitting or blowing pigment over them.

38,000 BCE

Last Neanderthals
Following a period of extreme climate change, Neanderthals became extinct. With the disappearance of the last Neanderthals, *Homo sapiens* was the only human species on Earth.

50,000 ▶   **10,000** ▶ ▶▶

50,000 BCE

First sea voyages
Modern humans from Asia made the earliest known boat journeys, crossing the sea to settle Australia. There, they found unfamiliar new animals, including the Giant Kangaroo and many large flightless birds. Many of these became extinct following the arrival of humans.

15,000 BCE

Into America
Modern humans from Asia crossed into the Americas, following herds of game. They were able to do this because the lower sea levels created a land bridge between the two continents, where today the Bering Strait divides Russia from Alaska.

14,000 BCE

First pots
Hunter-gatherers in Japan made the first pots—clay copies of woven baskets called "Jomon" (cord patterned) ware. In most other places, pottery was only invented once people became settled farmers.

40,000 BCE

Cro-Magnons
The first modern humans in Europe are called Cro-Magnons, after a site in France. They were the first people to make tailored clothes using bone needles.

Jomon pot

The Hall of Bulls in the Lascaux caves, France

Magical creatures

Around 17,000 years ago in Lascaux, France, early people decorated a network of caves with paintings of 2,000 animals, including horses, aurochs (wild oxen), bison, and stags. Perhaps these paintings were used in ceremonies to bring good hunting. We do not know. But when they were illuminated by the flickering light of stone lamps, the beasts must have seemed to have magical powers.

"Most people don't realize how *huge* some of the paintings are. There are pictures of animals there that are ten, fifteen feet long, and more. "

Ralph Morse, US photographer, who took the first photos of the Lascaux caves, in 1947.

10,000 ▶ 3000 BCE

7300 BCE   CATALHÖYÜK

The earliest-known town is Catalhöyük, in what is now Turkey. The settled lifestyle enabled farmers to grow a surplus to support craftworkers and to trade. People imported cowrie shells, obsidian (volcanic glass), and copper, and exported obsidian daggers, mirrors, and jewelry.

Cowrie shells

Obsidian

Crowded town
People lived in mud-brick houses that were tightly packed together. There were no doors, and houses were entered through ladders from the roofs.

▶▶ **10,000**

9000 BCE

Gobekli Tepe
Thought to be the world's oldest place of worship, this prehistoric temple in modern-day Turkey is older than the ancient Egyptian pyramids by around 6,500 years. Excavated in 1995, the site is made up of rings of monumental stone blocks surrounding T-shaped pillars that are carved with pictures of animals, such as snakes and vultures.

Reptile carving on a stone pillar from the Gobekli Tepe

9500 BCE

First farmers
People in Egypt and the Near East became the first farmers. With the arrival of farming, a new period called the Neolithic (New Stone) Age began. In other parts of the world, where people still lived as hunter-gatherers, the Mesolithic (Middle Stone) Age continued.

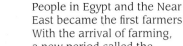

Deer disguise
This deer antler headdress was worn by a Mesolithic hunter in northern Britain in around 7500 BCE. It may have been worn as a disguise when stalking game, or for ritual dances, perhaps to contact the spirits of the deer.

The Poulnabrone dolmen in Ireland

4000–2500 BCE
Tomb builders
Farming people in Europe set up large stone tombs. The earliest, called dolmens, used standing stones supporting a horizontal tablestone. Originally, dolmens would have been covered with earth mounds. A tomb of the ancestors showed the right of the living to hold the land.

4000–3000 BCE
First cities
The first cities emerged in Mesopotamia (modern-day Iraq). Each city was ruled by a king on behalf of a local god, who was worshipped in a great temple.

Mesopotamian temple door plaque

King is shown larger than his family

5000 BCE
Copper tools
People in Central Europe and western Asia made the first metal tools, from copper. Stone tools remained the most commonly used, and so historians call this period of prehistory the Chalcolithic (Copper-Stone) Age.

4000–3000 BCE
Horse riders
People began to ride horses, on the steppes, or grassy plains, of Europe and Asia. They lived as shepherds, leading flocks of sheep across the steppes in search of fresh grazing.

3500 BCE
Chinese bronze
In China and western Asia, people discovered that by mixing tin with copper they could make a much harder metal – bronze.

6000 — **3000** ▶▶

3300 BCE — ÖTZI THE ICEMAN

In 1991, hikers in the Ötzal Alps, between Austria and Italy, discovered the body of a man in melting ice. At first they thought he was a modern-day victim. In fact, he was around 5,300 years old. The man, nicknamed Ötzi, had died after being shot with an arrow.

Handle is 60 cm (2 ft) long, and made from yew

Copper axe
Ötzi's axe had a copper blade bound to a wooden handle with leather thongs. This is the only complete prehistoric axe ever found.

Clothing and equipment
The body was found wearing a bearskin hat, clothes of deer and goat hide, and deer and bearskin shoes stuffed with grass. Ötzi also had a bow and arrows, a copper axe, a flint dagger, a fire-making kit, and berries for food.

3300 BCE
First writing
The Sumerians invented an early writing system called cuneiform. Around the same time Egyptians invented another writing system called hieroglyphic. It used picture signs, which stood for words, ideas, and sounds.

3100 BCE
The first kings
The first kings ruled in Egypt. The earliest we know was called Narmer, shown on a carving wearing the white and red crowns of Upper (southern) and Lower (northern) Egypt. Narmer may have united the two lands in a single kingdom.

Here the king wears the white crown of Upper Egypt

Narmer strikes his enemies with his mace.

Narmer palette

The first farmers

From 9500 BCE, people in Egypt and western Asia learned how to sow, harvest, and store crops. They also domesticated animals, such as goats, sheep, cattle, and pigs – they had become farmers, beginning a new period called the Neolithic (New Stone) Age. In East Asia and the Americas farming was adopted later, and different native crops were grown.

The Fertile Crescent
Farming began in an area known as the "fertile crescent" (shown in green above), which stretched from the Mediterranean to the Persian Gulf. It followed the courses of three great rivers – the Nile, the Tigris, and the Euphrates – which flooded regularly, depositing silt to make the soil fertile. Here grew wild grasses, ancestors of wheat, barley, rye, and other food crops.

Changing wheat
The wild ancestors of wheat had brittle heads that shattered when ripe, releasing grains to be spread by the wind. By harvesting plants with larger, more intact ears, people gradually changed wheat. It evolved into bread wheat, a plant whose grains wait on the plant to be harvested.

A flint sickle for harvesting grasses

Hard labour
Farming people had to work harder than hunter-gatherers. Women spent long hours grinding grain by pushing a small stone backwards and forwards on a large stone, called a quern. Skeletons from this period show that kneeling at the quern caused arthritis and damaged toes and ankles.

An early variety of wheat

An Egyptian woman grinding grain on a stone called a quern

Key events

9500 BCE
First farming began in Egypt and western Asia, as people settled to cultivate wild grasses.

8500 BCE
Goats and sheep were domesticated in the Near East.

8000 BCE
In Mesoamerica, people learned to grow squash. Rice was first domesticated in China.

7000 BCE
Pigs were domesticated in Turkey and cattle in the Near East. Maize was developed from wild teosinte in Mexico.

6500 BCE
Chinese farmers grew millet, along the Yellow River, and rice, by the Yangtze.

Settled life

Farming allowed people to stay in one place, settling in villages which then grew into towns. Settling down changed many aspects of daily life, bringing with it advantages and disadvantages.

Pros

- Easier to raise bigger families
- Life was more comfortable
- There was access to goods, through trade
- Potential for wealth and power, for some

Cons

- Overcrowding
- Risk of disease, caught by living alongside other people and animals
- Disposal of rubbish and sewage was a problem
- Farmers' wealth attracted attackers

Ancestor worship

Living in one place, farming people became aware of the ancestors who had lived before them. They believed that the dead watched over them. In 'Ain Ghazal, Jordan, statues of people, perhaps ancestors, were found buried in pits beneath houses. This may have been part of a ritual of ancestor worship.

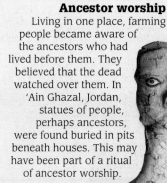

High-rise living

In many early settlements, people lived on top of one another.

'Ain Ghazal statue

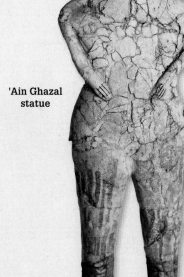

Practical pots

Most pottery was too heavy and fragile to be carried by hunter-gatherers, but when people settled, pots revolutionized their lives. They could use them to carry liquids, store grain, and cook food over a fire. Pottery was also decorative, and became a way of displaying wealth.

American farmers

Around 8000 BCE farming was developed in Mesoamerica (today Mexico and Central America) and South America. There were few large animals suitable for farm work, so Americans never invented wheeled transport or the plough. Many different native crops and animals were found in this region:

★ **Maize**
Domesticated in Mesoamerica from a wild grass called teosinte.

★ **Potatoes**
Wild potato species grew across the Americas.

★ **Llamas and alpacas**
Used for their meat, wool, dung (for fuel and fertilizer), and also as pack animals.

★ **Guinea pigs**
These animals are a major meat source in the Andes.

Teosinte

Animal adaptation

Animals changed when they were domesticated. Cattle and sheep became smaller and more docile than their wild ancestors. Sheep lost their long horns and developed a thick woolly fleece.

6000 BCE
In Sumeria, Mesopotamia, the cultivation of crops occurred on a large scale.

5000 BCE
Farming spread across Europe, West Asia, and North Africa.

5000 BCE
In the Andes mountains of South America, llamas were tamed.

4000 BCE
Paddy field cultivation of rice began in China. In the Mediterranean, vines and olives were farmed.

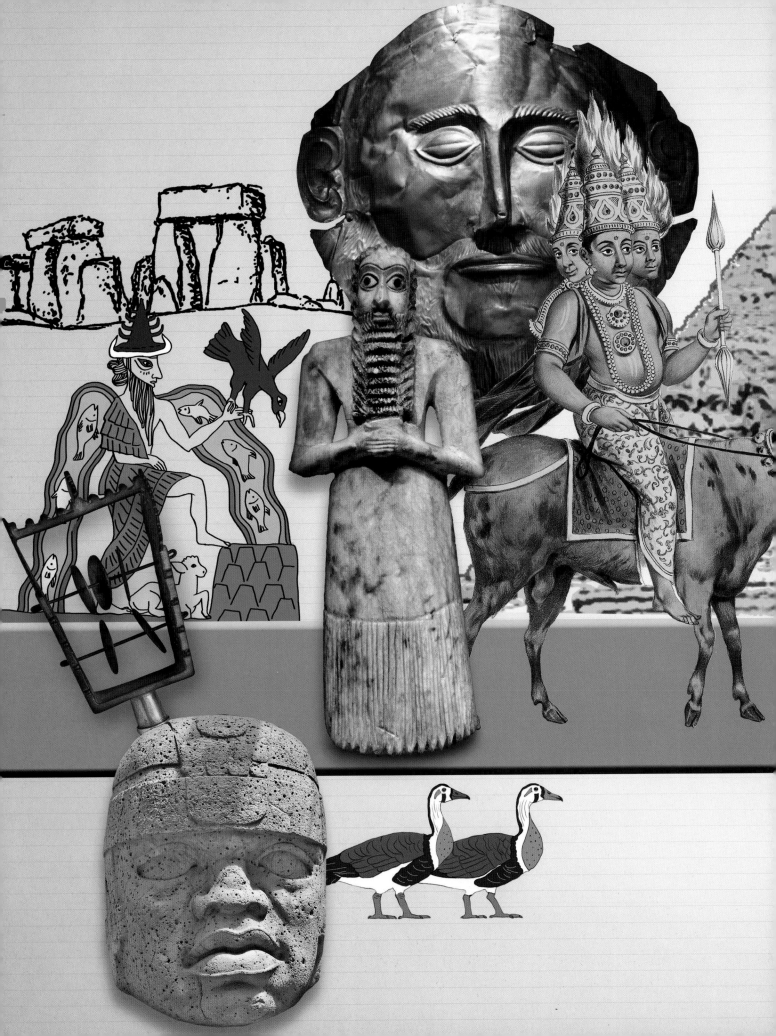

3000–700 BCE
Really ancient history

The invention of farming changed human life forever. People now lived a settled life that could support many more people than hunting and gathering. As the population exploded, villages grew into towns and cities, and different classes appeared. The earliest civilizations developed in Egypt and Mesopotamia, with kings, organized religion, and writing. A great advance was made when people learned how to use metals, for tools, weapons, and jewellery. Competition over land and resources also led to the first wars.

2686–2181 BCE   OLD KINGDOM, EGYPT

During the Egyptian Old Kingdom, a series of pharaohs built the largest stone tombs in history. Each pyramid tomb acted as an eternal home for the dead king, and a place where he was thought to change into an immortal god. The tallest of them, The Great Pyramid, stood 147m (481 ft) high.

Kingdom of the Nile

The civilization of Ancient Egypt grew up beside the desert along the banks of the River Nile. Each year the river flooded, depositing fertile soil along the banks where people were able to farm. The first period of Ancient Egyptian civilization, known as the Old Kingdom, was a time of peace and prosperity.

Mediterranean Sea
LOWER EGYPT ● Memphis
River Nile
UPPER EGYPT   Red Sea
SAHARA DESERT

Step pyramids

Pharaoh Djoser (ruled 2670–2651 BCE) built the first pyramid, with six stepped levels. This was the world's first large building made of stone.

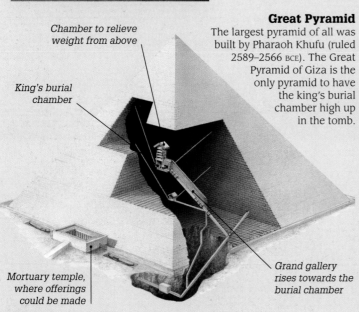

Great Pyramid

The largest pyramid of all was built by Pharaoh Khufu (ruled 2589–2566 BCE). The Great Pyramid of Giza is the only pyramid to have the king's burial chamber high up in the tomb.

Chamber to relieve weight from above

King's burial chamber

Mortuary temple, where offerings could be made

Grand gallery rises towards the burial chamber

3000 BCE

First state

In Egypt, pharaohs created the world's first state. The king was seen as divine, a living representative of the sky god, Horus. Pharaohs were the first rulers to wear crowns.

3000 BCE

Stonehenge

In Britain, farming people began to build Stonehenge, a ceremonial centre, aligned with the midwinter sunset. It began as a circular ditch and bank. The first stones were erected in 2600 BCE, followed by larger uprights with horizontal stones in 2500 BCE. How Stonehenge was used remains a mystery.

3000   2900

Longshan pot

3000 BCE

Chinese towns

Along the Yellow River, people built the first large walled towns in China. The Longshan people, named after the town where the first excavations took place, made beautiful pottery and silk textiles from moth cocoons.

Life after death

The Ancient Egyptians preserved the bodies of the dead for a life they believed existed after death. Bodies were mummified – embalmed, wrapped, and placed in cases covered in religious symbols for protection.

The Ancient Egyptian civilization continued, with few changes, for almost 3,000 years.

2800 BCE

Caral

The earliest American civilization developed in Peru. The people of the Norte Chico civilization built the first large towns in the Americas. One of the biggest was Caral (right), which had huge ceremonial platform mounds.

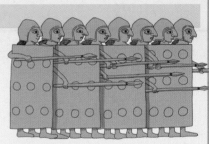

| 2800 | 2700 | 2600 | 2500 |

4000–2000 BCE MESOPOTAMIA

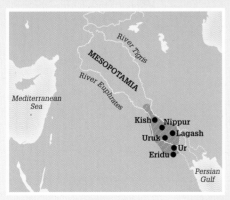

The first great civilization emerged in Mesopotamia, on the fertile flood plains of the Tigris and Euphrates rivers. The earliest dynasties were in the region of Sumer. The Mesopotamians are believed to have invented the wheel, the plough, and writing.

Men of war

Unlike Egypt, Mesopotamia was not a single state, but made up of city-states, each ruled by a king on behalf of a god. The cities competed for control, and are thought to have recruited the first armies in history.

Between two rivers

Mesopotamia means "between the rivers" and lay in roughly the area of modern Iraq. The region of Sumer is shown in pink. The dotted line on the map above shows the coastline at this time, which has retreated over the centuries.

Royal tombs

From 2600 BCE, the rulers of the city of Ur were buried in tombs filled with treasures and everyday items for the next life, such as this gaming board.

Into battle!

This mosaic reveals how, five thousand years ago in Mesopotamia, rival armies from city-states battled for supremacy. At the top, prisoners are dragged before the king, who has stepped down from his chariot. Below, ranks of infantry advance, and other soldiers kill the enemy with axes, and lead away prisoners. At the bottom, soldiers in chariots, each pulled by four donkeys, trample the dead.

Mosaic panel from a box found in a royal
tomb in the city of Ur in Mesopotamia

"The asses at the rear walk sedately,
while those drawing the other cars become
more and more excited as they encounter the
corpses strewn on the ground, until those at
the front have broken into a gallop which
threatens the balance of the riders."

Sir Leonard Woolley, the British archaeologist
who discovered the fragments of the mosaic,
from his book *Ur of the Chaldees*, 1929

Gods and temples

The ancient civilizations of Egypt and Mesopotamia were among the first to practise organized religion. People worshipped many gods, each one responsible for a different area of life. Gods were worshipped in large temples, staffed by priests. In these and in other early civilizations, organized religion was a powerful unifying force.

Egyptian gods
Egyptian gods took the form of animals, humans, and sometimes a mixture of the two. Re-Horakhty, above, combined the features of Ra and Horus.

★ **Ra**
God of the Sun, shown in many different forms, often with a solar disc on his head.

★ **Horus**
God of the sky and protector of the Pharaoh, shown as a falcon or a falcon-headed man.

★ **Thoth**
God of wisdom and writing, shown as a baboon or an ibis, or a man with their heads.

★ **Khnum**
God of pottery who made the first humans out of clay, shown with a ram's head.

★ **Hathor**
Goddess of joy and music, shown as a woman with the ears or head of a cow.

A painting of the columns of the Great Hypostyle Hall, Karnak

The Temple of Karnak
The most famous Egyptian temple, at Karnak, was dedicated to the creator god Amun-Re, his wife Mut, and Montu, the war god. Over hundreds of years, the temple was enlarged by succeeding pharaohs to become one of the largest religious complexes in the world.

Festivals
Gods each had their own festivals, when their statues were carried in processions. Music played a major role. The sistrum, a metal rattle, was used in ceremonies for the goddesses Hathor and Isis (goddess of motherhood and magic).

Sistrum rattle

Key events

5300 BCE
The oldest-known Sumerian temple, to Enki, the god of fresh water, was built in Eridu, Mesopotamia. It was called the "House of the Cosmic Waters".

2600 BCE
Temple of Ra, the Egyptian Sun god, was built in Heliopolis. Ra was the most important god worshipped during the Old Kingdom.

Egyptian priests perform a ritual

Mesopotamian gods

The gods of Mesopotamia were represented in human form. Although there were hundreds of them, the most important were the patrons of major cities. The gods are known by two names. They have a Sumerian name, which was used until the second millennium BCE, and then later an Akkadian name.

Enki / Ea
God of fresh water, mischief, and crafts and patron of the city of Eridu.

Inanna / Ishtar
Goddess of love, war, and the planet Venus, and the patron of Uruk.

Nanna / Sin
God of the moon, patron of Ur, and known as father of the gods.

Ningirsu / Ninurta
God of war and rainstorms and patron of the neighbouring cities of Girsu and Lagash.

Incense

Both the Egyptians and the Mesopotamians believed that their gods loved sweet-smelling incense. This was a mix of resin, wood, herbs, and spices imported from Arabia, which they burned. Its fragrant smoke was an offering to the gods.

Incense resin

Worshipper statues

Ordinary Mesopotamians visited their temples with offerings, such as animals to sacrifice, to please their gods. They left behind worshipper statues, which would pray continually to the god on their behalf. These reveal that the Mesopotamians clasped their hands together when praying.

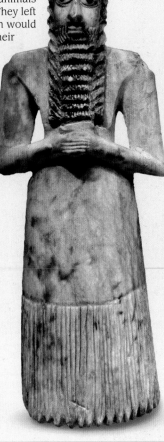

"I offered incense in front of the ziggurat…The gods smelled the sweet scent, and collected over the sacrifice like flies. "

The Epic of Gilgamesh, a Mesopotamian poem from the 18th century BCE

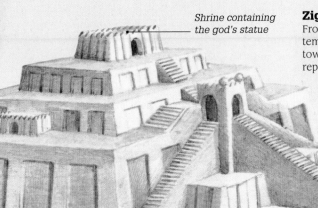

Shrine containing the god's statue

Ziggurat of Ur

From around 2200 BCE, Mesopotamian temple complexes included tall stepped towers called ziggurats. These may have represented a sacred mountain, or a ladder for the god to climb up to heaven. They dominated the flat landscape, a visible reminder of the power of the god and the people who had built the temple.

Great Ziggurat of Ur

2200 BCE
The first ziggurats were built in Mesopotamia. They were made of mudbricks, faced with glazed bricks and tiles.

Mesopotamian musician, followed by a priest

2055–1985 BCE
The earliest-known temple to Amun-Re, Mut, and Montu, was built at Karnak in Thebes.

1550–1295 BCE
During the New Kingdom, when Thebes became the capital of Egypt, Amun-Re became chief god and his temple at Karnak was massively enlarged.

605 BCE
King Nebuchadnezzar II of Babylon rebuilt the ziggurat dedicated to Marduk, which had been destroyed by the Assyrians.

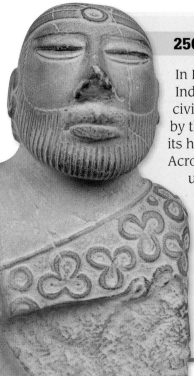

2500 BCE   INDUS CIVILIZATION

In Pakistan and northwest India, the mysterious civilization that grew up by the Indus River was at its height around 2500 BCE. Across the region, a uniform way of life was created – with shared measures and the same pottery styles.

Priest king
There is no evidence of kings or organized religion in the Indus. However, archaeologists called this imposing statuette the "priest king".

Indus lands
The Indus region was big enough to hold both Mesopotamia and Egypt, but we know very little about it.

Mohenjo-daro
Indus people built the first large planned cities, using standard-sized bricks. Every house had its own water supply, bath, and toilet. This is a view of the ruins of Mohenjo-daro, the most important Indus city, in what is now Pakistan.

2500   **2400**   **2300**

2500 BCE

Norte Chico
In Peru, the Norte Chico civilization continued to flourish, lasting until 1800 BCE. Unusually for an urban civilization, the Norte Chico people did not make pottery. There is also no evidence of art.

Bronze head of an Akkadian ruler, believed to be Sargon I

> ❝Sargon marched to Kazallu and turned Kazallu into a ruin heap, so that there was not even a perch for a bird left. ❞
>
> Babylonian Chronicle of Early Kings

2334 BCE

First empire
In Mesopotamia, King Sargon of the region of Akkad began his conquest of the region of Sumer, creating the world's first empire. As a result, Akkadian, a semitic language, related to Arabic and Hebrew, replaced Sumerian as the language of Mesopotamia.

Ziggurat of Ur today – the lowest level has been reconstructed.

2200 BCE

Chinese kingdom

According to legends, the first kingdom, ruled by the Xia dynasty, appeared in northwest China. It is thought to have been founded along the Yellow River by Yu the Great.

2112 BCE

Ziggurat of Ur

King Ur-Nammu of Ur (ruled 2112–2095 BCE) made his city the most powerful in Mesopotamia. He also built a great ziggurat temple, dedicated to the moon god Nanna/Sin.

Gods and temples
See pages 26–27

2180 BCE

End of the Old Kingdom

Following a period of famine, caused by low Nile floods, the Egyptian Old Kingdom fell apart. A period of disorder followed, with many rulers governing different parts of Egypt.

2040 BCE

Middle Kingdom

Mentuhotep II, ruler of Thebes, defeated his rivals and reunited Egypt, beginning the Middle Kingdom, which lasted until 1650 BCE. During this period, the cult of Osiris, god of the dead, became increasingly important.

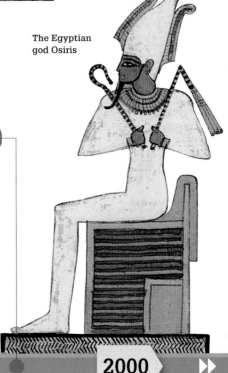

The Egyptian god Osiris

2200 — 2100 — 2000 ▶▶

2100 BCE

Minoan prosperity

On the island of Crete, in the Mediterranean, a people we call the Minoans flourished. They built large palaces, including a particularly fine example at Knossos. These were also religious and industrial centres, with workshops for metalworkers and other craftsmen. A wall painting from Knossos (left) shows a ritual in which people leap over a bull and perform acrobatic stunts. It is thought that athletes would grasp the bull's horns and then vault over its back.

Wall painting from Knossos showing acrobats bull-leaping

 The Minoans are named after Minos, a legendary king of Crete. We do not know what they called themselves.

The first writing

In different parts of the world, as civilizations grew more complex, people started to write. The earliest systems were invented by the Egyptians and the Sumerians of Mesopotamia. Their reason for inventing writing was to record commercial transactions. Later, writing was used for letters, religious texts, law codes, and to record historical events. With the coming of writing, history begins. For the first time, we know the names of ancient peoples and their rulers, and we can read their stories, written in their own words.

Reed signs

A writing technique used in the Middle East between 2500–330 BCE was called cuneiform, meaning "wedge-shaped". The signs were formed by pressing a pointed reed into wet clay, each time producing a wedge shape. The resulting picture signs stood for words, sounds, ideas, and objects.

Hieroglyphs

Egyptian hieroglyphs (sacred signs) were pictures of everyday objects to represent objects, ideas, and sounds. The names of pharaohs, shown in oval shapes called "cartouches", included the signs of the gods they claimed as relatives. Each pharaoh had two royal names. On the right are the names of Pharaoh Tuthmosis III, with a red disk for Re, and an ibis bird for Thoth.

Two names

Tuthmosis III was called Menkheperre, meaning "Eternal is the form of Re", and Tuthmosis Neferkheperu, meaning "Born of Thoth, beautiful of forms".

Hieroglyphs from the Temple of Hatshepsut in Luxor

Re   Men   Kheper
Re   Eternal   Forms
Menkheperre

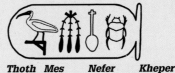

Thoth   Mes   Nefer   Kheper
Thoth   Born of   Beautiful   Forms
Tuthmosis Neferkheperu

Key events

3300 BCE

The Egyptians used hieroglyphs on bone and ivory tags to label goods. These are among the oldest surviving examples of writing.

3300 BCE

The Sumerians were writing with cuneiform (wedge shaped) script on clay tablets. The first signs were pictures of animals and objects, later simplified to patterns of wedges.

2600 BCE

Indus people of northwest India and Pakistan invented a script. The only texts known to exist are very short, and written on merchants' seals.

1800 BCE

The Minoans of Crete invented a writing system, called Linear A, with 90 picture signs, standing for syllables and objects. It has not been deciphered.

Egyptian scribe

Indus stone seal

The impression when the seal is pressed in clay

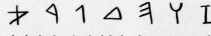

Oracle bone

Indus seals

The Indus people invented a writing system that has not been deciphered. Indus writing, using 300 picture signs, only survives on stone seals, used to identify goods and their owners.

Scatter   Book

Jaguar   Snake

Mayan glyphs

The Mayans of Mesoamerica invented a writing system with signs, called glyphs, which represented syllables and ideas. They wrote religious texts in screenfold books, called codices, made from fig tree bark.

Chinese oracle bones

The oldest surviving Chinese writing is on "oracle bones", used for divination (telling the future). A diviner wrote questions, such as when crops should be planted, on ox shoulder-blade bones or turtle shell. These were then heated and the diviner interpreted the cracks that appeared to give the answers.

Sun   Moon

Some early Chinese characters

Mountain   Rain

Phoenician alphabet

Around 1050 BCE, there was a huge advance, when the Phoenicians began using an alphabet, a system with signs standing for consonants. The advantage of this was that there were just 22 signs to learn. It was now easy for ordinary people to learn to read and write.

aleph beth gimel daleth he waw zayin

heth teth yodh kaph lamedh mem nun samekh

ayin pe tsade qoph resh shin taw

Adapting the alphabet

The Phoenician alphabet was copied by the Greeks who added new signs for vowels. This was then adapted by the Romans, who created the alphabet we use today.

Mayan painted codex (book)

1250 BCE

The Chinese wrote on "oracle bones", using picture signs called "ideograms", each standing for an idea or an object. There are no sound signs.

1050 BCE

Phoenicians began using an alphabet. There were earlier alphabets in the Near East, but it was the Phoenicians who spread the idea.

900 BCE

Some archaeologists believe that the first written texts in the Americas date from around 900 BCE, based on a carving from Veracruz in Mexico, which appears to have 28 signs.

300 BCE

The Mayans used glyphs (signs) to carve monumental inscriptions, paint texts on vases, and write books.

2000 ▶ 1500 BCE

Minoan pot

1800 BCE
Peruvian advances
Major advances in northern Peru led to the introduction of pottery, weaving, and intensive farming. The population grew and new urban centres were built.

◄◄   **2000**   **1900**   **1800**   ●

2000 BCE
Minoan seafarers
The Minoan civilization, on the island of Crete, dominated the eastern Mediterranean. The Minoans were great seafaring traders, exchanging Cretan goods, such as olive oil, wine, and decorated pottery, for Egyptian ivory and copper from Cyprus. They also founded trading settlements on other islands, such as Karpathos and Thera (Santorini). Minoan pottery (above) was often decorated with marine creatures, such as octopuses.

 Minoan palaces were fitted with sophisticated plumbing systems and flushing toilets.

1760 BCE
Babylonian empire
King Hammurabi of Babylon conquered Mesopotamia, creating a short-lived empire. He is best known for his law code, inscribed on a stele (stone) that he had set up in public so all could see it. The carving (left) shows him receiving his laws from Shamash, god of justice.

"To the end of days, forever, may the king who happens to be in the land, observe the words of justice which I have inscribed."

King Hammurabi, Law Code

Stele of Hammurabi

The kings of the Shang dynasty ruled China from 1600 BCE. People worshipped ancestors, and the massive gulf between rulers and ordinary people grew. When a king or noble died, he was buried with hundreds of slaves or prisoners, executed by beheading, to serve him in the next life.

Burial customs
Found among the items in a Shang royal tomb were this chariot, and the skeletons of two charioteers and the horses to pull it.

Age of bronze
The bronze industry flourished at this time. Skilled craftsmen made tools, weapons, musical instruments, and ritual items, such as this blade.

Mycenaean gold mask

1650 BCE
Egypt invaded
The Hyksos, a people from western Asia, conquered the Egyptian delta, fighting from horse-drawn chariots later adopted by the Egyptians.

1600 BCE
Mycenae
The Mycenaean civilization rose to power in Greece. They were influenced by the Minoans, copying their art and fashions, but were much more warlike. They built fortified palaces and conquered Crete in around 1450 BCE.

1700   **1600**   **1500** »

1650 BCE
Hittite conquerors
The Hittites conquered an empire that encompassed most of Asia Minor, also known as modern-day Turkey. They rode into battle on chariots, and were one of the first peoples to use iron, from around 1550 BCE. They traded iron goods, but kept the technology secret for 300 years.

1628 BCE
Thera eruption
A massive volcanic eruption on the Greek island of Thera buried Minoan settlements on the island. It also set off tidal waves which devastated nearby islands, and coastal settlements on Crete.

1550 BCE
New Kingdom
Pharaoh Ahmose drove Hyksos invaders out of Egypt and a new period of rule began, known as the New Kingdom. Pharaohs, ruling from Thebes, later conquered an empire in Asia. It was a time of prosperity, during which the huge temple complex at Karnak was built.

Fresco from Thera of a boy with fish

The temple complex at Karnak today

The metal ages

People made a huge advance when they learned how to use metals. Metal tools were easier to shape than stone ones, and they could be mass-produced using moulds. Unlike a stone axe, useless when broken, a copper or bronze one could be melted down and recycled. Shiny metals, such as gold and silver, were also perfect materials for jewellery and coins.

Copper is heated over a fire by Egyptian metalworkers.

Smelting copper
Around 6500 BCE, people learned to extract copper from ores (rocks containing minerals and metals), which they recognized by their bright green colour. They heated the rocks until the red metal flowed out – a process called smelting. The molten metal could then be poured into moulds.

Brilliant bronze

By 3200 BCE, people learned that, by mixing a small amount of tin with copper, they could make a much harder metal called bronze. Tin is a scarce metal, which made bronze extremely valuable.

The age of iron
Although iron is the commonest metal, it was the last to be used by people. It has a much higher melting point than other metals, which makes it difficult to extract and work. It could not be poured into a mould, but has to be hammered into shape. It is often heated in an extremely hot furnace, called a forge, which makes it easier to work.

Greek ironworker at a forge

Using moulds
Like copper, bronze was cast: heated until it melted, then poured into a mould to make items, such as this pin from Morigen, Switzerland, which is 3,000 years old.

Chinese metalwork
The most skilled early bronzeworkers were the Chinese, who used casting techniques to make sculptures, vessels, and weapons such as this axe blade.

Key events

7000 BCE
Gold and copper, from naturally occurring nuggets, were used to make jewellery in western Asia and Egypt.

6500 BCE
People in southeastern Europe and western Asia learned to extract copper from mineral ores by smelting.

5000 BCE
At Varna, Bulgaria, wealthy people were buried in tombs containing 3,000 gold artefacts.

3200 BCE
In western Asia, people learned how to make bronze by mixing copper and tin.

Copper ore

Pure iron
Iron's hardness made it the perfect material for tools and weapons. This dagger dates from around 100 BCE–100 CE. The top handle is shaped like a human face.

Bull-shaped gold ornament from Varna

Gold was often recycled, so ancient gold jewellery usually only survives in graves.

Glorious gold
Gold, which is beautiful and scarce, has always been prized all over the world. Soft and easy to work, it does not tarnish or rust, and is the perfect material for jewellery. Some of the world's oldest gold jewellery, dating from 5000 BCE, was found in graves in Varna in Bulgaria.

American metal
In the Americas, people made jewellery, statuettes, and masks from gold, silver, and copper, but did not discover how to work the harder metals. This gold mask comes from a royal tomb in Sipan, Peru, dating from 250 CE.

Choose your metal
Each metal was used for different purposes, according to its availability and properties, such as hardness or colour.

Greek silver coin

★ **Gold**, the most valuable metal, was made into royal funeral masks and jewellery for the rich.

★ **Silver**, the second-most-prized metal, was used for jewellery, cups, and coins.

★ **Copper**, an attractive red metal, was used for decorative items and tools, such as axes and chisels. Copper is soft, so these needed regular resharpening.

★ **Bronze** was used for high-status objects, such as swords, spearheads, shields, helmets, brooches, and mirrors.

★ **Iron**, the hardest and most common metal, was used for weapons and everyday items, such as tools, nails, and wheel rims.

1550 BCE
Iron was first smelted in the area that is now Turkey, beginning the Iron Age.

Reaping hook

1200 BCE
The Chinese used bronze to make the world's first life-size statues of people.

1200 BCE
Iron-working reached western Europe. The coming of iron weapons led to an increase in warfare.

Bronze razor from Cambridge, England, 500 BCE

500 BCE
Chinese metalworkers learned how to heat iron until it melted, creating the first cast iron.

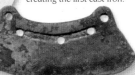

"All eyes are on your beauty until you set. All work ceases when you rest in the west."

"All eyes are on your beauty until you set. All work ceases when you rest in the west."

Akhenaten, Hymn to the Aten

The Olmec were making rubber from the sap-like fluid of trees 3,000 years ago.

Gods and temples
See pages 26–27

1400 BCE

The Olmec
The first Mesoamerican civilization developed in the jungles of the north coast of Mexico. The Olmec built earth mounds and temples, and carved colossal sculptures of the heads of rulers, ancestors, or gods – all wearing helmets.

1352 BCE

Sun worshipper
Pharaoh Akhenaten tried to make the Egyptians worship a single god, the Aten or Sun-disc (right). He founded a new capital, Akhetaten, with open-air temples for worshipping the Sun. On his death, around 1334 BCE, the old religion was restored.

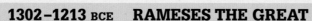

| 1500 | • | • | • | 1400 | • | • | • | 1300 | • |

1302–1213 BCE   RAMESES THE GREAT

Rameses II, known as Rameses the Great, ruled Egypt for 66 years. His long reign brought stability and prosperity to the Egyptian empire, and he was a major figure in the Middle East. He even claimed to have defeated single-handedly the threat from the Hittite empire in the north, at the battle of Kadesh. In fact the battle was inconclusive.

Father of many
It is said that Rameses had seven wives and fathered more than a hundred sons. His favourite wife was his first, Nefertari, whom he married at the age of 15.

Famous face
Rameses built a huge number of monuments and temples, which often included colossal statues of himself, such as the temple at Abu Simbel (right).

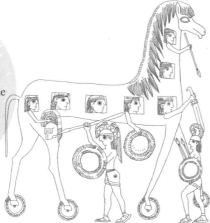

Trojan horse
A Bronze Age legend tells of the siege of Troy. The Greeks built a huge wooden horse, hid soldiers inside, and pretended to sail away. When the Trojans took the horse into the city, the soldiers crept out, and opened the gates to the Greeks, who captured the city.

1000 BCE

The Aryans
Since the middle of the second millennium, a people called the Aryans had been settling in northwest India. They brought with them an early form of Hinduism. Most of what we know of them comes from their collection of religious poems, the Vedas. Their language, Sanskrit, is closely related to many European languages.

Agni, one of the most important Vedic gods

1250–1100 BCE   BRONZE AGE COLLAPSE

From 1250–1100 BCE, the eastern Mediterranean was in turmoil. There was a mass movement of peoples looking for new lands to settle, and some of the great Bronze Age civilizations, including the Mycenaeans and Hittites, were violently destroyed by unknown enemies. Only Egypt was strong enough to beat off foreign invaders, whom the Egyptians called the "Sea Peoples".

Greek Dark Age
Some time around 1100 BCE, Mycenae (right) and the other fortified palaces in Greece were sacked and burned. A period now called the Greek Dark Age followed. The knowledge of writing was lost, and population levels fell.

1000

Egypt endures
Pharaoh Rameses III defeated a great seaborne invasion by the Sea Peoples in the Nile delta in 1178 BCE. Rameses had scenes of his victory carved on temple walls, showing a captive people called the "Peleset". They later settled on the coast of Canaan, where they gave their name to Palestine. We know them from the Bible as the Philistines.

1046 BCE

Zhou dynasty
In China, King Wu of Zhou defeated the last Shang emperor in battle, and founded the Zhou dynasty. Under the Zhou, iron-working was introduced to China.

Phoenicians
After the Bronze Age, the Phoenicians, who lived on the coast of modern-day Lebanon and Syria, became the leading seafaring merchants of the Mediterranean. They traded in purple dye, extracted from the murex sea snail.

A panel on the back of Tutankhamun's gold throne shows the king being anointed with scented oil by his queen, Ankhesenamen.

Hidden treasures

For seven years, archaeologist Howard Carter had been searching the Valley of the Kings in Egypt for the lost tomb of a little-known pharaoh called Tutankhamun. Then, in November 1922, the team uncovered some steps leading down to a sealed door. With trembling hands, Carter made a tiny opening in the doorway, and peered in by the light of a candle. Before him lay the greatest collection of Egyptian treasures ever discovered. Never before had a royal tomb been unearthed that had not been emptied by grave robbers. The treasures had remained in the tomb for 3,000 years, since they were buried with the young pharaoh Tutankhamun, for use in the afterlife.

"As my eyes grew accustomed to the light, details of the room within emerged slowly from the mist, strange animals, statues, and gold – everywhere the glint of gold."

Howard Carter, *Tomb of Tutankhamun*, 1923

An Egyptian scribe

Children in Ancient Egypt were usually taught at home, and expected to do the same work as their parents, usually farming. Only the sons of scribes and nobles went to school, where they learned writing and accountancy. Scribes kept all the official records in Egypt, and could become very successful. However, their training was long and rigorous.

An early start
From the age of four, a boy went to scribal school, where he would train for up to ten years. Lessons began early in the morning, and pupils would take with them their midday meal of bread and beer. The boys sat cross-legged on the floor, ready to learn.

Tools of the trade
One of the boys' first lessons was to make pens. They learned how to chew the ends of reeds to separate the stiff fibres into delicate nibs. The pens were kept in a wooden palette, along with cakes of red and black ink. Scribes wrote on paper made from the papyrus plant, which grows in the Nile marshes. However, to save papyrus, pupils practised on slabs of limestone or broken pieces of pottery.

Lots to learn
Students had to learn more than 700 hieroglyphic signs, as well as simplified versions of the symbols, used in everyday letters and accounts. The boys copied out literary texts to practise writing, and also studied mathematics and accountancy.

Best behaviour
Young scribes must have envied other children their own age, who did not have to go to school. For them, discipline was strictly enforced and unruly or lazy pupils were often beaten. They were also reminded of the benefits of the life ahead of them. A scribe could look forward to authority, freedom from manual labour, and exemption from taxes in times of flood.

Ostracon
Pieces of stone or pottery used for writing were called ostraca. This ostracon shows a copy of a classic poem from Egyptian literature, written in hieratic script.

> **"By the hypnotic process of repetition, the boy was filled with elaborate repertoire of form and phrase that made up the literary language of the state."**
>
> Extract from Egyptologist John Romer's book, *Ancient Lives*, 1984

Wooden palette
This palette of pens is inscribed with the name of Rameses I, indicating that the scribe who used it worked for the pharaoh's palace.

> **"The ears of a boy are on his back. He hears when he is beaten."**
>
> School text quoted by the historian Adolf Arman in *The Literature of the Ancient Egyptians*, 1927

Goose census
This scribe is counting geese for taxation records. His palette of pens is tucked under his arm, and he keeps his scrolls in the basket-work "briefcase" in front of him.

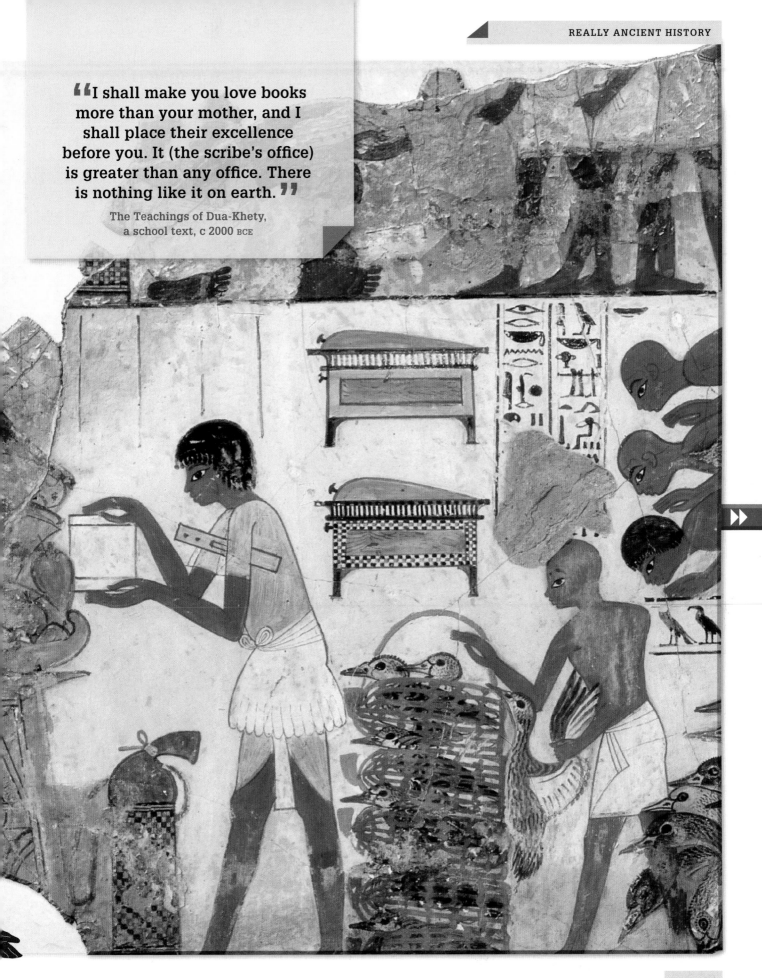

"I shall make you love books more than your mother, and I shall place their excellence before you. It (the scribe's office) is greater than any office. There is nothing like it on earth."

The Teachings of Dua-Khety, a school text, c 2000 BCE

1000 ▶ 700 BCE

965 BCE

Solomon's Temple
David's son, Solomon, built a temple in Jerusalem, a site still sacred to Jews today. On Solomon's death the kingdom split into two: Israel, in the north, and Judah in the south.

> **"In the fourth year of Solomon's reign over Israel, in the month of Ziv, the second month, he began to build the temple of the Lord."**
>
> The Bible: 1 Kings: 6

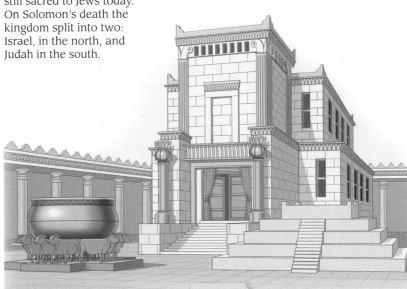

1000 BCE

City of Jerusalem
According to the Bible, Jerusalem was conquered by the Israelite King David (ruled c 1006–965 BCE). This painting shows the Ark of the Covenant, a portable shrine, being carried into the city. Jews believe that the Ark held stone tablets, inscribed with ten commandments written by God.

1000 ● ● ● **900** ● ●

960–600 BCE ASSYRIAN EMPIRE

By the 9th century BCE, the Assyrians, from northern Mesopotamia, had become the most feared military power in the near East. Their armies conquered both Judah, whose kings had to pay tributes of gold and silver, and Israel, whose people were resettled in Assyria. The Assyrians' enemies, led by the Babylonians, later joined forces to destroy the Assyrian empire.

ASSYRIA ●Nineveh
Mediterranean Sea ISRAEL
JUDAH ●Babylon
EGYPT BABYLONIA

From Egypt to Iraq
This map shows the Assyrian Empire in 670 BCE, when it stretched from Egypt to Iraq. Within the empire, peoples who rebelled against Assyrian rule were ruthlessly punished.

In Ancient Assyria, lion hunting was the sport of kings.

Lion hunt
The Assyrians loved hunting as much as they loved warfare. This relief carving, from the Palace of Nineveh, in modern-day Iraq, shows King Ashurbanipal hunting lions from his chariot.

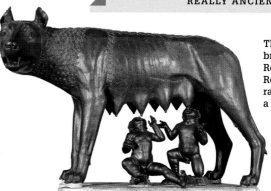

The twin brothers Romulus and Remus were raised by a she-wolf.

750 BCE   GREEK WRITING

The Greeks adopted an alphabet, from the Phoenicians. Not long after, *The Iliad* and *The Odyssey*, two long poems by the poet Homer, were first written down. This marks the beginning of western literature.

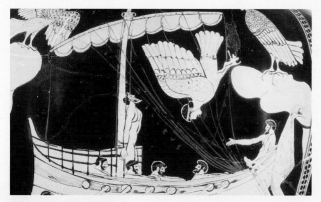

The hero Odysseus
The Odyssey tells the story of Odysseus, returning home from war. Here, he has encountered the menacing sirens, half-women, half-birds, who try to lure the ship to its doom.

753 BCE

The founding of Rome
According to Roman legend, Rome was founded by the twin brothers Romulus and Remus in 753 BCE. Archaeology shows that the city really began as a humble farming settlement in the 9th century BCE.

750 BCE

Greek colonies
The Greeks founded colonies around the Mediterranean and Black Seas. These include Massilia (Marseilles in France), Neapolis (Naples in Italy), and Tripolis (Tripoli in Libya).

800

700

800 BCE

Chavin de Huantar
The Chavin civilization dominated Peru at this time. The most important site was Chavin de Huantar, a political and religious centre filled with carvings of jaguars (below), eagles, and supernatural beings.

776 BCE

Olympic games
The Olympic Games, held in honour of the chief Greek god, Zeus, were first held in Greece. During the games, people from all over the Greek world gathered to compete.

Arctic hunters
In the Canadian arctic, from 800 BCE, people hunted seals and walruses through holes in the ice, using elaborately carved bone harpoons. These hunters are called the Dorset people.

 Wars were often stopped so people could travel to the Olympic Games in safety.

The Ancient Greek pentathlon included discus and javelin throwing, jumping with weights, running, and wrestling.

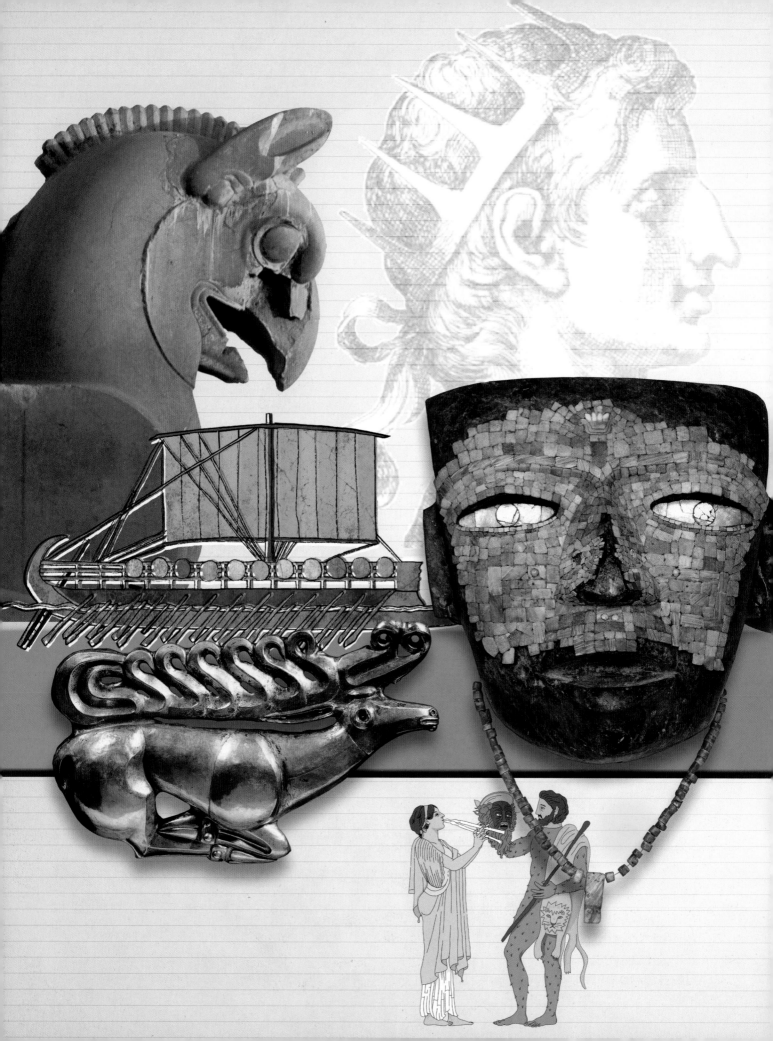

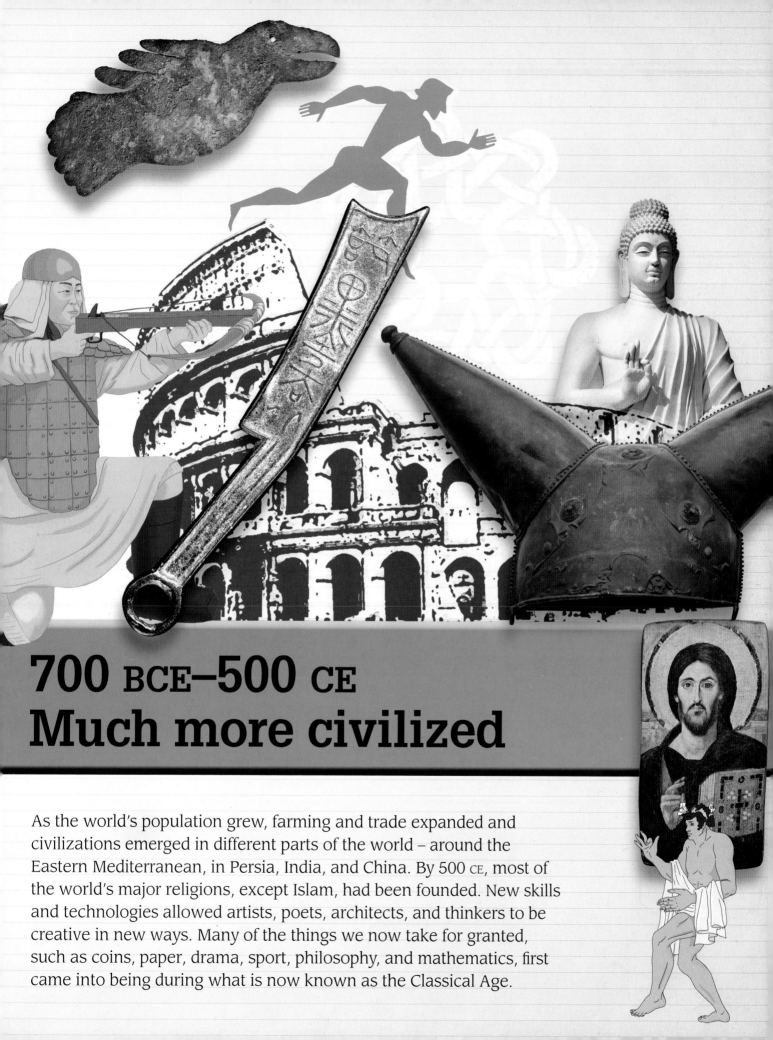

700 BCE–500 CE
Much more civilized

As the world's population grew, farming and trade expanded and civilizations emerged in different parts of the world – around the Eastern Mediterranean, in Persia, India, and China. By 500 CE, most of the world's major religions, except Islam, had been founded. New skills and technologies allowed artists, poets, architects, and thinkers to be creative in new ways. Many of the things we now take for granted, such as coins, paper, drama, sport, philosophy, and mathematics, first came into being during what is now known as the Classical Age.

700▶600 BCE

689 BCE

Babylon sacked

Assyria was still the dominant civilization in Mesopotamia after its armies destroyed the city of Babylon. During the reign of Ashurbanipal (ruled 668–627 BCE), Assyria even conquered Egypt, but its empire had collapsed by 612 BCE.

King Ashurbanipal is shown here helping to rebuild a temple in Babylon.

Mysterious Etruscans

The Etruscans of northern Italy lived in cities and built elaborate tombs. They left many beautiful objects, such as this head overlaid with gold. However, their written script is difficult to decipher, so they remain a mystery.

660 BCE

First emperor

According to legend, Jimmu became the first emperor of Japan in 660 BCE. He was said to be descended from Amaterasu, the Japanese goddess of the Sun.

700   •   •   ●   •   **680**   •   •   •   **660**   •

685–668 BCE   THE RISE OF MILITARY SPARTA

After the Greek city-state of Sparta crushed the neighbouring land of Messenia, Sparta forced the Messenians to become slaves (helots). But the helots outnumbered the Spartans. The risk of a revolt turned Sparta into a military state ruled by two kings and a Council of Elders.

Battle-ready troops
Sparta became the strongest military power in Greece. Sparta never bothered to build defences against invaders. Its strength lay in its formidable army. All adult male Spartans were full-time soldiers, ready to fight for their city at any time.

Killer looks
Beneath their bronze helmets, Spartan soldiers wore their hair long to appear more ferocious. Their tunics were dyed red to hide any bloodstains.

Bronze helmet

652 BCE

Scythian success

The Scythians defeated the Medes tribes of northern Iran. The Scythians were nomads from Central Asia who migrated west to found a powerful empire in what is now Ukraine and southern Russia. They were skilled horsemen and buried their leaders in large mounds called *kurgans*.

Growing up in Sparta
See pages 48–49

Golden stag from a Scythian shield

46

Painting from the *Chronicles of Japan*, 1891, showing Jimmu (standing) spying a sacred bird

"Draco's code was written not in ink but in blood."

Plutarch, Greek historian

620–600 BCE   FIRST USE OF COINS

The world's first true coins were produced in the kingdom of Lydia in Anatolia (Turkey). They were made of electrum, a mixture of gold and silver. Before this, metal bars and ingots (blocks) were used for money. Coins were more portable, and the Greek city-states around the Mediterranean quickly adopted the idea.

Lydian coin made of electrum

621 BCE
Draco's laws
A man called Draco gave Athens, Greece, its first set of laws. Because he prescribed the death penalty for nearly every crime, his name lives on – harsh laws have come to be described as "draconian".

616 BCE
King of Rome
Tarquinius Priscus, who was an Etruscan by origin, became the fifth king of Rome (the first, Romulus, was said to rule from 753 to 716 bce). Tarquinius Priscus won a series of battles over the neighbouring tribes of Sabines, Latins, and Etruscans to make Rome the most important power in central Italy.

640   **620**   **600**

 When a Scythian leader died, his wife, servants, and horses were sacrificed. They were buried in a circle around his body.

600 BCE
African round-trip
According to the historian Herodotus, writing 160 years later, the Egyptian Pharaoh Necho II sent a Phoenician fleet to explore the east coast of Africa. The Phoenicians were traders from Lebanon, admired for their seafaring know-how. Their ships sailed on round the tip of Africa into the Atlantic, reaching the Mediterranean Sea three years later.

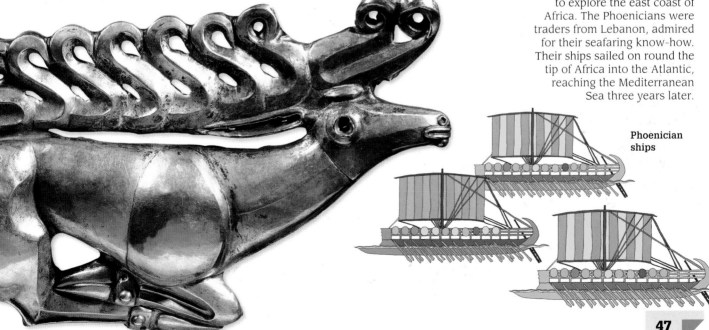

Phoenician ships

47

Growing up in Sparta

From the moment he or she was born, every Spartan boy or girl belonged to the state. A council of elders would inspect the newborn baby to see if it was healthy and strong. If it seemed weak, it would be left to die on a hillside. The lives of both boys and girls were dedicated to the military power of Sparta.

To the barracks

At the age of seven, a boy was taken from his family and sent to military school to be turned into a soldier. The boys lived and slept in barracks, where they were taught the arts of war. Their sisters started their education at the same age. They learned to wrestle, run, and throw the javelin. The Spartans believed that this training would produce strong mothers, who would give birth to strong sons.

Toughening up

Young Spartans were trained to be tough. The boys were made to go barefoot at all times – which would have been painful over rough, thorny ground – and were kept permanently short of food. Once a year, they were taken to the sanctuary of the goddess Artemis and publicly whipped to test their resilience.

Everything to prove

Before he became a citizen, a young Spartan had to prove his courage and ferocity in a special ritual. He was sent out alone into the countryside at night, armed with only a dagger and allowed to kill any helot he came across. Helots were despised slaves, who were forced to farm the land for the Spartans.

Life as a warrior

At the age of 20, a Spartan man became a full-time soldier called a hoplite, a name derived from his large heavy shield, called a hoplon. From then on, he lived as part of a pack of 15 men who ate, drank, trained, and fought together. He would have to marry by the age of 30, to produce the next generation of warriors.

Tough training
This 19th-century woodcut depicts young Spartans in training. They are naked, as was usual in Greece.

> **❝After they were 12 years old, they were no longer allowed to wear a tunic and were given one cloak a year; their skin was hard and they had practically no baths.❞**
>
> The Greek scholar Plutarch, c 95 CE

Sturdy dagger
A typical Greek dagger was about 40 cm (1.3 ft) long, with a blade 7.5 cm (3 in) wide.

> **❝Son, either with this [shield] or on it!❞**
>
> This was a Spartan mother's traditional farewell to her son, urging him to be brave. Only cowards lost their shields. Fallen heroes were carried home on theirs.

Running girl
This bronze figurine from about 500 BCE shows a Spartan girl, wearing a short tunic, taking part in a running race.

Vase painting
This vase painting from around 510 BCE shows a Spartan footsoldier carrying his shield.

"A Spartan boy stole a young fox and hid it under his coat. He let it tear out his intestines with its teeth and claws, and died upon the spot, rather than be found out."

Story told by the Greek scholar Plutarch

600 ▶ 500 BCE

559–486 BCE   THE PERSIAN EMPIRE

In a little over 30 years, King Cyrus the Great of Persia (ruled 559–530 BCE), a small unimportant kingdom in what is now southern Iran, conquered the largest empire the world had yet seen. It was known as the Achaemenid Empire, from the name of its ruling dynasty. Under King Darius I (ruled 522–486 BCE), the empire set its sights on the lands of Greece.

The city of Persepolis
Darius I built Persepolis as his ceremonial capital. Its magnificent pillared halls reflected the might and splendor of the empire.

585 BCE
Solar eclipse
Thales of Miletus, a Greek city-state in Anatolia (modern-day Turkey), correctly predicted a solar eclipse. Thales was one of the earliest Greek philosophers—thinkers who asked questions about the natural world.

590 BCE
African pharaohs
The kings of Nubia, a kingdom on the Nile in what is now Sudan, made their residence at Meroe. The Nubian rulers modeled themselves on the pharaohs. They wrote in a type of hieroglyphs and buried their dead in pyramid tombs.

600 • ● ● ● **580** • • • ● **560** •

587 BCE
Nebuchadnezzar
When the Jews rebelled against Babylonian rule, Nebuchadnezzar II ordered the destruction of their temple in Jerusalem. The city was burned and thousands of Jews were sent to Babylon.

563 BCE
Birth of the Buddha
According to tradition, Siddhartha Gautama was born a prince in northern India. He was so distressed by human suffering that he gave up his life of luxury and fasted beneath a tree for six years until he reached enlightenment. He became known as the Buddha, the "enlightened one," whose teachings are followed by millions of people today.

550 BCE
Birth of Confucius
Confucius (Kung Fuzi) was a Chinese philosopher and teacher whose writings stressed respect for family elders, authority, and tradition. Confucianism, the way of life based on his teachings, would have great influence on Chinese ideas and politics.

Wheel of life symbol on each sole

> **"Even death is not to be feared by one who has lived wisely."**
> The Buddha (563–483 BCE)

Carving of the Buddha's footprints, 1st century BCE

550 BCE
Rise of the Celts
In central Europe, the Celts began spreading out from their original heartland in the northern Alps (Austria and Switzerland). They controlled long-distance trade in salt and iron, and their rich burials included luxury goods of Greek and Etruscan origin, traded through the city of Massilia (Marseilles, France).

Celtic warriors
See pages 56–57

The Royal Road was a 1,600-mile (2,575 km) highway that ran from the city of Susa in Persia all the way to Sardis in western Turkey.

Persian lands

Cyrus the Great's conquests stretched from Anatolia (Turkey) in the west, to Afghanistan in the east. His son Cambyses (ruled 530–522 BCE) added Egypt, and Darius I added Thrace (the southeast Balkans).

> **"I am Cyrus, King of the World, Great King, Mighty King!"**
>
> Cyrus the Great, 538 BCE

Immortal Persians

These soldiers, who once decorated the walls of Darius's palace, represent the Immortals, elite troops who formed the king's personal bodyguard. In real life, the king had 10,000 Immortals—if one was killed, a new recruit immediately replaced him.

507 BCE

People power

The city-state of Athens chose a new form of government: democracy (meaning "rule of the people"). All male citizens were able to vote on major decisions affecting the city. Women, foreigners, and slaves were excluded.

---

540   **520**   **500**

---

535 BCE

Battle at sea

Phoenicians founded the city of Carthage (modern Tunis) in 814 BCE. Growing rivalry with the Greek city of Massilia led to a sea battle at Alalia, off Corsica. The Greeks lost, leaving Carthage in control of the western Mediterranean.

The Roman Empire
See pages 68–69

509 BCE

Roman Republic

Rome was still a tiny city-state when its citizens decided to throw out their kings and govern themselves. They set up a republic headed by two consuls—elected magistrates who ruled with the help of the Senate.

Emblem of the Roman Republic. In Latin, SPQR stands for *Senatus Populusque Romanus*, which means "Senate and People of Rome."

Sporty Greeks

This bronze discus belonged to an athlete named Exoidas, who won a sporting contest with it. The Greeks competed in many sports, including running, discus, boxing, wrestling, and javelin-throwing.

The Greek-Persian wars

In the early 5th century BCE, the Persians twice attempted to conquer Greece. The Greek city-states, especially Athens and Sparta, were always squabbling with each other but they united against the Persians. Though hugely outnumbered, the Greeks finally fought the Persians off.

Hoplites on the run
This vase painting shows Greek soldiers (hoplites). The Greeks fought on foot in formations called phalanxes, of 8 to 50 ranks (rows). With their shields locked tightly together to form a protective wall and the spears of those in front pointing toward the enemy, the phalanx advanced at a run.

Quick-moving Persian
The Persians had greater mobility on the battlefield thanks to their lighter equipment. This archer is wearing a soft felt cap and mail coat in contrast to the heavy bronze helmets and body armor of the Greeks. The Persians fought at a distance, using their archers to break up the advancing enemy and bringing in cavalry to ride them down.

Persian archer painted on a cup, c. 300 BCE

Modern copy of a hoplite sword

Key events

547 BCE

Cyrus the Great, king of Persia, conquered the Ionian city-states of Anatolia (modern-day Turkey).

499 BCE

During the reign of Darius I, the Ionian city-states revolted against Persia. Athens came to their aid.

490 BCE

Darius I sent a huge army to punish Athens. The Athenians defeated the Persians at Marathon.

484 BCE

Two years into his reign, Xerxes began preparations for a massive invasion of mainland Greece.

483 BCE

The Athenian general Themistocles persuaded Athens to start building a fleet.

"Come and get them!"

Leonidas's answer to Xerxes when he ordered the Spartans to lay down their weapons at Thermopylae

Who's who?

Xerxes
Darius I's son, Xerxes, became king of Persia in 486 BCE. Six years later, he invaded Greece in revenge for his father's defeat at Marathon.

Artemisia
Queen of Halicarnassus (a city on the site of Bodrum, Turkey), Artemisia sent five ships to join Xerxes' fleet. She took part in the Battle of Salamis.

Leonidas
Known as Leonidas the Brave, this king of Sparta led an elite force of 300 Spartans on a suicide mission at Thermopylae.

Major battles

490 BCE Marathon
This battle was fought on the plain of Marathon, north of Athens. Led by the Athenian general Miltiades, a much smaller Greek army defeated Darius I's invasion force.

Forces
Greeks: 10,000 hoplites: 9,000 from Athens, 1,000 from Plataea
Persians: 25,000 foot soldiers; 1,000 cavalry; 600 ships

480 BCE Thermopylae
As Xerxes' invasion force moved south into Greece, the outnumbered Greeks met it at a mountain pass. They held it up for two days before the Persians found a route around.

Forces
Greeks: 7,000, including 300 elite Spartan troops
Persians: Up to 250,000, including 10,000 "Immortals" (elite infantry)

480 BCE Salamis
Themistocles, commanding the Athenian fleet, lured the Persian fleet into an ambush off the island of Salamis. King Xerxes watched from the shore as his much larger fleet was rammed and destroyed.

Forces
Greeks: 378 ships
Persians: 800 ships

479 BCE Plataea
The Greek and Persian armies clashed on Theban territory. A surprise Spartan phalanx charge made the Persian army turn and flee, giving the Greeks final victory.

Forces
Greeks: 40,000
Persians: 120,000 (including Greek allies)

The Battle of Thermopylae
This 19th-century painting shows the heroic Spartan king Leonidas. The Greeks met Xerxes' invasion force at a narrow mountain pass. Knowing defeat was inevitable, Leonidas sent the rest of the Greeks away while he and his Spartan force delayed the Persian advance. They all died.

Marathon man
Pheidippides was a Greek messenger who ran all the way from Athens to ask the Spartans for help before the Battle of Marathon but they refused to come. Another story says that he ran 25 miles (40 km) from Marathon to Athens to announce the Greek victory—the origin of the modern marathon.

480 BCE
Xerxes crossed the Hellespont into Europe to march on Greece.

Persian ship

480 BCE
The Persians reached Athens and burned the city.

479 BCE
The Persians were defeated at Plataea and never invaded Greece again.

477 BCE
Athens headed an anti-Persian alliance of city-states. Sparta refused to join.

c. 440 BCE
The history of the Greek and Persian wars was written down by Herodotus, the ancient Greek historian.

500 ▶ 400 BCE

King Xerxes looks across the sea toward Greece

500 BCE

Rise of the Zapotecs
The Zapotec people of southern Mexico built a ceremonial center at Monte Albán, in the Oaxaca valley. The site stayed in use for 1,000 years. This clay burial urn (left) was crafted in the shape of a Zapotec god.

494 BCE

Trouble in Rome
The plebs (ordinary people) of Rome went on strike until the patricians (nobles) agreed to let them elect two of their own officials. These two elected magistrates were called tribunes.

480 BCE

Xerxes at the Hellespont
The Persian king Xerxes assembled a huge army to invade Greece. At the Hellespont, the stretch of water that separates Asia from Europe, Xerxes ordered a bridge to be built by lashing lines of boats together so that his army could cross.

The Greek-Persian wars
See pages 52–53

 500 ◆ ● ● ● **480** ◆ ● ● ● **460** ◆ ●

475 BCE

Warring China
China, which was much smaller then than it is today, entered the Warring States period. The Zhou kingdom broke up into seven states, whose princes competed with each other for dominance. It was a time of great technological advances both in warfare and agriculture.

484–405 BCE THE GOLDEN AGE OF ATHENIAN THEATER

Drama originated in Athens with plays put on each year at a festival to honor the god Dionysus. From there, it spread across the Greek world. The works of three Athenian dramatists—Aeschylus, Sophocles, and Euripides—are still performed today.

Funny face
Both tragedies and comedies were put on. The actors in comic plays wore grotesque masks. This mask is of a slave, a popular butt of jokes.

Acting in the open air
Each city had its own theater. Ancient Greek theaters consisted of tiers of stone seats built in a semicircle into a hillside. The action took place in the central area, called the orchestra.

Ancient Greek actors

THE PARTHENON

When the Persians attacked Athens in 480 BCE, they burned the temples on the Acropolis, the sacred hill overlooking the city. The Athenians never forgave this act of blasphemy. They built a new temple on the site, the Parthenon, dedicated to the goddess Athena.

Classical architecture

The Parthenon, one of the most famous works of classical architecture, was constructed at the height of Athens's power in the mid-5th century BCE.

"Xerxes the King will cross you, with or without your permission."

Xerxes defies the Hellespont after a storm has destroyed his first bridge

400 BCE

Celts on the move

Groups of Celts began to migrate into the Po valley in northern Italy, where they attacked the Etruscan cities, and into southeast Europe.

440 ● ● ● **420** ● ● ● **400** ▶▶

431 BCE

Greeks at war

The Peloponnesian War broke out between Athens and its allies on one side, and Sparta and its allies on the other. Athens was successful at first, but its army and fleet were destroyed in a misguided attack on Syracuse, in Sicily, in 415–413 BCE. It surrendered to Sparta in 404 BCE.

Athenian warships at the Battle of Syracuse

Chinese money

Ancient Chinese money was cast in bronze or copper. It was made in the shape of tools, such as knives and spades, and pieces often had a punched hole, so that several of them could be strung together.

 In 430–429 BCE, a plague swept the city of Athens. Its victims included the Athenian leader and general Pericles.

Celtic warriors

The Celts (called "Gauls" by the Romans) were not a single people but consisted of scattered tribes ruled by warrior chiefs. Originally from an area north of the Alps, some tribes migrated south after 400 BCE, clashing with the Greeks and Romans. Archaeologists call the Celtic culture of this period La Tène, after a Swiss site. By 100 BCE, the La Tène culture had spread throughout Europe.

Celtic gods

Celtic religion was tied in with the farming year and nature. Hundreds of gods were worshipped under different names throughout the Celtic world. Here are four:

Belenus
The god of sun and fire, Belenus was associated with the Beltane festival on May 1, when fires were lit to purify cattle.

Brigit
Also known as Brigantia, Brigit was the goddess of healing, poetry, and fertility. In Ireland, she was later adopted as a Christian saint.

Cernunnos
This horned god was associated with fertility, nature, harvest, and the underworld.

Epona
The goddess Epona (left) was the protector of horses. Roman soldiers adopted her, and built her a temple in Rome.

The world of the druids
Celtic priests were called druids. The druids carried out many rituals and may have offered up human sacrifices to the gods. This picture shows a druid using a golden sickle to cut mistletoe in a grove of oak trees. Mistletoe was a sacred plant to the Celts.

Celtic hero
This Celtic head, found at a site near Prague, in the Czech Republic, has staring eyes and a swept-back mustache. Around its neck is a torc—the metal neck ring worn by Celtic warriors. The Romans admired the courage of the Celts, but thought they were boastful and drank too heavily.

Key events

400 BCE
Groups of Celts invaded the Po Valley in northern Italy and settled there.

390 BCE
The warrior leader Brennus led an army of Gauls to attack and capture the city of Rome.

279 BCE
An army of Celts invaded Greece and sacked the sacred shrine of Delphi.

Sacred mistletoe

225 BCE
The Romans defeated the Gauls of northern Italy at the Battle of Telamon.

A horned helmet, probably for ceremonial use

Wild warriors

Brennus
This chieftain led an army of Gauls to attack Rome in 390 BCE. Guard geese sounded the alarm, but the Romans had to give Brennus gold to make him leave.

Caractacus
From his Welsh hideout, Caractacus resisted the Roman invasion of Britain for six years, but eventually he was captured and taken to Rome.

Boudicca
Queen of the Iceni, a tribe in eastern England, Boudicca (right) led a rebellion against the Romans in 61 CE.

Working in metal
The Celts were skilled craftspeople, working in gold, bronze, and iron. They loved to decorate their metalwork with intricate patterns of circles, curves, whorls, and spirals, and with animal and plant motifs.

A bronze mirror with a richly decorated back

A bronze brooch of two coiled hoops

> **"Some shave their cheeks but leave a moustache that covers the whole mouth and, when they eat and drink, acts like a sieve, trapping particles of food."**
>
> Diodorus of Sicily describing the Celts, c. 35 BCE

A fortified Celtic village in Anglesey, North Wales

After the Romans
In Gaul and Britain, Celtic culture merged with that of the occupying Romans. After the Romans left, Germanic invaders pushed the surviving Celts back into Brittany in France, and into Wales, Cornwall, and southwest Scotland in Britain.

101 BCE
The Roman general Marius defeated the invading Cimbri at the Battle of Vercellae.

58–51 BCE
Julius Caesar fought a series of campaigns to conquer Gaul (France and Belgium).

43 CE
Emperor Claudius sent an army to begin the Roman conquest of Britain.

Celtic shield

61 CE
Boudicca led a revolt of the Celtic tribes of Britain against the invading Romans.

400 ▶ 300 BCE

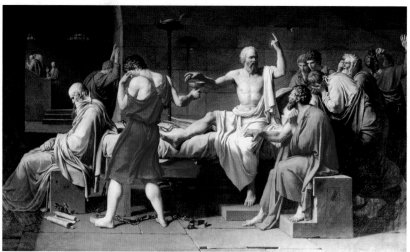

Socrates takes the cup of hemlock

"The hour of departure has arrived, and we go our ways."

Socrates, on learning of his death sentence

350 BCE
Crossbows
Handheld crossbows came into use in China. The ancient Greeks also had a type of crossbow called a gastraphetes. Crossbows were used in warfare for hundreds of years.

399 BCE
Death by hemlock
The Greek philosopher Socrates was sentenced to death by swallowing poisonous hemlock. He had been found guilty of corrupting young Athenians with his ideas—a charge brought by his political enemies.

400 ● ○ ○ ○ **380** ● ○ ○ ○ **360** ● ○ ○

378 BCE
Coup in Thebes
Led by their general, Epaminondas, the Thebans drove a Spartan garrison out of their city. Thebes now became the most powerful Greek city-state. It headed a Greek uprising against Alexander the Great, who destroyed the city in 335 BCE.

390 BCE
Goose alarm
Cackling geese sounded the alarm when an army of Gauls (Celts) tried to seize the Capitoline Hill in Rome. The geese woke the guards, but the warning came too late to save the rest of the city, which was sacked.

Terracotta sculpture of knucklebone players, c. 330–300

400 BCE
Chavin culture
The Chavin people, who lived in the Andean highlands of Peru, were flourishing at this time. They domesticated the llama and made pottery vessels of jaguars, monkeys, and other animals.

Classic game
Knucklebones was a very popular game among both Greek men and women (who played it separately from the men, as they were not allowed to mix). It was similar to jacks but the pieces were animal bones.

356–323 BCE   ALEXANDER THE GREAT

One of the finest generals in history, Alexander became king of Macedon, in northern Greece, at age 20 after his father Philip II was murdered in 336 BCE. Alexander fulfilled Philip's plan to invade Persia. In eight years, Alexander created an empire that stretched from Greece to northern India. When he died, at age 32, his warring generals carved up his empire among themselves.

Legendary hero
Alexander's military exploits made him a legend in his own lifetime. He founded and named many cities after himself, including Alexandria in Egypt, and believed he was a god. However, he died before producing an heir (his son was born after his death).

The lighthouse at Alexandria

KEY DATES

334 BCE *Alexander invaded Asia at the head of an army of 37,000 men.*

332 BCE *Alexander conquered Egypt and made himself pharaoh.*

331 BCE *He returned to Persia, defeated King Darius, and destroyed Persepolis.*

326 BCE *After reaching northwest India, his men refused to go any farther east.*

323 BCE *Alexander died suddenly in Babylon after drinking with his companions.*

305 BCE

Pharaoh Ptolemy
Ptolemy, one of Alexander the Great's Macedonian generals, made himself pharaoh, founding the last dynasty to rule Egypt. He began work on building the lighthouse at Alexandria, one of the Seven Wonders of the Ancient World.

300

305 BCE

War elephants
Chandragupta Maurya, founder of the Mauryan Dynasty of north India, gave 500 war elephants to Seleucus, another of Alexander's generals, in exchange for most of Afghanistan. Seleucus used them in his wars against his rivals.

Battle of Issus
This Roman mosaic shows Alexander at the Battle of Issus (333 BCE), where he defeated his rival Darius III for the first time. He is riding his favorite warhorse, Bucephalus, whose name meant "ox head." By 330 BCE, Alexander had conquered all of the Persian Empire.

Terracotta statue of a Mauryan war elephant

 The Greek philosopher Aristotle was a tutor of the 13-year-old Alexander the Great.

300 ▶ 200 BCE

Stone gateway carved with scenes from the Buddha's life

The Great Stupa at Sanch, India

The Roman Empire
See pages 68–69

290 BCE
Roman domination
The city of Rome ruled nearly all of Italy after winning a 50-year war against the Samnites. Only the north (occupied by the Gauls) and a handful of Greek cities in the south remained unconquered.

The term "Pyrrhic victory" is named after a Greek king, Pyrrhus. He defeated the Roman army in 280 BCE, but with such terrible losses that he soon retreated.

262 BCE
Buddhist ruler
Appalled by the violence of war, the Mauryan emperor Ashoka (ruled 268–232 BCE) became a convert to Buddhism. He built the Great Stupa at Sanchi to house relics of the Buddha.

| 300 | 280 | 260 |

300 BCE
Peruvian mummies
Hundreds of mummies from around 300 BCE have been found in the dry Paracas Peninsula of Peru. The bodies were seated and wrapped in long layers of brightly colored cloth. It is believed that the cultures of the Andes treated the mummies of their ancestors as sacred objects.

280 BCE
Colossal statue
The Colossus was a vast statue erected in the harbor of the Greek island of Rhodes. The giant bronze statue of the sun god, Helios, stood for only 56 years before being toppled by an earthquake.

Paracas mummy from Peru

An 18th-century artist's impression of the Colossus of Rhodes

221 BCE

First emperor of China

Zheng, ruler of the kingdom of Qin, conquered the other six warring states of China and proclaimed himself Qin Shi Huangdi ("First Emperor"). This portrait comes from an 18th-century album of Chinese emperors.

Archimedes in his bath

Tomb army See pages 62–63

212 BCE

Death of Archimedes

The Greek mathematician Archimedes was killed by Roman soldiers at the siege of Syracuse. A great scientist, he is supposed to have set fire to the Roman ships using a large mirror to reflect the Sun's rays. Archimedes is also said to have figured out how to measure volume while sitting in his bath.

240 • • 220 • • 200 ▶▶

264–146 BCE **THE THREE PUNIC WARS**

The Punic Wars were fought between Rome and the city of Carthage in North Africa for control of the western Mediterranean. The Third (149–146 BCE) resulted in the final destruction of Carthage. "Punic" derives from *Poeni*, the Latin name for the Carthaginians.

War at sea

The First Punic War (264–241 BCE) was fought for control of Sicily. The Carthaginians were expert sailors, but the Romans built a fleet and defeated them at sea to win the war.

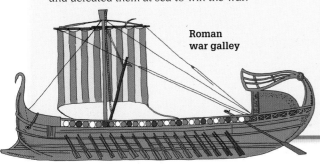

Roman war galley

Hannibal crosses the Alps

In 218 BCE, the Carthaginian general Hannibal crossed the Alps with a large army and 37 elephants to attack Rome from the north. He destroyed the Roman army at the Battle of Cannae, but Rome went on to win the Second Punic War in 201 BCE.

Tomb army

In 1974, men digging a well near the ancient Qin capital in China broke into a large pit that contained thousands of life-size clay soldiers. The statues were guarding the tomb of Qin Shi Huangdi, the First Emperor. Records say that it took more than 700,000 men to build his massive tomb. Qin Shi Huangdi united China and made everyone obey the same laws. He standardized weights and measures and even established how wide the axles on wagons should be. He claimed that his Qin Dynasty would rule for 10,000 generations. In fact, it only lasted from 221 to 206 BCE.

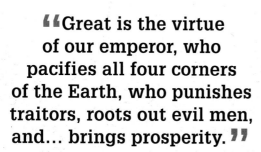

"Great is the virtue of our emperor, who pacifies all four corners of the Earth, who punishes traitors, roots out evil men, and... brings prosperity. "

Inscription on a tower built on Mount Langya, Anhui Province, to glorify Qin Shi Huangdi

Ranks of warrior soldiers

200 ▶ 100 BCE

164 BCE
Jewish revolt
Judah Maccabee, a Jewish freedom fighter, captured Jerusalem and rededicated the temple to God, an event commemorated each year by the Jewish festival of Hanukkah. Maccabee and his followers were fighting to regain the independence of Judea (Israel) from a tribe called the Seleucids.

A 15th-century depiction of the fight for Jerusalem, where the men resemble medieval knights

171 BCE
Powerful Parthian
Mithridates I, king of Parthia (northeastern Iran), seized Mesopotamia from the Seleucids, the dynasty that ruled western Asia. His victory created an empire that stretched from Iraq to Afghanistan.

Silver coin showing Mithridates

146 BCE
Mighty Rome
On the orders of the Senate, a Roman army destroyed the city of Carthage in North Africa, burning it to the ground. That same year, Rome captured Corinth and completed its conquest of Greece.

200

150

150 BCE
Bactrian king
Menander, king of the Indo-Greek kingdom of Bactria (Afghanistan), converted to Buddhism. His reign was a time of great prosperity, but the Bactrian kingdom collapsed soon after his death in 131 BCE. Sakas (Scythians) invaded the region from Central Asia.

200 BCE–800 CE   PACIFIC VOYAGERS

Polynesian settlers were venturing from the islands of Fiji and Tonga far across the Pacific. Using their knowledge of the stars, currents, and the flight patterns of birds to navigate the vast ocean expanses, they reached Rapa Nui (Easter Island) by 300 CE and Hawaii by 800 CE.

Polynesian canoe
The Polynesians' sailing canoes were made of two wooden hulls lashed together with rope. Floats called outriggers helped keep them stable.

Stick chart
The Polynesians made sea charts using sticks to show the currents and shells to represent the islands.

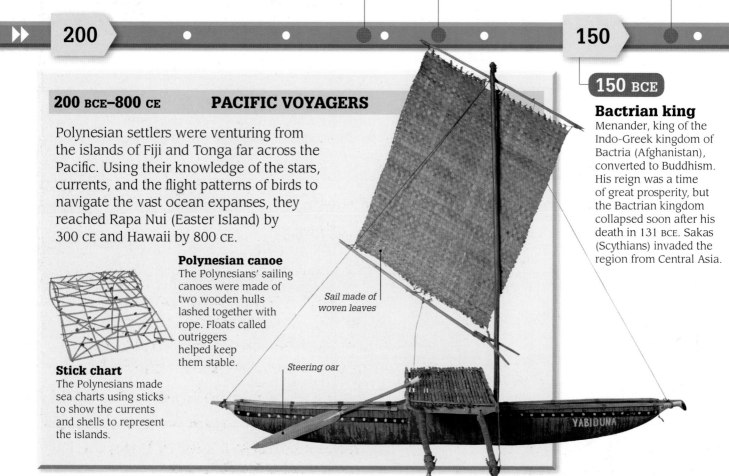

Sail made of woven leaves

Steering oar

Outrigger

📢 **The Hopewell people were gardeners. They grew plants such as sunflowers for their tasty seeds.**

Copper crow
This bird sculpture was made by the Hopewell people who flourished in eastern North America from 200 BCE to 500 CE. They built ceremonial mounds and crafted objects of copper.

110 BCE

Silk Road from China
The Silk Road, the land trade route that ran across the mountains and deserts of Central Asia to the Mediterranean, and named for the silk trade, was busy at this time. Only the Chinese knew the secret of making silk, which was highly prized in Rome.

100

121 BCE

Han emperor
Emperor Wudi expelled the Hsiung-Nu, nomadic raiders from Mongolia who had invaded China. Wudi was the seventh emperor of the Han dynasty, which had come to power in 202 BCE. He was a strong ruler, who built up the authority of the emperor at the expense of the nobles and made Confucianism the state religion.

A 17th-century silk painting showing Emperor Wudi greeting a Confucian scholar

105–101 BCE ROME'S NEW ARMY

Rome's unending wars of conquest were causing difficulties – only land-owning citizens were allowed to fight in the army and they were reluctant to leave home for long periods. Gaius Marius, an ambitious general and politician, changed this by opening up the army to all citizens, turning it into a disciplined, professional force. With his new army he won victories in North Africa and northern Italy.

Woollen cloak
Leather bottle for water or wine
Dish and pan
Pack containing three days' rations
Mattock for digging ditches
Turf cutter for building ramparts

Roman soldier's kit
Marius expected his soldiers to carry their own kit and cook their own food. A soldier's pack could weigh as much as 40 kg (90 lb).

"[Gaius Marius] vied with the common soldiers in frugality and endurance, thereby winning much goodwill among them."
Greek scholar Plutarch (46–120 CE) in his book *Lives*

📢 **Wudi sent an explorer to bring back horses from Central Asia.**

The Roman Empire
See pages 68–69

100–44 BCE · JULIUS CAESAR

Born into a noble family, Julius Caesar was an ambitious politician who rose to power in the midst of civil war. After conquering Gaul, he returned to Rome, defeated his main rival, Pompey the Great, and had himself named dictator, an office giving him extraordinary powers.

Caesar in charge

As dictator, Caesar carried out many reforms. The Julian calendar is named after him. But in 44 BCE he was declared dictator for life, leading his enemies to fear that he planned to make himself king of Rome.

Assassination of Caesar
A group of around 60 senators conspired against Caesar. On 15 March (a feast day known as the Ides of March) he was publicly stabbed to death in the Senate.

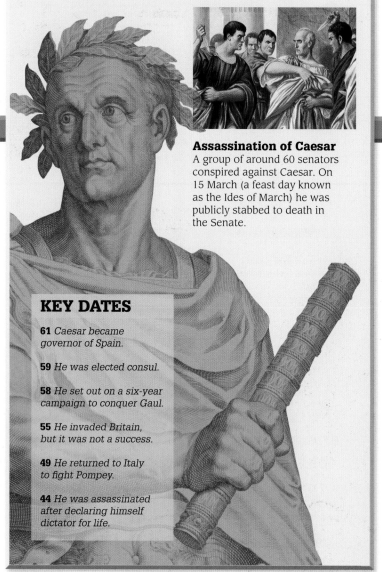

KEY DATES

61 *Caesar became governor of Spain.*

59 *He was elected consul.*

58 *He set out on a six-year campaign to conquer Gaul.*

55 *He invaded Britain, but it was not a success.*

49 *He returned to Italy to fight Pompey.*

44 *He was assassinated after declaring himself dictator for life.*

73 BCE
Slaves' revolt
Spartacus, an escaped gladiator, started a revolt of slaves near Naples in southern Italy. More than 70,000 slaves flocked to join him. The rebels roamed Italy for two years before being crushed by a Roman army led by Crassus. Some 6,000 rebels were nailed on crosses as a warning to others.

100 ● **80** ▶ ●

100 BCE
Hill forts
Around this time, the Celts (Gauls) of northwest Europe and southern Britain were building large hilltop settlements surrounded by lines of ditches and stockades. These forts served as tribal capitals, and some held several thousand inhabitants. The Romans called them oppida (towns).

Celtic offering
This bronze shield, discovered in the River Thames, London, may have been thrown into the river as an offering to a Celtic god.

The story of Silla
King Pak Hyokkose is said to have founded the Korean kingdom of Silla in 56 BCE. According to legend, Pak Hyokkose had hatched from a large red egg brought to Earth by a flying horse.

Vercingetorix throws down his arms in defeat to Caesar, seated.

In 53 BCE, 9,000 Parthian (from Persia) archers defeated a Roman army of 40,000 at the Battle of Carrhae (Turkey).

52 BCE
Last of the Gauls
Vercingetorix, war leader of the Gauls, surrendered to Julius Caesar after the siege of Alesia, a hill fort in eastern France. Caesar had Vercingetorix sent to Rome, paraded through the streets, and then strangled. Vercingetorix's defeat ended the wars in Gaul.

"Vercingetorix rode out… and made a turn about Caesar."

Plutarch, the Greek historian, describes the surrender in his *Lives*, c 100 CE

27 BCE
First Roman emperor
Octavian was granted the title of Augustus, in effect making him emperor. Octavian, Caesar's adopted nephew, had taken control of the Roman world after winning the war against Caesar's assassins and defeating his former ally, Mark Antony.

60 • **40** • **20** • **1** ▶▶

69–30 BCE CLEOPATRA

Cleopatra (ruled 51–30 BCE) was the last of the Macedonian dynasty that ruled Egypt for 300 years. At first she shared power with her brother, Ptolemy XIII, but later she overthrew him. After Cleopatra's death, Egypt became a Roman province.

Egyptian beauty
Cleopatra had affairs with Caesar, who supported her against her brother, and with Mark Antony, a Roman general. Antony and Cleopatra's political enemies feared the couple would found a powerful new dynasty.

Death by poison
When she learned of Mark Antony's death, Cleopatra killed herself with a bite from a snake.

4 BCE
Birth of Jesus Christ
Nobody knows for certain, but many historians believe that Jesus Christ was born in this year. The star of Bethlehem, described in the Gospel of Matthew, may have been a comet visible in the night sky.

15th century painting of the birth of Christ

The Roman Empire

The Roman Empire grew slowly at first – it took 500 years for the small city of Rome to conquer the whole of Italy – but by the 1st century CE its frontiers stretched from Spain in the west to Syria in the east. This vast empire of more than 60 million people was held together by a strong and efficient system of provincial government, backed by the army.

Enemies of Rome

Samnites
The Samnites lived in the mountains of south Italy. They were always ready to make trouble for the Romans, who fought three major wars against them in the 4th and 3rd centuries BCE.

Carthaginians
The Carthaginians were Rome's bitterest enemies in the 3rd century BCE. Their empire, which at times included North Africa, Spain, Corsica, Sardinia, and most of Sicily, blocked Roman expansion in the Mediterranean.

Parthians
The Parthians, who ruled Persia from the 3rd century BCE, were a threat on the eastern frontier. The Romans never forgot their humiliating defeat by the Parthians at Carrhae (Harran, Turkey) in 53 BCE.

Cimbri and Teutones
The Cimbri and Teutones were two tribes from northern Europe who threatened northern Italy in the 2nd century BCE. The Cimbri defeated two Roman armies at Arausio (Orange, France) in 105 BCE.

Marcomanni
The Marcomanni, a Germanic tribe from north of the Danube frontier, invaded Roman territory in the 2nd century CE. Emperor Marcus Aurelius expelled them but had to fight a lengthy war against them.

Head of Rome
Standard coins were issued across the empire. They were stamped with the head of the emperor to show who was in charge.

The Roman world
Shown in red in the map above is the Roman Empire in 118 CE, during the reign of Emperor Hadrian. The empire was divided into around 45 provinces, each headed by a governor.

Brilliant engineers
The Romans built this impressive aqueduct to carry fresh water across the River Gard to the city of Nemausus (Nîmes) in southern France. The Romans were skilled engineers. Their network of paved, all-weather roads linked towns and cities right across the empire.

Key events

753 BCE
The city of Rome was said to have been founded by twins, Romulus and Remus.

509 BCE
The people of Rome overthrew their king, Tarquin the Proud, and formed a republic.

209 BCE
Rome had overcome its neighbours and become the dominant power in Italy.

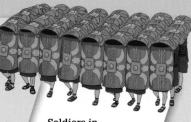

Soldiers in tortoise formation

27 BCE
Octavian founded the Roman Empire. He ruled as its first emperor, under the name Augustus.

Famous generals

Scipio Africanus

Leading the fight against the Carthaginians in the Second Punic War, Scipio took the war to Africa, where he defeated Hannibal at the Battle of Zama (202 BCE).

Pompey the Great

A famous general of the 1st century BCE, Pompey won victories in the east and in Spain. In 67 BCE he defeated the pirates who had been terrorizing traders in the Mediterranean.

Trajan

Born in Spain, Trajan became emperor in 98 CE. He conquered Dacia (Romania) and part of Mesopotamia, and his victories are displayed on Trajan's Column in Rome.

Roman society

In the reign of Augustus (ruled 27 BCE–14 CE), only a tenth of the empire's population were full citizens – women and slaves were among those excluded. People's place in society depended on their birth – whether they were a patrician (noble) or pleb (ordinary citizen) – and their wealth.

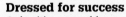

Dressed for success

Only citizens could wear a toga – this toga's purple stripe indicates that the man is a senator. His wife wears a *stola* (dress) and *palla* (cloak).

Soldier and captive

Prisoners taken in war were sold into slavery. They might become gladiators and fight in the arena, or be sent to row in war galleys.

Former slaves

Many working people in Rome were former slaves who had been freed by their masters. Their children automatically became citizens.

Roman gods

The Romans had hundreds of gods and goddesses associated with every aspect of life. These are some of the major ones:

★ Jupiter, king of the gods
★ Juno, queen of the gods
★ Mars, god of war
★ Venus, goddess of love and beauty
★ Neptune, god of the sea
★ Apollo, god of the Sun and the arts
★ Diana, goddess of the Moon and hunting
★ Minerva, goddess of wisdom
★ Vulcan, blacksmith of the gods
★ Vesta, goddess of the hearth

Neptune in his sea chariot

---

1 CE

The population of the city of Rome reached around one million, making it the world's largest city.

117

The Roman Empire reached its fullest extent, thanks to Trajan's conquests in the east.

Roman war galley

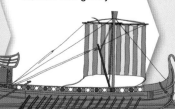

212

Emperor Caracalla granted full Roman citizenship to all free adult males living in the empire.

476

Barbarians overthrew the Western Roman Empire. The Eastern (Byzantine) Empire lasted until 1453.

The four Roman emperors who followed Augustus – Tiberius, Caligula, Claudius, and Nero – all died violent deaths.

63 BCE–14 CE   EMPEROR AUGUSTUS

Augustus, the name Octavian took in 27 BCE, meant "revered one". Augustus's great achievement was to end the civil wars and bring peace and stability to the Empire. He rebuilt Rome and reorganized the government and the army. When he died aged 75, he was succeeded by his stepson, Tiberius.

> **"I found Rome a city of bricks and left it a city of marble."**
>
> **Emperor Augustus**

A clean custom

The Romans built heated baths all over the Empire. Instead of using soap, they cleaned their skin with olive oil, which they scraped off with metal strigils (curved tools).

Flask of olive oil

Metal strigil

43

Into Britain

Emperor Claudius sent an army of 40,000 to invade Britain. The conquest of Britannia (the Roman name for Britain) took 40 years to complete and most of Scotland was never subdued.

---

1 — **20** — **40**

23

China in turmoil

A rebel army overthrew the emperor Wang Mang, who had seized the throne for himself in 9 CE. China was plunged into chaos until a Han prince, Liu Xiu, took control. Ruling as Emperor Guang Wudi, he managed to reunite China by 36 CE, and founded the Eastern Han dynasty.

High-rise house

This model of a multistorey building buried in the tomb of a Chinese noble shows architecture during the Han dynasty. Animals lived at ground level, living quarters were in the middle, and there was a watchtower on top.

c 33–300   CHRISTIANITY

In 33 CE Jesus Christ, a charismatic Jewish religious leader, was put to death in Jerusalem. His followers believed that he was the Son of God. They founded a new religion, Christianity, which spread to many parts of the Roman Empire. Christians were persecuted because they refused to make sacrifices to the Roman gods.

Jesus Christ

Four of Christ's early followers, Matthew, Mark, Luke, and John, recorded his life and teachings. Their accounts were written down in four books, the Gospels, some decades after his death.

The fort of Masada in modern-day Israel

In 64 CE a fire swept through Rome. Emperor Nero blamed the Christians, but many said he started it himself so he could build a palace.

80

Open for business
Emperor Titus laid on 100 days of gladiator fights and wild animal hunts to mark the opening of the magnificent Colosseum in Rome. It had taken eight years to build.

66

Jewish revolt
A Jewish revolt broke out in the Roman province of Judea. Vespasian (who became emperor in 69 CE) and his son Titus crushed the rebellion, destroying the Temple in Jerusalem. Jewish resistance fighters retreated to the hilltop fort of Masada, which fell to the Romans in 73 CE.

60 ● ● ● ● **80** ● ● ● **100** ▶▶

79

Vesuvius erupts
The sudden eruption of the volcano Vesuvius buried the Roman towns of Pompeii and Herculaneum, in Italy, under thick layers of ash and mud. Thousands were killed by burning clouds of gas.

100

Pyramid building
Work began on the enormous Pyramid of the Sun in the city of Teotihuacán, Mexico. When it was finished, about 100 years later, it stood 63 m (207 ft) high.

Paul's journey
Like Jesus himself, the first Christians were Jewish. St Paul, a Jew and a Roman citizen, became a Christian after seeing a great light while travelling to Damascus. Paul spread the new religion to non-Jews (Gentiles), journeying around the eastern Mediterranean and writing letters (the Epistles) to groups of Christians. He was probably executed in Rome around 67 CE.

On the road to Damascus, St Paul is blinded by a light from heaven.

Volcanic debris raining down on the people of Pompeii

Wall painting from a house in Pompeii, depicting fans rioting in 59 CE

Riot in Pompeii

In 59 CE, spectators from the nearby town of Nuceria poured into Pompeii to watch a gladiatorial show in the town's amphitheatre. A scuffle broke out between rival fans, and many people died in the fighting that followed. Emperor Nero ordered the Senate to carry out an investigation, and after hearing the report's findings he banished the riot ringleaders and closed the amphitheatre for ten years. It must have seemed a harsh penalty to the Pompeiians who – in common with people across the Empire – loved going to see the gladiator fights.

"A serious fight... arose out of a trifling incident at a gladiatorial show – abuse led to stone-throwing and then swords were drawn. The people of Pompeii, where the show was held, came off best. "

The Roman historian Tacitus describing the riot in *Annals*, c 116 CE

100 ▶ 200

Moche mask
This copper-and-gilt mask was made by a Moche craftsman. The Moche were a warlike people who emerged in northern Peru between 100 and 200. They were also skilled workers in gold and pottery.

122
Hadrian's Wall
The first emperor to visit every part of the Roman Empire, Hadrian ordered the building of a stone wall to defend Britain's northern frontier from the Celtic tribes of Scotland. It took two years to construct the 122 km (76 mile) wall. Much of it is still standing today.

130
Wealthy Kushans
Under King Kanishka, the Kushan Empire extended from Afghanistan into northern India. The Kushans prospered from their control of the Silk Road, the ancient trade route between China and the Mediterranean.

Sculpture of a Kushan prince's head

```
100 • • • 120 • • 140 •
```

105 THE INVENTION OF PAPER

Cai Lun, a Chinese court official, is credited with inventing paper in 105. In fact, paper was already being made in China – Cai Lun reported on the process to Emperor He and a note of it was made in the records. Paper was used both for writing and for wrapping. The Chinese even had toilet paper.

Chinese writing
The Chinese wrote on paper and silk. Ink came in a hard stick that the writer ground against a stone and then mixed with a little water. He applied the ink with a brush like this one.

Making paper
Paper was made from plant fibres. In this 19th-century engraving, two men beat and split bamboo stems, then a third soaks the bundles in water.

121–180 MARCUS AURELIUS

Roman emperor Marcus Aurelius was a peace-loving man who was constantly at war. First of all he had to fight the Parthians on the eastern frontier. Then he had to deal with an invasion by the Marcomanni, Germanic tribes who lived north of the Danube river. He left the Empire in good shape on his death.

KEY DATES

161 *Marcus Aurelius became emperor, ruling at first with his adopted brother, Lucius Verus.*

166 *The Romans won the Roman-Parthian War.*

179 *Marcus Aurelius defeated the Marcomanni near Vindobona (Vienna).*

180 *Marcus Aurelius died, and his son Commodus became emperor.*

Philosopher emperor
A lifelong lover of learning and philosophy, Marcus Aurelius wrote down his thoughts about life in a book called the *Meditations*.

Flesh and blood
Marcus's son Commodus had no interest in government and spent all his time at the games. He took part in staged animal hunts in the Colosseum, supposedly slaying 100 lions in one day.

---

160 · · · **180** ● ● · **200** ▶▶

184

192

200

Yellow Turban revolt
Up to 400,000 rebels wearing yellow turbans went on the rampage in China. They were crushed but the authority of the Han emperor was fatally weakened. Cao Cao, a warlord, took over as the real power behind the throne.

> **"I'd rather betray others than have others betray me."**
>
> Saying attributed to Cao Cao

Champion Chams
The kingdom of Champa arose in Vietnam. The Chams were seafaring people who traded with India and adopted Hinduism. They came to rule most of present-day Vietnam and spent much of their time fighting the Chinese.

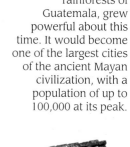

The Maya
See pages 88–89

Mayan city
The city of Tikál, deep in the tropical rainforests of Guatemala, grew powerful about this time. It would become one of the largest cities of the ancient Mayan civilization, with a population of up to 100,000 at its peak.

A ruined Hindu temple in the Champa city of My Son

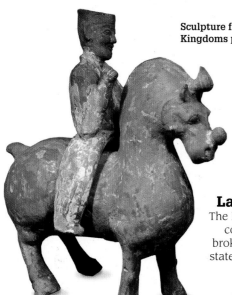

Sculpture from a Three Kingdoms period tomb

Ardashir I

Artabanus V being trampled by Ardashir's horse

The god Ahura Mazda holding out the ring of kingship

220

Last of the Han
The Han dynasty finally collapsed and China broke up into separate states during the Three Kingdoms period. In 280, China was reunited under the western Jin dynasty.

224

Persian coup
Ardashir I overthrew the Parthian emperor of Persia, Artabanus V, to found the Sasanian (or Sassanid) dynasty of rulers. A symbolical scene carved on a cliff face at Naqsh-e Rustam in Iran shows Ahura Mazda, high god of the ancient Persians, making Ardashir a king.

The Maya
See pages 88–89

200 • • • **220** • • • **240** •

100–600 TEOTIHUACÁN

Teotihuacán in Central Mexico was the largest city of ancient America. Built between 100 and 250, it covered an area of more than 30 sq km (11.5 sq miles). Its people traded widely and its influence was felt as far as Guatemala. The city was at the peak of its power around 500, but fell into decline a century later.

Face to face
This impressive stone mask was probably made for the statue of a god to wear. Skilfully worked, it is covered with turquoise, obsidian, and coral, and the staring eyes are of mother-of-pearl.

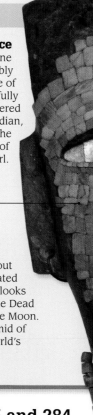

Turquoise mosaic pieces

City of the gods
Teotihuacán was laid out as a sacred site, dedicated to the gods. This view looks down the Avenue of the Dead from the Pyramid of the Moon. On the left is the Pyramid of the Sun, one of the world's largest pyramids.

  There were 25 Roman emperors between 235 and 284.

Third-century ceremonial bronze bell from Japan

250

Japanese kingdom
In Japan, a kingdom was emerging in the Yamato region of Honshu Island. Its rulers extended their control across most of Japan over the next two centuries.

260

Empire in crisis
The Roman Empire was plunged into crisis after Emperor Valerian was taken prisoner by the Sasanian king Shapur I. Meanwhile, barbarian invaders threatened the Empire's northeastern frontiers, and a usurper set up a breakaway Gallic Empire in the west.

The Roman Empire
See pages 68–69

Lord of Sipán
This intricate ornament is one of hundreds of precious items buried with a Moche warrior-king. His coffin at Sipán in northern Peru has been dated to about 290.

260 • • • 280 • 300 ▶▶

269

Warrior queen
Zenobia, queen of Palmyra, a wealthy city in Syria, took advantage of the Roman Empire's weakness. She carved out an independent kingdom for herself in Syria and Egypt. Defeated by Emperor Aurelian in 272, she was taken as a captive to Rome, where she died.

Statue of the Empire's four tetrarchs (co-emperors)

285

Empire of two halves
Diocletian, a wise and efficient emperor, decided the Empire was too large for one man. He appointed Maximian to rule the west, while he ruled the east. In 293, each emperor took a junior colleague, making a rule of four (tetrarchy).

19th-century portrait of Queen Zenobia

"Her eyes were black and powerful... and her beauty incredible."

Description of Zenobia in the *Historia Augusta*

77

"How she clung to her father's neck! How she loved her nurses, her tutors, her teachers! How studiously and intelligently she read..."

The author Pliny describing a friend's daughter, Minicia Minata, 106 CE

CHILD OF THE TIME

A Roman girl's life

When a Roman girl was eight days old, she was placed on her father's knee. If he did not accept her, she was put outside to die. This happened to boys too, if they were sickly, but more often to girls. Usually, however, the birth of a baby of either sex was a welcome event, and parents hung garlands on the front door of their house in celebration.

A charmed childhood

At eight days old, the baby had a naming ceremony. Her father placed a charm called a *bulla* around her neck, which she wore until she married. The baby was dressed in restricting swaddling clothes up to the age of two and, if she came from an upper-class family, was looked after by slaves.

School days

Like their brothers, well-off girls went to school from the age of seven to 11 to learn reading, writing, and maths. But not all girls went to school. Most received just a basic education, after which they were taught household skills by their mothers. The daughters of slaves had to work from an early age.

Time for fun and games

Although Roman children were dressed like miniature adults, there was plenty of time for fun with balls, hoops, spinning tops, and wooden toys. Children also played games together with marbles, dice, and nuts. Girls had dolls. Some lucky children might have kept a pet, such as a small dog, rabbit, or even a goose.

Growing up and leaving home

On the eve of her wedding, a girl marked the end of childhood by dedicating her favourite doll to the household gods. Girls could marry at 12, though 15 was the usual age. As a wife, her duties would be to run the household, manage the slaves, and have children. However, wives could own property and many were successful businesswomen.

"During the time that I lived, I enjoyed myself and I was always loved by everyone. In fact, believe me, I had the face of a little boy, not of a girl... of pleasing and noble appearance, with red hair, short on top and long behind..."

From an epitaph to a five-year-old Roman girl who died in the 1st century CE

Girl with a stylus
This girl taps her stylus (pen) to her mouth as she ponders what to write on the wax tablet. She appears on a wall painting in Pompeii, Italy, that dates from the first century.

Golden locket
Wearing a bulla *signified that a child was born free, not a slave. The charm was also believed to ward off evil spirits.*

"My daughter is very close to my heart... For what has nature wanted to be more delightful to us, what has nature wanted to be more dear to us than our daughters?"

The Roman politician Cicero, c 70 BCE

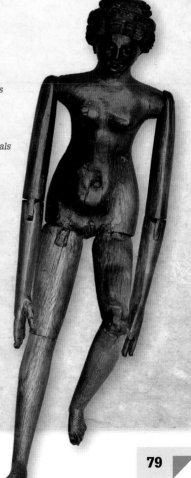

A precious doll
This wooden doll was found in the tomb of a Roman girl called Crepereia Tryphena. The fact that it was buried with her, reveals that she died before reaching adulthood.

Buddha head from Gupta, India

272–337   CONSTANTINE THE GREAT

Constantine I was proclaimed emperor in the west in 306 but was immediately plunged into civil wars against his co-emperors and rivals. He claimed that the Christian God helped him secure victory for the control of Rome against the usurper Maxentius in 312, and the next year he and his co-emperor Licinius issued the Edict of Milan, allowing freedom of worship throughout the empire. For Christians, this put an end to the constant threat of persecution.

Sole emperor
In 324 Constantine became sole emperor after defeating Licinius and ordering his execution. Constantine continued to support Christianity and ordered the building of churches throughout the empire. However, he was not formally baptized a Christian until just before his death.

320
Indian ruler
Chandragupta I became king of the small state of Gupta in northern India. Conquering far and wide, he founded the Gupta Empire that dominated India for 200 years.

317
China divides
Northern China was overrun by nomads and broke up into 16 kingdoms. The Eastern Jin dynasty (317–420) established itself in the south of the country, ruling from Nanjing.

300 ● **320**

KEY DATES

306 *Constantine was proclaimed emperor.*

312 *He won the Battle of the Milvian Bridge.*

313 *Constantine ended the persecution of Christians.*

324 *Constantine founded Constantinople as a new capital to rival Rome.*

337 *He was baptized as he lay on his deathbed.*

Constantinople
Constantine's greatest legacy was the city of Constantinople (Istanbul), the new capital he founded for the Eastern Empire. This medieval map shows some of its early churches and monuments.

Changes in Tikál
In 379 Yax Nuun Ayiin, an invader from Teotihuacán, became ruler of the Mayan city of Tikál. This sculpture of a god holding a severed human head was found in his tomb.

> **"By this sign [of the cross], conquer!"**
>
> **Words that Constantine is said to have seen written in the sky at the Battle of the Milvian Bridge**

Obelisk in Aksum, Ethiopia

An early Christian couple

391

Theodosius I

Having made Christianity the official religion of the Roman Empire in 380, Theodosius I went on to outlaw pagan sacrifices in 391. He ordered the destruction of many pagan temples.

The last Olympic Games of the ancient world were held at Olympia in 393.

340

African convert

King Ezana of Aksum (modern Ethiopia) was converted to Christianity by a Syrian missionary, Frumentius. The burial places of the kings of Aksum were marked by tall granite obelisks. This one is 24 m (78 ft) high.

361

Return of the gods

Civil wars followed the death of Constantine I. His nephew Julian, who became emperor in 361, tried to restore paganism in the empire, but died fighting the Persians two years later.

340 — **360** — **380** — **400** ⏵⏵

376–395   BARBARIAN ATTACK

When the Huns, nomads from Central Asia, migrated into eastern Europe, they caused panic among the Germanic tribes on the edge of the Roman Empire. In 376 the Goths asked to settle within the Empire. They were refused and Emperor Valens died fighting them. They entered anyway and were given land in the Balkans. In 395 Alaric led the Goths in an uprising against Rome.

Heavy iron head to cause maximum injury

Combat weapon

The favourite weapon of the Franks was a throwing axe that they hurled at the enemy.

Visigothic warrior

The Goths later split into two groups – Visigoths and Ostrogoths. The Visigoths went west, invaded Gaul, and later founded a kingdom in Spain. The Ostrogoths (eastern Goths) founded a kingdom in Italy.

Germanic tribes

The Romans gave the name "barbarian" to all peoples from outside the empire. The Germanic tribes originally lived to the north and east.

⚔ **Goths** This tribe migrated south from Scandinavia to the Black Sea area.

⚔ **Franks** This group of tribes settled on the lower Rhine (northern Germany).

⚔ **Vandals** This people eventually set up a kingdom in North Africa.

⚔ **Jutes, Angles, and Saxons** These peoples invaded England from Denmark and northern Germany.

400 ▶ 500

A scramasax, a single-edged knife carried by the Angles and Saxons

Leather sheath

410–453 ATTILA THE HUN

Attila was the leader of the Huns – nomadic warriors from Central Asia who had settled in what is now Hungary. Attila united the Huns and led them on a series of raids, plundering everything in their path and striking fear into the hearts of the Romans.

Troublemaker
Attila was nicknamed the "scourge of God", meaning that he wanted to make trouble. His long skull was due to the Huns' custom of binding babies' heads.

KEY DATES

433 *Attila became the ruler of the Huns.*

441 *He began raiding the Eastern Empire.*

451 *Attila was defeated at the Battle of Châlons.*

453 *He died of a nosebleed on his wedding night.*

407
Britain, farewell!
Constantine III, a general serving in Britain, declared himself emperor. He crossed to Gaul, taking the troops remaining in Britain with him. Britain no longer had links with the Roman Empire. After 450, Angles, Saxons, and Jutes from Denmark began migrating into southern and eastern Britain.

400 ● ●● ● ● **420** ◉ ● ● **440** ▶ ●

406
Rhine crossing
On the last day of the year, a barbarian horde crossed the frozen River Rhine from Germany to invade the Roman Empire. They swept through Gaul until they reached the Pyrenees.

410
Sack of Rome
Alaric, leader of the Visigoths, invaded Italy and captured Rome. He asked for gold and silver in return for sparing it. When this was refused his troops looted the city. In 455 Vandal raiders from North Africa sacked Rome even more thoroughly.

425
Japanese burial mounds
The Yamato rulers of Japan were building large, keyhole-shaped burial mounds (*kofun*). The largest, the Daisen-kofun, was said to be that of Emperor Nintoku. Yamato Japan had close links with China and Korea.

Alaric riding into Rome

Guardian boar
When the Yamato rulers were buried, large clay figures of animals such as boars, horses, and chickens were placed in and around the *kofun* mounds. These guardian figures are known as *haniwa*.

Fierce warriors

The Huns attacked the Eastern Empire year after year, draining it of men and resources to defend itself. Superb riders, the Huns controlled their horses at speed as they rained arrows and javelins on their enemies. In 451 Attila invaded Gaul but left after being defeated by an army of Romans and Goths at the Battle of Châlons in central France.

> **"** ... the best horsemen of the whole Hunnic race rode around in a circle... and recited his deeds in a funeral chant. **"**
>
> A Roman historian, Priscus of Panium, describes Attila the Hun's funeral

Theodoric on a gold coin

493
Ostrogoths take over

Theodoric, ruler of the Ostrogoths, invaded Italy and replaced Odoacer as king after a three-year campaign. He made his capital at Ravenna on Italy's Adriatic coast, and adopted Roman customs.

---

460   480   500 ▶▶

476
Rome falls

Italy was virtually the only part of the Western Empire still under imperial rule. Odoacer, a barbarian general in the Roman army, overthrew the last emperor, a young boy called Romulus Augustulus, to make himself king of Italy. After 500 years, the Roman Empire in the west was at an end. The Eastern, or Byzantine, Empire with its capital at Constantinople, survived until 1453.

The Roman Empire See pages 68–69

500
Town in Africa

Jenné-Jene on the River Niger in present-day Mali was the first town to emerge south of the Sahara in West Africa. The inhabitants were farmers who built mudbrick houses and knew how to make iron.

400–650   THE NAZCA LINES

The people who lived in the Nazca desert of southern Peru made huge pictures of birds, animals, and geometric shapes on the ground. They created the outlines by removing the reddish pebbles from the surface to uncover the whitish soil underneath. The designs can only be viewed from the nearby foothills and no one knows why they were made.

Desert spider

The dry, windless conditions have preserved the mysterious lines in the desert. This photograph of a giant 46-m- (150-ft-) long spider is taken from a plane.

500–1450
The marvellous Middle Ages

The end of the Roman Empire plunged Europe into the Dark Ages, but by 1000 powerful kingdoms had formed, trade had revived, and medieval Christianity was flourishing. The birth of Islam saw the creation of a dynamic Arab Empire that stretched from Spain and North Africa as far as India. Mighty China was way ahead of the West in technology, but the Mongol invasions and Black Death brought widespread destruction to both Asia and Europe. In the Americas, great civilizations such as the Aztecs and Incas were at their height.

500 ▶ 600

A mosaic portrait of Justinian

Eagle brooch
This beautiful brooch belonged to an Ostrogoth noblewoman – or perhaps a princess. The Ostrogothic kingdom of Italy held out against Justinian's armies for 20 years, but was finally conquered in 553.

507
Frankish victory
Clovis, king of the Franks, defeated the Visigoths at the Battle of Vouillé and began to drive them out of southwest France into Spain. This 15th-century painting shows Alaric II, the defeated Visigothic king, kneeling before Clovis.

532
Riot in Constantinople
Justinian, the Byzantine (Eastern) emperor, seemed in danger of losing his throne after rioting in Constantinople. However, the riot was crushed and the 30,000 rebels killed. Two years later, Justinian's position was made even stronger when his general Belisarius retook North Africa from the Vandals.

500   **520**   **540**

Boy monk
See pages 104–105

529
Monastic life
Benedict founded a monastery at Monte Cassino in Italy. He laid down rules for how the monks should live, dividing the day between prayer and work. Monasteries following St Benedict's Rule spread across Europe and were centres of learning during the Dark Ages.

542
Plague!
An outbreak of bubonic plague struck the city of Constantinople. It had broken out two years earlier in Egypt and spread around the Mediterranean, probably carried on grain ships by infected rats. The huge loss of life weakened the empire and in particular the army, overstretched by Justinian's campaigns in Italy and North Africa.

According to the historian Procopius, at the height of the plague 10,000 people a day were dying in Constantinople.

A 13th-century plaque of St Benedict

Silk woven in Constantinople
in the 9th century

The world of Islam
See pages
96–97

570

Birth of Muhammad

The Prophet Muhammad was born in Mecca, in what is now Saudi Arabia. A member of the minor Quraysh clan, he was orphaned at the age of seven and brought up in the household of his uncle, Abu Talib. At that time, the people of Arabia worshipped many gods.

553

The secret of silk

A silk-making industry developed in Constantinople with the arrival of the first silkworms. The insects were said to have been smuggled from Persia by two monks, who hid them inside their hollow canes. Before this, silk had to be imported at great cost because the Chinese refused to reveal the secret of silk production.

593

Buddhist prince

Prince Shotoku, one of Japan's great cultural heroes, became regent, ruling on behalf of his aunt, Empress Suiko. A devout Buddhist, Shotoku encouraged the spread of Buddhism, which became the state religion. He also wrote down a document that set out the principles that should govern Japanese society.

560 • • • **580** • • • • **600** ▸▸

581

China reunited

Emperor Wendi, founder of the Sui dynasty, made himself sole ruler of China, reuniting the country after three centuries of division and instability. Under his successor, Emperor Yangdi, work began on the 2,000-km- (1,240-mile-) long Grand Canal network. Linking the south and north of the country, it is still the longest canal system in the world.

597

Augustine's mission

After encountering a group of Anglo-Saxon slaves in a market, Pope Gregory I sent Augustine, a Roman churchman, to Britain to convert the Anglo-Saxons to Christianity. Augustine baptized King Ethelbert of Kent, whose wife was already a Christian, and founded a church at Canterbury.

❝Not Angles, but angels.❞

Pope Gregory I, on seeing fair-haired Anglo-Saxons in a Roman slave market

A silk painting showing boats on the Grand Canal

Mayan ruins

The Maya built complex stone buildings without metal tools or wheeled transport. Ruins are known at more than 40 sites.

Uxmal
A dwarf is said to have built the Magician's Pyramid at Uxmal in a day. In reality, it was built over 400 years.

Palenque
This city in northern Mexico was covered by jungle until restoration began in the 1920s. Its Temple of the Sun is well preserved.

Chichen Itzá
This site is home to an impressive 24-m- (78-ft-) high stepped pyramid. Each side had a staircase leading to the Temple of Kukulkan at the top.

Temple of Kukulkan

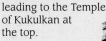

The Maya

The Mayan people lived in the forests of Central America, in cities of 5,000 to 15,000 inhabitants. These cities, ruled by "god-kings", were constantly at war with each other. The Maya had the most advanced writing system in ancient America, which used symbols called glyphs. Around 300 the Maya began to erect stone monuments that recorded the deeds of their god-kings. After 800, many Mayan cities collapsed, probably due to famine.

Mayan nobleman
Each Mayan city was ruled by its own noble family. Mayan nobles spent a lot of time on their appearance – this pottery figure shows a nobleman in all his finery, with a heavy bead necklace, feather headdress, and earplugs.

"There was neither man, nor animal, birds, fishes, crabs, trees, stones, caves, ravines, grasses, nor forests, there was only the sky."

From the Maya account of creation

Key events

250
The Classic Mayan civilization emerged in the central lowlands of Guatemala. They began to build magnificent temples and keep records of their kings.

450
Tikál, in Guatemala, was now the largest and most important of the Mayan cities. Its closest rival was Calakmul, with which it was constantly at war.

750
The warring between the Mayan cities was at its height at this time.

800
The Classic Mayan cities of the central lowlands began to decline.

869
Construction stopped at Tikál as the city entered its final days.

A Mayan bloodletting ritual

Blood sacrifices

The Maya believed that their rulers could communicate with the gods and their dead ancestors through bloodletting rituals. They also believed that the gods wanted sacrifices of human blood.

★ The Maya pierced their tongue, lips, or ears with sting-ray spines, pulled a thorny rope through their tongue, or cut themselves with an obsidian (stone) knife.

★ One reason for fighting wars was to collect prisoners who could be sacrificed to satisfy the gods.

★ The victim in a human sacrifice had his or her heart removed. Sometimes the skin was flayed (cut off) and worn by the priest. Parts of the body might be eaten.

★ Men, women, and children were drowned in sacred wells or hurled from cliffs to appease the gods.

Gods of the Maya

The Maya worshipped hundreds of gods, who had multiple personalities – some good and some bad. Mayan gods could morph between human and animal shapes.

Ah Bolon Tzacab

This leaf-nosed god of farming was associated with royal power and the offering of human blood. Kings often held a sceptre in the shape of this god.

Ah K'in

Also known as Kinich Ahau, Ah K'in was the god of the Sun and controlled drought and disease. He was often shown as a man with a hooked nose.

Buluc Chabtan

This was the god of war, violence, and sudden death (including human sacrifices). He was usually portrayed with a black line down one cheek.

Chac

The rainmaker god, Chac was often shown covered in scales and with fangs and a hooked snout. He carried a serpent as a symbol of lightning.

Ah Puch

The god of death and the underworld, Ah Puch was often depicted as a skeleton or rotting corpse.

Other cultures

Olmec (1500–400 BCE)
The Olmec inhabited Mexico's Gulf Coast region, and are known for carving colossal stone heads.

Teotihuacans (200 BCE–700 CE)
These mysterious people from northern Mexico built the largest city in ancient America.

Zapotecs (1500 BCE–700 CE)
The centre of the Zapotec Empire was at Monte Albán in the Oaxaca valley of southern Mexico.

Mixtecs (900–1400)
The Mixtecs rose to power after the decline of the Zapotecs and took over at Monte Albán.

Toltecs (900–1187)
The warlike Toltecs from northern Mexico captured the Mayan city of Chichen Itzá in 987 and ruled it for 200 years.

Aztecs (1325–1521)
The Aztecs migrated into Mexico in the 12th century and ruled the last great civilization of ancient Mexico.

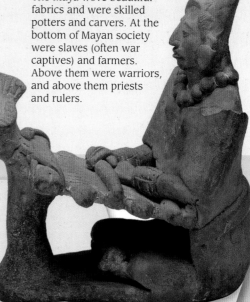

Aztec nobleman

Daily life

The Maya wove beautiful fabrics and were skilled potters and carvers. At the bottom of Mayan society were slaves (often war captives) and farmers. Above them were warriors, and above them priests and rulers.

Figure of a woman weaving

987
The Toltecs took over in Chichen Itzá, controlling the city until 1224.

1527–1546
The Spanish led three campaigns to conquer the Mayan people of the Yucatán peninsula.

1697
The very last Mayan outpost, Tayasal on Lake Petén Itzá, fell to the Spanish.

Muhammad's successors, the first four caliphs

618
Tang takeover
Li Yuan, regent to the last Sui emperor, a boy, had him murdered and seized power for himself. He reigned as Gaozu, the first emperor of the Tang dynasty. In 626 Gaozu's son Taizong forced his father to step down. Taizong's reign was the start of a golden age in China.

606
Indian empire
Harsha, king of a small Indian state, united the whole of northern India. Literature and culture flourished, but his empire broke up soon after his death in 647.

China's golden age
See pages 92–93

637
Arab conquests
Following Muhammad's death in 632, the Arabs, united by Islam, embarked on a campaign of conquest. By 637 they had seized Jerusalem and Damascus from the Byzantine Empire, and soon they had conquered the Persian Empire. Syria, Palestine, and Egypt fell next, and by 698 they controlled the whole of North Africa.

| 600 | | | | 620 | | | | 640 | |

610
Greek replaces Latin
Heraclius became the Byzantine (Eastern) emperor, ruling until 641. He saw off the Persians, who were threatening to invade. As most people in the Eastern Empire spoke Greek rather than Latin, he made it the official language of government.

610–629 THE BIRTH OF ISLAM

Muhammad was a merchant in Mecca, Saudia Arabia, before he grew discontented and took up a life of contemplation. In 610, aged about 40, he received a series of divine revelations and began preaching the message that there is one God: Allah. His revelations are contained in the Qur'an, which is for Muslims the direct word of God. The new religion that Muhammad taught, Islam, means submission to God.

Heraclius on horseback

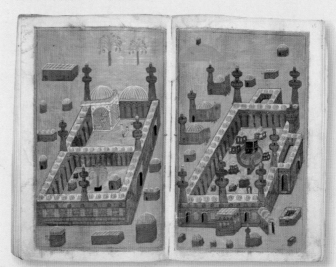

Medina and Mecca
The people of Mecca turned against Muhammad and in 622 he fled to Medina. That journey marks the start of the Islamic era. In 629 Muhammad returned to Mecca. Today, both cities are holy for Muslims.

12th-century illumination of Medina (left) and Mecca (right)

A ship sprays Greek fire

673
Secret weapon
When Arab ships reached Constantinople, the Byzantines brought out a new weapon – bronze tubes that fired a strange liquid. Known as "Greek fire", the liquid caught light on the water and produced raging flames. The weapon saw off the Arabs and saved the city.

"[Kallinikos] had devised a sea fire which ignited the Arab ships and burned them with all hands. "

Byzantine historian Theophanes, c 810

690
Empress Wu
Wu Zetian became the only woman in Chinese history to rule as emperor in her own name. She ruled from 690 to 705 but had also been the real power in Tang China during the reigns of her husband Gaozong (649–683) and son.

Royal helmet
This is a replica of a magnificent helmet that may once have belonged to an Anglo-Saxon king. He was buried in a ship in around 625 with this and other treasures at Sutton Hoo, eastern England.

660 · · · · · 680 · · · 700 ▶▶

683
Warrior king
Pakal was a political ruler and living god of the Mayan city of Palenque. Dying at the age of 80 after a 68-year reign, he transformed Palenque into a powerful city with new palaces and temples, including his own tomb, the Temple of Inscriptions.

700
End of a city
Teotihuacán in Mexico, once the greatest city in ancient America, collapsed, bringing 600 years of history to a close. Drought, crop failures, and famine probably weakened the city and left it vulnerable to attack.

Crown from Silla

668
Golden success
Silla conquered the neighbouring kingdoms of Paekche and Koguryo to take sole control of Korea. Silla had grown rich on gold. Its rulers, several of whom were women, were buried in tomb mounds with fabulous golden finery.

Funeral jade mask of King Pakal

The Maya
See pages 88–89

China's golden age

Two dynasties, the Tang (618–907) and the Song (960–1279), dominated medieval China, a time of great artistic and technological developments. The Tang period is often called the Golden Age of China. The Tang emperors were successful at fighting wars and Chinese influence spread into Central Asia. After a period of disunity, the Song dynasty brought a return to prosperity before it fell to the Mongols.

Four Tang emperors

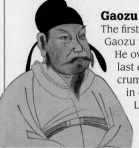

Gaozu
The first Tang emperor Gaozu was born Li Yuan. He overthrew the last emperor of the crumbling Sui dynasty in 618, but his son Li Shimin forced him to step down in 626.

Taizong
Li Shimin took the imperial name of Taizong. He was one of the greatest emperors in Chinese history, and his reforms brought lasting prosperity and stability to China. He died in 649.

Gaozong
Reigning from 649 to 683, Gaozong was a weak emperor. After suffering a series of strokes, he left affairs of state to his wife, Wu Zetian. She later took the title of *huangdi* ("emperor") for herself.

Xuanzong
The longest-serving Tang emperor was Xuanzong, who reigned for 43 years from 712 to 756. Art and culture flourished during his reign, which is considered the highpoint of Tang success.

Curvy camel
The Bactrian camel was the principal form of transport along the Silk Road. Camel caravans carried glass, jade, crystal, and cotton into China, and silk, tea, paper, and fine ceramics out of China. Ceramic figures of camels and horses, standing about 50 cm (20 in) tall, were often placed in the tombs of Tang nobles and important officials.

A palace concert
Elegant ladies of the Tang court drink tea while they play and listen to music. A small dog is curled up under the table. This painting by an unknown Tang artist is done in inks on silk.

Key events

618
The Tang dynasty was founded by Li Yuan, who rebelled against the Sui.

Li Yuan on horseback

659
The Tang expanded into Central Asia, making the Silk Road safer for travellers.

751
The Arabs defeated a Chinese army at the Talas River (present-day Kyrgyzstan).

755–763
A rebellion led by General An Lushan weakened Tang rule.

907
The fall of the Tang plunged China into the "Five Dynasties" period when China broke up into different kingdoms.

Tang capital
Chang'an (Xi'an), a busy trading city that attracted merchants from all over Asia, had a population of around two million people. Little survives of the Tang city today.

> **"Before my bed, the moon is shining bright I think that it is frost upon the ground. I raise my head and look at the bright moon, I lower my head and think of home. "**
>
> **"Thoughts on a still night" by Li Bai (701–762), a major poet of the Tang dynasty period**

There were 30 cards in a standard pack.

Chinese pagoda
The Iron Pagoda of Kaifeng was built in 1049 under the Song. It owes its name to the iron-red colour of its glazed bricks. Pagodas were associated with Buddhism, which was widespread in China.

Cards were made of thin, flexible cardboard.

Traditional Chinese playing cards

Tang and Song inventions

Woodblock printing
Developed around 650, woodblock printing involved carving text onto a block, which was then pressed in ink and then onto paper.

Paper money
When it appeared, around 800, paper money was called "flying money" because the notes could easily blow away.

Mechanical clock
The first record of a clock with a mechanical device to keep time accurately was in China and dates to 725.

Porcelain
The Chinese had discovered the art of making porcelain (very hard, fine white pottery) by 900.

Magnetic compass
The Chinese were using magnetized iron needles to find north on land by the 1040s and at sea by the 1120s.

Playing cards
Ladies at the Tang court enjoyed a game called the "leaf game", played with cards.

960
Song Taizu, founder of the Song dynasty, reunited China, bringing a return to stability.

1127
The Song dynasty moved south after Jurchen nomads overran northern China.

1234
Mongol armies conquered northern China and began attacking the Southern Song.

Mongol warrior

1279
The Mongol conquest of China was completed after the last Song emperor drowned in battle.

93

700 ▶ 800

Gospel book
About 130 calfskins were used in the making of the Lindisfarne Gospels. This beautiful and richly decorated illuminated manuscript was written and decorated by one monk, Eadfrith, in northeast England around 715.

732

Battle of Tours
A Muslim army from Spain advanced as far as Tours in central France before being beaten by the Franks, led by Charles Martel. Though not a king himself, Charles Martel founded the Carolingian dynasty of Frankish kings.

Charles Martel

731

English historian
Bede, a monk at Jarrow in northern England, wrote the *Ecclesiastical History of the English People*. Bede, an outstanding scholar, has been called "the father of English history".

750

Andean city
Tiwanaku, a city on the *altiplano* (high plains) of present-day Bolivia, was at its height. The Tiwanaku people built stone monuments and terraced the mountain slopes for farming.

| 700 | 720 | 740 | 760 |

711

Muslims in Spain
Tariq ibn Ziyad, a Berber from North Africa, came ashore at Gibraltar at the head of a large Muslim army. Within a year he had overrun all of Spain, except for the small kingdom of Asturias in the northwest.

 The name of Gibraltar comes from the Arabic *Jebel al-Tariq*, meaning "the hill of Tariq".

750

The Abbasids
Abu al-Abbas, head of a clan descended from Muhammad's uncle, overthrew the Umayyad caliphs, rulers of Islam since 661. Only one member of the Umayyad dynasty, Abd ar-Rahman, escaped – he fled to Spain and established an emirate at Cordoba. The new Abbasid caliph defeated a Chinese army at the Battle of Talas River near Samarkand in 751.

The world of Islam
See pages 96–97

Abu al-Abbas being proclaimed caliph

Byzantine empress Irene

797

Mother love
Banished from court in 790, when her son Constantine VI was proclaimed sole ruler, Empress Irene returned in 792 to resume her position as co-ruler of the Byzantine Empire. In 797, along with the Bishops and courtiers, she had her son blinded and declared herself Empress.

793

Raiders from the sea
Vikings, warriors from Scandinavia, attacked and looted Lindisfarne monastery in northeast England. The first recorded Viking raid, it came without warning and caused widespread horror and alarm.

780 | ● ● ● | **800**

786

Cultured caliph
Haroun al-Rashid became the fifth Abbasid caliph (head of state). He made the Abbasid capital of Baghdad a centre of learning and encouraged scholars to translate ancient Greek and Roman texts into Arabic. Some stories in the *Thousand and One Nights* relate to him.

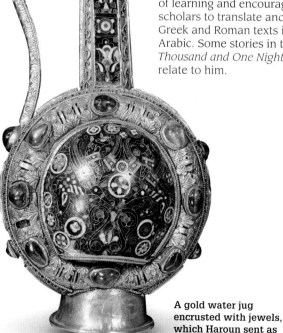

A gold water jug encrusted with jewels, which Haroun sent as a gift to Charlemagne

748–814   CHARLEMAGNE

Charlemagne, the grandson of Charles Martel, became sole ruler of the Franks in 771. He was the greatest of the Frankish kings – Charlemagne means "Charles the Great". In 30 years of campaigning, he doubled the size of the kingdom, conquering the Lombards of north Italy and the Saxons of northern Germany. Although he encouraged learning, he never learned to read.

Crowned as emperor
On Christmas Day 800 Pope Leo III crowned Charlemagne as emperor in Rome. It was an unprecedented event. Charlemagne was the first emperor in the West for nearly 400 years.

KEY DATES

774 *Charlemagne conquered the Lombards of north Italy.*

778 *His army was defeated at the Battle of Roncesvalles in Spain.*

804 *The war against the Saxons came to an end.*

814 *Charlemagne died in his palace at Aachen, Germany.*

> **"He took constant exercise in riding and hunting, which is natural to a Frank."**
>
> Frankish historian Einhard, c 830

Legendary hero
This medieval manuscript shows Charlemagne and his knights in pitched battle against the Muslims in Spain. One of Charlemagne's knights was the hero of the poem "The Song of Roland", a popular romance of medieval times.

The world of Islam

In the seventh century, Arab armies swept out of Arabia to conquer a vast empire that eventually stretched from Spain deep into Central Asia. They carried with them the religion of Islam revealed to the prophet Muhammad. Influenced by the Byzantine and Persian civilizations they conquered, the Arabs adopted new styles of art and architecture and ways of farming. Islamic scholars kept the study of philosophy, mathematics, medicine, and philosophy alive.

Who were they?

Umayyads
The Ummayads were the first dynasty of hereditary caliphs, leaders of the *ummah* (Islamic community) from 661.

Abbasids
This dynasty ruled the Muslim world from 750 to 1258, though after 900 many areas broke away.

Fatimids
The Fatimids created an independent kingdom in Egypt and North Africa from 908 to 1171.

Almoravids
The Almoravids were Berbers from North Africa. In the 11th century, they founded an Islamic empire that included Muslim Spain.

The Dome of the Rock

Completed in 691, the Dome of the Rock in Jerusalem is one of the earliest surviving Islamic buildings. Its design was clearly influenced by Byzantine architecture but already possessed distinct Islamic features.

Gilded wooden dome, 20 m (65 ft) across

Tiles added in the 16th century

The Qur'an

Muslims believe that the Qur'an is a flawless record of God's word as revealed to Muhammad by the angel Jibril (Gabriel). It consists of 114 chapters, each known as a *sura*.

Key events

622
Muhammad fled from the town of Mecca to Medina in what is now Saudi Arabia, marking the start of the Muslim era.

632
On Muhammad's death, his father-in-law Abu Bakr became caliph (leader of Islam), the first of the four "rightly guided" caliphs.

638
The Arabs conquered Jerusalem. In the next 60 years, their armies overran Syria, Palestine, Persia, Egypt, and North Africa.

644
The standard version of the Qur'an was made on the orders of Caliph Uthman. It was sent to every Muslim province.

661
Ali, the fourth caliph, was assassinated. Mu'awiya, first of the Umayyad Dynasty, became caliph.

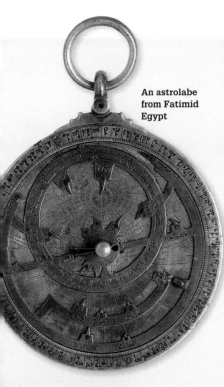

An astrolabe from Fatimid Egypt

Arab gifts to the world

■ **Numerals**
Today, Arabic numerals are used all over the world. Based on the Indian number system, they were adopted by Muslim scholars as they were simpler for calculations than Roman numerals.

■ **Astrolabe**
Arab astronomers developed the astrolabe, a device for measuring the height of the Sun and stars. It helped them to calculate the direction of Mecca.

■ **Chess**
The game of chess was first played in ancient India. The Arabs learned it from the Persians. Popular in Muslim Spain, it spread from there across Europe.

■ **Coffee**
Sufis (mystics) in Arabia took up drinking coffee to keep them awake at night when they were praying. Coffee eventually reached Europe through Istanbul in the 1600s.

Muslims playing chess around 1238

Muslim scholars

Ibn Sina (980–1037)
Known as Avicenna in the West, Ibn Sina wrote hundreds of works on all areas of knowledge, including mathematics, astronomy, philosophy, and medicine.

Ibn Rushd (1126–1198)
Ibn Rushd (Averroes) was a great thinker. His writings on Plato and Aristotle, translated into Latin, revived the West's interest in classical philosophy.

Al-Jazari (1136–1206)
An inventor and engineer, Al-Jazari described more than 100 extraordinary machines in his great *Book of Knowledge of Ingenious Mechanical Devices*.

A mechanical boat invented by Al-Jazari

Five Pillars of Islam

Every Muslim is obliged to perform five basic deeds, the Five Pillars, in his or her lifetime. They are:

Shahadah To recite: "There is no god but God (Allah) and Muhammad is the Messenger of God".

Salat To perform prayers five times a day, facing towards Mecca.

Zakat To support the poor and needy by setting aside some income.

Sawm To fast (go without food and drink) from dawn to sunset during the month of Ramadan.

Hajj To make the pilgrimage to Mecca at least once in his or her lifetime.

680
Islam split into two branches: Sunnis, who accepted the leadership of Abu Bakr, and Shiites, who only followed the teachings of Muhammad and his descendants.

711
A Muslim army from North Africa, led by Tariq ibn Ziyad, invaded Spain and overthrew the Visigothic kingdom.

750
The Abbasids overthrew the Umayyad caliphate. Their first caliph, Abu-al-Abbas, moved the capital from Damascus to Baghdad (in present-day Iraq).

Abbasid mosque at Samarra

970
The Seljuk Turks of Central Asia converted to Islam and began migrating into Persia (present-day Iran).

1055
The Seljuk sultan Tughril seized power in Baghdad and took control of the Arab Empire.

800 ▶ 900

843
Treaty of Verdun
Charlemagne's empire was split between his three warring grandsons. Charles the Bald gained West Francia (modern France), Louis gained East Francia (modern Germany), and Lothair gained Lotharingia, the central region from the Netherlands to north Italy.

802
Khmer king
Cambodia's Khmer Empire was founded by Jayavarman II, who proclaimed himself "king of the world". He would dominate this part of Southeast Asia for 500 years.

Charlemagne's empire divided into three

850
Gunpowder
The Chinese invented gunpowder, an explosive mix of sulphur, charcoal, and saltpetre. They used it to launch flaming arrows from tubes. Gunpowder did not appear in Europe for another 500 years.

| ▶▶ | 800 | ● | • | 820 | • | 840 | ● | ● | ● | 860 |

---

825 — TEMPLE OF BOROBUDUR

The temple of Borobudur on the Indonesian island of Java is the largest Buddhist monument in the world. It was built around 825 by the Sailendra dynasty, originally from Kalinga in east India. The temple was built in three tiers. Each of the openwork stupas (domed shrines) contains a seated statue of Buddha, and there are 504 Buddha statues in all.

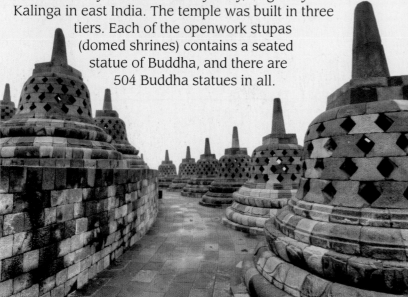

850
Viking raids
Viking longships were raiding right along the Atlantic coast and up rivers to attack towns and monasteries. Viking traders had settled in Dublin, Ireland, and warrior bands began to overwinter in England and France. Over the next two decades Viking raids intensified.

858
Clan Japan
Ruling on behalf of his grandson, the child-emperor Seiwa, Fujiwara Yoshifusa became regent. His Fujiwara clan was now the dominant power in Japan.

The Vikings
See pages 100–101

Viking longship

Brother monks
Cyril and Methodius converted the Slavs of Bulgaria to Christianity. They invented a script to write the Bible in Slavic. It became the Cyrillic script in which all Slavic languages, including Russian, are written today.

 A copy of a Buddhist text known as the *Diamond Sutra*, which dates from 868, is thought to be the oldest surviving printed book in the world.

880 ● ○ **900**

869

The end of Tikál
The last-known building was erected in Tikál. The city was abandoned about 50 years later, bringing an end to the Mayan civilization in lowland Guatemala.

882

Swedish Vikings
Oleg, a Rus chieftain, became ruler of Kiev on the River Dnieper. The Rus were Viking traders from Sweden who travelled down the rivers of Russia to the Black Sea. Some continued to Constantinople, where they served as bodyguards to the Byzantine emperor.

Vikings carrying their boat between Russian rivers

849–899   **ALFRED THE GREAT**

Alfred became king of Wessex, by then the largest of the Anglo-Saxon kingdoms of England, at a time when Danish Vikings looked set to take over. He succeeded in halting their advance by allowing the Danes to settle in north and east England, an area that came to be known as the Danelaw.

"He was warlike beyond measure and victorious in all battles."
The Welsh monk Asser describing Alfred in 893

Wise ruler
Alfred built fortified towns to defend Wessex. Well-educated for the time, he made laws and founded schools.

Legends of Alfred
There are many colourful tales of Alfred. He is said to have spied on the Danes in their camp disguised as a minstrel. Another tells of how he was given shelter by a peasant woman who asked him to watch her cakes cooking and he let them burn.

KEY DATES

871 *Alfred succeeded his brother as king of Wessex.*

877 *The Danes attacked, forcing Alfred into hiding.*

878 *Alfred defeated the Danes at Edington.*

c 888 *Alfred and Guthrum, the Danish leader, divided England between them.*

Gold jewel
The inscription on this tiny gem of crystal and gold, known as the Alfred Jewel, says "Alfred ordered me to be made".

Guthrum
A Danish Viking, Guthrum was the ruler of the Danelaw (eastern England). He fought many battles against King Alfred the Great of Wessex in the 870s.

Eric the Red
An outlaw and a smooth-talker, Eric managed to convince a group of Icelanders to sail to Greenland in 985 and establish a colony there. It thrived for more than 450 years.

Harald Hardrada
Harald III of Norway, known as Harald Hardrada, travelled as a young man to Constantinople. He was killed in 1066, fighting King Harold for the English throne.

Guthrum greeting Harald I of Norway

The Vikings

The Vikings – pagan pirates from Denmark, Norway, and Sweden – burst upon Europe in the 790s, creating terror wherever they went. The Viking Age had dawned. Over the next two centuries, many Vikings settled in the lands they conquered in Britain, Ireland, and France, while some crossed the Atlantic to colonize Iceland and Greenland. Other Viking adventurers travelled down the great rivers of Russia to settle and trade with the Arab and Byzantine empires.

Farmers and raiders
The Vikings were farmers as well as raiders. The women wove woollen cloth and took care of the crops and animals when the men were away.

Men's dress
Viking men wore baggy, woollen trousers and a cloak fixed at the shoulder. They had helmets for battle, but these never had horns.

Women's dress
Viking women wore a linen cap and a long, linen tunic. Over the tunic was a wool pinafore, fastened on each side with a brooch.

Sails were square and made from wool cloth.

Longships
Viking ships were built of overlapping planks of wood, nailed together. They were powered by oars or by the wind. The sails were probably woven from wool.

> **"I have never seen more perfect physical specimens, tall as date palms, blond and ruddy... Each man has an axe, a sword, and a knife, and keeps them by him at all times."**

Ibn Fadlan, a tenth-century Arab traveller, describes Viking traders he met on the River Volga

Steering oar at the back

Key events

793
Vikings unexpectedly attacked a monastery on Lindisfarne, off the northeast coast of England.

841
Vikings from Norway founded a trading settlement on a swampy site in Ireland. It would become the city of Dublin.

Viking longship

862
The city of Novogorod in Russia was founded by Swedish Vikings trading down the rivers of Russia to the Black Sea.

866
Vikings captured the town of York in north England. They named it Jorvik and made it their kingdom's capital.

Fine jewellery
A high-ranking Viking woman would have worn this gold-and-silver brooch, which comes from Gotland, Sweden. Viking craftspeople created beautifully intricate jewellery.

Norse gods
The Vikings were Germanic peoples, and their gods and goddesses had their roots in the mythology of northern Europe.

 Odin The god of war, Odin rode an eight-legged horse, and gathered up the bodies of fallen warriors to carry them to his hall, Valhalla.

 **Thor** The god of the sky and thunder, Thor was armed with a great hammer, *Mjolnir*, for fighting off dragons and demons.

 Baldr The son of Odin and Frigg, Baldr was known as "the beautiful". His blind brother, Hodr, killed him with a mistletoe arrow.

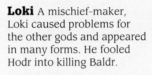 **Loki** A mischief-maker, Loki caused problems for the other gods and appeared in many forms. He fooled Hodr into killing Baldr.

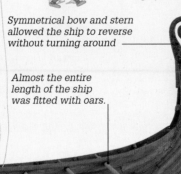 **Heimdall** Possessor of the *Gjallarhorn*, a very loud horn, Heimdall will blow into it to mark the arrival of *Ragnarok*, the final day.

Symmetrical bow and stern allowed the ship to reverse without turning around

Almost the entire length of the ship was fitted with oars.

Remote settlements

Orkney and Shetland Islands
These island groups off the north coast of Scotland were settled by Viking farmers from Norway in the ninth century.

Faroe Islands
Viking settlers reached these North Atlantic islands around 825. They called them *Faereyjar* (Sheep Islands).

Iceland
Settlers arrived in Iceland from Norway around 870. Within 60 years the population had grown to more than 20,000.

Greenland
Icelanders led by Eric the Red settled here in 985. At that time the climate was warm enough to grow crops and raise livestock.

Vinland
Leif Ericson found a land he called Vinland to the west of Greenland. It is thought to have been Newfoundland, Canada.

Reconstructed Viking houses on Newfoundland

Viking games
The Vikings were fond of playing board games such as *Hnefatafl* (king's table), played with pegs or counters. Chess became popular later.

A walrus-ivory chess piece

Viking warriors

885
A large Viking army besieged Paris, France, for several months. Viking attacks weakened the kingdom of the West Franks.

960
King Harald Bluetooth of Denmark was the first of the Scandinavian Vikings to convert to Christianity.

1014
Sweyn Forkbeard, king of Denmark, conquered England. His son Cnut would rule both England and Denmark.

1450
The Viking settlements in Greenland were abandoned about this time, as the climate became harsher and colder.

900 ▶ 1000

The Great Mosque at Cordoba

Coyote head
This magnificent mother-of-pearl headdress is in the form of a Toltec coyote-god. The warlike Toltecs had their capital at Tula in central Mexico, a city they founded around 900.

929
Caliph of Cordoba
Abd al-Rahman III, emir of Cordoba in Spain and descendant of the Umayyads, took the title of caliph. He united all of Al-Andalus (Muslim Spain) under his rule, halted the advance of the Christian kingdoms in the north, and rebuilt much of the Great Mosque at Cordoba.

900 • • ● • **920** • ● ● • **940** •

911
Normandy on the map
Charles III, king of the West Franks, gave Rollo, a Viking leader, land at the mouth of the River Seine on condition he gave up raiding and became a Christian. The area came to be known as Normandy (land of the Norsemen).

The Vikings
See pages 100–101

Stone ancestors
A row of statues with large heads, thought to be ancestor figures, stand guard on Easter Island. Called *moai*, they were erected by Polynesian settlers, who had reached the island by the tenth century.

930
First parliament
Viking settlers in Iceland held their first *Althing* – an outdoor assembly that was open to all free men. The *Althing* is claimed to be the world's oldest parliament.

After 991, the English paid the Danish Vikings to stay away. This annual tribute was known as the Danegeld.

960

Danish convert
Following the conversion of King Harald Bluetooth, Denmark became the first Viking kingdom to adopt Christianity. Harald built roads, bridges, and forts across Denmark.

962

German emperor
Otto I, king of Germany, was crowned emperor in Rome, reviving the idea of a Western Empire that had died with Charlemagne. Otto's empire came to be known as the Holy Roman Empire.

Otto being crowned by the Virgin Mary (in reality, Pope John XII crowned him)

960 • **980** • **1000** ▸▸

985

Going to Greenland
Viking explorer Eric the Red persuaded settlers from Iceland to sail west with him to Greenland. The Viking colony on Greenland survived until around 1450.

988

Baptism of Vladimir
Prince Vladimir of Kiev agreed to adopt the Greek Orthodox faith in return for marrying the sister of the Byzantine emperor, Basil II. His baptism sealed Russian ties with the Byzantine Empire and decided Russia's future religion.

960

China reunited
The 60 years of chaos that had followed the fall of the Tang dynasty finally ended when an army general, Zhao Kuangyin, seized power. He ruled as Taizu, the first emperor of the Song dynasty. The Song capital was at Kaifeng in the north of China.

The golden age of China
See pages 92–93

Vladimir's baptism

Boy monk

With Christian faith the focal point of life during the Middle Ages, many parents were keen for their children to follow a religious calling. Boys were sent to monasteries and girls to convents from a young age. As well as being taught to sing the religious services, they learned to read and write in Latin, the language of the church and government. Later on, monastic schools developed to train boys for public life.

Entering a monastery
Boys entered monasteries from about ten years old. Parents brought their sons, sometimes taking monastic vows on their behalf if the boys were too young to take their own vows. The first vow was obedience to the abbot (head monk). Boys adopted the same clothing as the senior monks – a plain woollen tunic and sandals.

Daily worship
Monasteries followed a strict routine of study, work, and prayer. In between schooling, there was worship. With eight prayer times – beginning at midnight with matins and finishing at 9pm with compline – monastic life was regimented and must have been tiring for youngsters.

Copying manuscripts
As there were no printed works, all books had to be copied by hand. Senior monks helped the young boys in the art of replicating religious texts. Boys spent hours copying the Gospel books, psalms, works of theology, and lives of the saints. It was undertaken as a labour devoted to the service and glory of God.

Apprenticeship to adulthood
After years of study, it was time to decide on the future. Most young men became monks and remained in the monastery. Some went on to careers as officials in the church or clerks in the king's writing office.

Trainee tonsure
Here a young monk is being tonsured – having the top of his head shaved. This ritual showed he had been accepted into the monastic order.

> **❝If the boys commit any fault in the singing, either by sleeping or such-like transgression, let them be stripped and beaten in their shirt only.❞**
>
> Rules of the French medieval monastery, St Benigne of Dijon

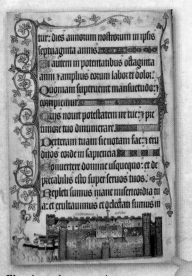

Illuminated manuscripts
Texts were copied onto fine parchment made of calf-, goat-, or sheepskin. In amongst the writing were decorative pictures (illuminations).

Oyster shells used as mixing palettes

> **❝Let the boys be present with praises of the heavenly king and not be digging foxes out of holes or following the fleeting courses of hares. He who does not learn when he is young does not teach when he is old.❞**
>
> Alcuin of York (735–804), writing to the monks of Jarrow, England

Coloured pigment to mix with water to produce ink

Scriptorium scribe
This young monk is carefully copying in the scriptorium ("writing room"). Monks used reed pens and fine brushes to produce their manuscripts.

"From the age of seven I have spent the whole of my life within that monastery devoting all my pains to the study of the scriptures."

The English monk and historian Bede (673–735)

1000 ▶ 1100

 The Anasazi complex of Pueblo Bonito contained more than 650 rooms.

1021
Courtly tale
Princess Murasaki Shikibu wrote *The Tale of Genji*, a story of love and intrigue set in the Heian imperial court. Considered by many to be the world's first full-length novel, it has about 400 characters, including the hero, Prince Genji.

Murasaki Shikibu

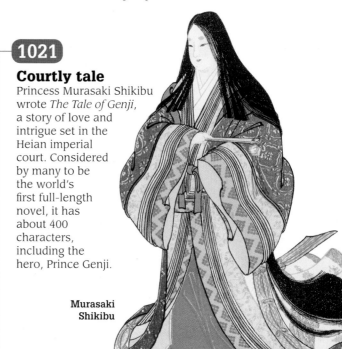

1000
High-rise living
The Anasazi people of New Mexico were living in pueblos (villages), which consisted of apartment-like complexes of multi-roomed dwellings that were sometimes several storeys high. The Anasazi built their houses from adobe (sun-baked mud).

1000 ● · · ● 1020 ● · · · 1040 ● ·

1002
Vinland
Leif Ericson, son of Eric the Red, may have been the first European in America. Sailing west from Greenland, he reached a place thought to be Newfoundland that he called Vinland. The name may have meant "grapevine land" or "pasture land".

Statue of Leif Ericson

1016
Danish rule
Cnut, a Dane, was crowned king of England after defeating King Edmund Ironside. He then secured the throne of Denmark, ruling both countries for the next 20 years.

1044
Burmese kingdom
Prince Anawrahta became king of Pagan, a Buddhist kingdom on the Irrawaddy River in Burma that became very powerful during his reign. He built the Golden Shwezigon Pagoda, said to house Buddha's tooth.

Gold leaf temples and shrines surround the central stupa of the Golden Schwezigon Pagoda.

The Vikings
See pages 100–101

Coronation cloak of the
Norman kings of Sicily

Chinese clock
Su Song, a Chinese
statesman, built a
12-m- (40-ft-) tall
water-powered
clock that kept time
and could be used
to make precise
astronomical
observations.

Modern replica of
Su Song's clock

1053

Normans in Italy
A number of landless knights from
Normandy went to Italy to seek
their fortunes in the 11th century.
One of them, Robert Guiscard,
carved a power base for himself
in southern Italy after winning
the Battle of Civitate against the
Pope. Between 1061 and 1091
the Normans conquered the
Italian island of Sicily.

1071

Turkish victory
The Seljuk Turks inflicted a
crushing defeat on the Byzantine
army at the Battle of Manzikert
before sweeping on to take most
of Anatolia (Turkey), Syria, and
Jerusalem. The Seljuks already
controlled Persia and Iraq.

The Crusades
See pages
110–111

1095

First Crusade
Pope Urban II
called upon the
knights of western
Europe to free
Jerusalem from the
Muslims. Fired by
religious zeal and
the prospect of
booty, thousands
"took the cross".

1060 ● **1080** ● **1100** ▶▶

1066–1087 THE NORMANS CONQUER ENGLAND

In 1066 William, duke of Normandy (in northern
France), conquered England after defeating Harold II.
He imposed Norman rule throughout the country and
gave the land to his leading barons, who built strong
stone castles. The Domesday Book, a list of all the
property in William's new kingdom, was compiled in 1086.

Decisive battle
The Bayeux Tapestry, made around 1080, tells the
story of William's victory at the Battle of Hastings
on 14 October 1066. Harold died on the battlefield.
Here Norman knights attack the king's bodyguard.

Harold II
Harold had become king
on 6 January 1066, after
King Edward the Confessor
died without an heir.

William I
William claimed that Edward
had promised the throne to
him. He became known as
William the Conqueror.

1100►1200

Angkor Wat

Inlaid turquoise

Sicán knife
This 9th–11th-century ceremonial gold knife, known as a *tumi*, was found in the tomb of a Sicán ruler from Peru. *Tumi*s may have been used to cut the throats of sacrificial victims.

1113
Temple mountain
The temple of Angkor Wat in Cambodia was built by the Khmer king Suryavarman II. The largest religious structure in the world, it was designed to resemble the Hindu sacred mountain of Meru.

1127
Southern Song
When nomads overran northern China and seized the Song capital of Kaifeng, a Song prince, Gaozong, escaped. He founded the Southern Song dynasty.

The golden age of China
See pages 92–93

| 1100 | 1120 | 1140 |

1137–1193   SALADIN

Saladin (Salah ad-Din in Arabic) was a great Muslim warrior. He began his career fighting for Nur ad-Din, the ruler of Syria. Having overthrown the Fatimid dynasty, Saladin used Egypt as his power base to attack the crusader kingdom of Jerusalem.

Chivalrous leader
Saladin won fame for being generous to his enemies. When the crusader Richard I of England lost his horse, Saladin sent him another.

KEY DATES

1152 *Saladin joined the service of Nur ad-Din.*

1171 *Saladin overthrew the Fatimids and made himself sultan of Egypt.*

1187 *Saladin recaptured Jerusalem, ending 88 years of crusader rule.*

1192 *Saladin and Richard signed a treaty, reducing the crusader kingdom.*

"His power was manifest, his authority supreme."

Saladin's secretary, Imad al-Din, c 1200

Fall of Jerusalem
In July 1187 Saladin's army defeated the crusaders at the Battle of Hattin, fought in blazing heat. Saladin went on to capture Jerusalem, prompting the Pope to launch the Third Crusade.

1150
Cahokia city
A city at Cahokia in the Mississippi Valley of North America may have held up to 30,000 people. At its heart was a massive earth mound topped by a wooden building, either a temple or a palace. It is one of more than 100 mounds built at Cahokia.

Aibak enters Delhi.

1192
First shogun
Minamoto Yoritomo took the title of shogun ("supreme commander"). He was now undisputed military ruler of Japan and the emperor was reduced to a figurehead.

1175
Muslims in India
Muhammad of Ghur, an emir (prince) from Afghanistan, established a great Muslim empire in northern India. It broke up after his death in 1206, but his general Qutb-al-Din Aibak founded the first sultanate of Delhi.

1160 — **1180** — **1200** ▶▶

1158
Seat of learning
The university of Bologna, Italy, was formally established, though its origins date back to 1088. Paris had a university by 1150 and Oxford by 1167. They developed out of cathedral schools where students would gather at the feet of a teacher.

1170
Unholy murder
Four knights, who claimed to be acting for King Henry II of England, murdered Thomas Becket, the archbishop of Canterbury. Henry was angry with Thomas, his former friend and advisor, for putting the rights of the church above those of the crown. Thomas was made a saint in 1173.

> **"The sword struck… and the crown of the head was separated from the rest."**
>
> *Life of St Thomas* by Edward Grim, 1172

The murder in Canterbury Cathedral

The Crusades

In 1095, after a plea for help from the Byzantine emperor, Pope Urban II called upon the Christian knights of Europe to travel to Jerusalem and recapture it from the Muslims. He believed the Muslims were denying access to Christian pilgrims. The mission was the first of the Crusades – a series of wars fought over the next two centuries between Christians and Muslims for Jerusalem, a sacred place to both religions.

Crusader castles
Crusaders built huge fortresses to house garrisons and also to guard the pilgrim routes. The Krak des Chevaliers ("fortress of the knights") in Syria was a base for up to 2,000 knights, who controlled the surrounding lands and raided Muslim territories.

Fighting monks
Some crusaders were knights who had taken religious vows.

Hospitaller Knights
Also known as the Order of St John of Jerusalem, they formed to care for sick pilgrims but later provided armed escorts.

Templar Knights
The Templars wore a white mantle (cloak) with a red cross in battle. The order grew wealthy as people gave the knights land and money.

Teutonic Knights
After the fall of the crusading kingdoms, this German order of knights began to convert the pagans of the Baltic area.

Clash of cultures
The crusaders called all Muslims "Saracens". The Arabs, who regarded the crusaders as barbarians, called them all *Franj* ("Franks") because so many came from France.

A 14th-century painting of a crusader and a Muslim jousting

Key events

1095
Pope Urban II proclaimed the First Crusade (1095–1099). Crusaders took Jerusalem and established four states in the Middle East: Edessa, Antioch, Jerusalem, and Tripoli.

1144
The crusader state of Edessa in Syria fell to Zengi. The Second Crusade (1145–1149), launched by the French churchman St Bernard of Clairvaux, failed to win back Edessa.

1187
Saladin defeated a crusader army at the Battle of Hattin. In the resulting Third Crusade (1189–1192), the Muslims were victorious.

Saladin

1204
The Fourth Crusade (1202–1204) never reached Jerusalem. The crusaders were diverted to Constantinople, where they sacked the city.

1217
The Fifth Crusade (1217–1221) tried but failed to seize Jerusalem by first conquering the Muslim state of Egypt.

Venice in the 1270s

West meets East
The crusaders learned a lot from Arab culture. They discovered foods such as dates, figs, ginger, and sugar. Venetian and Genoan ships carried pilgrims and soldiers to and from the Middle East, returning laden with cottons, silks, spices, and other exotic goods.

"There was such a slaughter that our men were up to their ankles in the enemy's blood."

A French eyewitness describes the fall of Jerusalem, 1099

Who's who

Peter the Hermit
French monk Peter the Hermit led an army of peasants to Constantinople before the First Crusade. However, they were killed by the Seljuk Turks on arrival in Asia.

Godfrey of Bouillon
A knight of the First Crusade, Godfrey was made the first king of the crusader kingdom of Jerusalem and the surrounding lands.

Zengi
The Turkish governor of northern Syria, Zengi started the Muslim comeback against the crusader states.

King Richard I
This king of England was known as Richard the Lionheart because of his fierce fighting in the Third Crusade.

Saladin
The greatest Muslim military leader of all, Saladin reclaimed Jerusalem in 1187, but ordered his soldiers not to kill, rob, or harm.

Peter the Hermit

Welcome home
Crusaders' wives had to look after their husbands' estates while they were away – and they often proved astute businesswomen. Thousands of men did not return.

Statue of a returning crusader and his wife

1229
Emperor Frederick II regained Jerusalem by making a treaty with the sultan of Egypt during the Sixth Crusade (1228–1229).

1248
Led by Louis IX of France, the Seventh Crusade (1248–1254) targeted Muslim Egypt again, but was another defeat.

1270
Louis IX of France (St Louis) and his son John Tristan died of fever in Tunis, North Africa, during the short-lived Eighth Crusade (1270).

1291
Muslims seized the port of Acre, the last major crusader stronghold in the Middle East. Europeans lost interest and the Crusades ended.

A 19th-century woodblock print showing Taira Tomomori and a drowned retainer (servant) at the bottom of the sea

Samurai battle

On 24 March 1185 two samurai (warrior) clans, the Taira and the Minamoto, fought a naval battle at Dan-no-Oura, on Japan's Inland Sea. The fighting lasted half a day, with fierce hand-to-hand combat. Rather than surrender, Taira Tomomori and other Taira leaders committed suicide by jumping into the sea – to this day, the crabs in the bay are said to hold the spirits of the drowned warriors. The Battle of Dan-no-Oura ended the five-year Genpei War. The victorious clan leader Minamoto Yoritomo took the title of shogun (ruler of Japan) in 1192.

"Then Hoichi [made his lute sound] like the straining of oars and the rushing of ships, the whirr and hissing of arrows, the shouting and trampling of men, the crashing of steel upon helmets."

A minstrel, Hoichi, tells the story of the Battle of Dan-no-Oura in *The Tale of Heike*

1200 ▶ 1300

Pope Innocent III

Mongol warriors
See pages
118–119

1209
War on heretics
Pope Innocent III launched a crusade against the Albigensians – the name given to the Cathars of southern France who held religious views unacceptable to the church. King Philip II of France used the Albigensian Crusade as a way to impose royal authority in the south. Thousands died in the savage persecution that followed.

1206
Mongol warlord
Temujin, a chieftain from the steppes of Mongolia, succeeded in uniting all the Mongol tribes under his command. He took the name of Genghis Khan ("Universal Ruler") before setting out on the first of his campaigns to conquer Asia.

1215
Magna Carta
In England, a barons' revolt forced King John to sign the Great Charter, or Magna Carta. An important document in the history of human rights, the Magna Carta stated that the king was not above the law. Resistance to royal power also led in 1265 to the first English parliament that included commoners as well as nobles.

King John's seal

1200 • • • • ⬤ | 1220 • • • | 1240 •

1204
Crusader rampage
The Fourth Crusade never reached Jerusalem. Short of money, the crusaders diverted to Constantinople, where a claimant to the throne promised to pay them if they helped him take power. They sacked the city and set up a "Latin Empire". The Byzantine Empire never fully recovered.

1212
Spanish reconquest
An army led by the kings of Aragon and Castile defeated a Muslim force at Las Navas de Tolosa. This marked a turning point in the struggle between Muslims and Christians in Spain. By 1248 most of Spain was in Christian hands.

1242
Battle of the Ice
Alexander Nevski, prince of Novgorod in Russia, defeated an army of Teutonic Knights (a German military order). The battle was fought on a frozen lake in what is now Estonia.

The crusaders
attacking Constantinople

The Crusades
See pages
110–111

Rose window
This beautiful rose window of coloured glass, one of three, is from Chartres Cathedral in France. The cathedral, constructed from 1194–1250, was built in the Gothic style that swept through Europe in the 13th century.

The Solomonids ruled Ethiopia for more than 700 years.

A fresco in St Mary's Church, Lalibela, built during Yekuno Amlak's reign

1271
Traveller's tales
Marco Polo, a Venetian merchant, set out on a journey into Asia. He was away for 25 years. On his return he wrote a memoir describing his adventures. His book opened up the unknown world of Asia to Europeans.

"I have not told half of what I saw."

Attributed to Marco Polo

Marco Polo at the court of the Mongol emperor, Kublai Khan

1270
Heirs of Solomon
Yekuno Amlak became emperor of Ethiopia, restoring the Solomonid dynasty of Aksum. The Solomonid kings claimed they were descended from the son of the biblical King Solomon and the Queen of Sheba.

1260 — 1280 — 1300 ▶▶

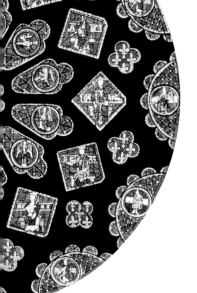

1270–1450   GREAT ZIMBABWE

Great Zimbabwe was the capital of a large empire in southern Africa, which had grown rich through its control of the trade in gold and ivory. The ruler and his entourage lived inside a walled palace called the Great Enclosure with walls up to 11 m (36 ft) high in places. The modern African country of Zimbabwe takes its name from this impressive site.

 The outer wall of the Great Enclosure at Great Zimbabwe contains about 900,000 stone blocks.

Baker boy
Here a master baker demonstrates how to cook bread. Though most apprentices were boys, girls were apprenticed as bakers as well as seamstresses (dressmakers) and cordwainers (shoemakers).

"I place [my son] for the purpose of learning the trade... to live at your house and to do work for you from the feast of Easter next for four continuous years, promising you... that my son does the said work and that he will be faithful and trustworthy."

Apprenticeship agreement made in Marseilles, France, c 1250

Young apprentices

As towns in medieval Europe grew, trades developed to provide goods and services. This resulted in opportunities for children. Many became apprentices, gaining valuable training and experience in a profitable trade from a skilled master for a fixed period of time, usually five to ten years.

Placing a child

Parents were anxious to place children with a good master craftsman. Popular trades included goldsmiths, stonemasons, carpenters, vintners (wine merchants), and apothecaries (chemists). Most children were boys aged from 10 to 15, and their parents paid a fee towards their care. The child was bound by law to work for his master for the apprenticeship.

Guild oaths

Every trade had a guild or association. Guilds controlled standards, set prices, protected their members, and also set the rules of apprenticeship. Apprentices had to take a ceremonial oath. This was a grand occasion, with guild officers dressed in liveries (robes) of velvet and fur. It was a daunting but very special moment for young apprentices.

Apprentice life

Most apprentices formed close bonds with their master and his family. They lived in the master's home, ate with the family, and wore clothes supplied by the master. But they were primarily there to learn. Most of the day was spent in the workshop. Hard graft was expected otherwise the master could release the apprentice and charge his family a fee.

Journeyman

At the end of the training, the apprentice became a journeyman ("day-worker"). He no longer lived in the master's household, and was free to travel around, building contacts and gaining experience. If he saved enough money, he could become a master himself, running his own business.

Workshops
On-the-job training took place in the master's workshop. Here, workers are busy in a goldsmith's workshop in Paris.

> **"And well and truly you shall serve your master for the terms of your apprenticeship. And ye shall be obedient under the wardens and to all the clothing [livery] of the fellowship. "**
>
> Guild oath of apprenticeship

Tools of the trade
Apprentices had to get to grips with the tools suited to their trade. Some were difficult and dangerous to use, but firsthand experience was the best way to gain confidence.

> **"[He] shall instruct and inform... and shall let him out reasonably and shall keep him in food and clothing, in shoes, and all other necessary things as other merchants do... "**
>
> Contract between a fletcher (someone who fits feathers to arrows) and his apprentice

Stonemason's chisel (top) and shoemaker's knife

Dick Whittington
The famous story of Dick Whittington is based on a real man. With no prospects of inheriting land, Richard Whittington (1354–1423) went to London and served an apprenticeship with a mercer (cloth trader). He was so successful that he ended up Lord Mayor of London.

Mongol warriors

In the 13th century, mounted Mongol warriors swept out of the steppes of northeastern Asia to terrorize the surrounding lands. Leading them was Genghis Khan, a soldier of genius who united the warring Mongol tribes and turned them into one of the most formidable fighting machines the world has ever known. It took the Mongols barely 50 years to conquer a vast land empire stretching from the Pacific Ocean to Eastern Europe.

Twin daggers

— *Ivory handle*

Warrior weaponry
Mongol warriors carried a bow and arrows, battle-axe, curved sword, and lance. These finely crafted daggers (above) belonged to an elite warrior.

Siege warfare
Here Genghis Khan lays siege to a Chinese town. The Mongols learned siege warfare from the Chinese. They attacked fortified cities with siege machines and used giant catapults to hurl firebombs, flammable liquids, or dead animals over battlements.

Key events

1206
Courageous leader Temujin was proclaimed Genghis Khan ("Universal Ruler") after uniting the Mongol tribes.

1215
Genghis Khan led an army to besiege and capture the Jin capital of Yanjing (Beijing) in northern China.

Mace used by a warrior of high status

1219
Genghis Khan invaded Persia and overthrew the Kharezmid Empire in a campaign notable for its great savagery.

1241
The Mongols destroyed a Hungarian army at the Battle of Liegnitz (Legnica in modern-day Poland).

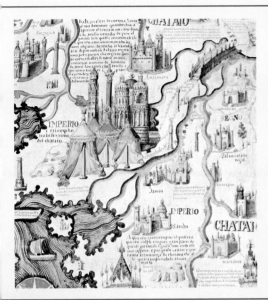

The khanates

On Genghis Khan's death, the empire was divided into khanates (territories) among his sons. The khan (ruler) of each was subject to the Great Khan, but the western khanates soon broke away.

★ **Khanate of Kipchak (Golden Horde) – Russia**

★ **Khanate of Chagatai – Central Asia**

★ **Khanate of Ilkhan – Persia**

★ **Khanate of the Great Khan – Eastern steppes and China**

A map showing the capital of the Great Khan at Dadu (Beijing)

The Great Khans

Ögedai Khan

The third son of Genghis Khan was the second Great Khan of the Mongol Empire, succeeding his famous father. He reigned from 1229 to 1241, and continued the expansion of the empire in the east.

Güyük Khan

Eldest son of Ögedai, Güyük ruled only briefly, from 1246 to 1248. His enthronement at Karakorum in Mongolia angered his cousin Batu, who had conquered Russia and wanted to be elected as Great Khan.

Möngke Khan

Grandson of Genghis, Möngke was the last Great Khan to base his capital at Karakorum. During his reign (1251–1259) he conquered Iraq and Syria.

Kublai Khan

Another grandson of Genghis Khan, Kublai took over in 1260. He expanded the empire in China and founded the Yuan Dynasty there, moving his capital to Dadu (Beijing) in 1271.

Kublai Khan

> ❝ **It is easy to conquer the world from the back of a horse.** ❞
>
> Saying attributed to Genghis Khan

Fearless fighter

Mongol cavalrymen adopted hit-and-run combat tactics, swooping in to fire multiple arrows at the enemy from the safety of the saddle. Another favourite trick was to pretend to retreat and then ambush an opponent in hot pursuit.

Life on the move

The Mongols were nomadic herdsmen and traders, moving from place to place with their herds of horses, camels, sheep, and goats. They lived in *ger*s or yurts, circular felt tents that could be erected and dismantled quickly. Genghis Khan ruled from a *ger* that was 9 m (30 ft) wide and richly hung with silks.

1258

The Mongols killed more than 200,000 prisoners during their siege and capture of the Abbasid capital, Baghdad.

1260

A Mamluk Muslim army defeated the Mongols at the Battle of Ain Jalut in the Jezreel Valley of modern-day Israel.

1271

Kublai Khan proclaimed himself emperor of all of China when he adopted the Chinese dynastic title of Yuan.

1281

Kublai Khan was prevented from invading Japan by a *kamikaze* ("divine wind") that destroyed his fleet.

Mongol bow

1300 ▶ 1400

📢 The Black Death, which originated in China, killed 73 million people in Asia.

1347

The Black Death
An epidemic of bubonic plague raged throughout Europe, killing 45 per cent of the population in four years. Victims suffered terrible swellings and internal bleeding. People thought God had sent the plague as a punishment and did all they could to seek his forgiveness.

A procession of penitents asking for God's forgiveness

1314

Victorious Scots
Robert the Bruce, king of Scotland, defeated the army of King Edward II of England at the Battle of Bannockburn. His victory spelled an end to English attempts to rule Scotland. One story tells how Robert, at an all-time low, took inspiration from a spider. Watching it spin its web, he realized that with perseverance he could succeed, too.

 1300 ● ● ● **1320** ●● ● ● **1340** ●●

1324

Gunfire!
Knowledge of gunpowder had reached Europe from China via the Mongols and Arabs, and cannons were used for the first time in Europe at the Siege of Metz (eastern France today). The coming of gunpowder would change the face of warfare.

1346

Longbow victory
The Hundred Years' War between England and France had broken out in 1337. King Edward III invaded France to pursue his claim to the French throne. He won a great victory at the Battle of Crécy, thanks to the deadly accuracy of the Welsh and English longbows.

1325

Fabled Timbuktu
Mansa Musa I, ruler of the gold-rich Mali Empire of West Africa, made the pilgrimage to Mecca. Under Mansa Musa, the Malian city of Timbuktu became a renowned centre of Islamic scholarship and culture.

Using cannons to attack the city of Afrique, Tunisia in 1390.

Mansa Musa on his throne

1300–1400 AN AGE OF LITERATURE

Literature flourished in 14th-century Europe, especially in Italy. The greatest writer of the age was the poet Dante Alighieri, author of *The Divine Comedy*. Fellow poets Petrarch and Giovanni Boccaccio were also celebrated for their verse. Boccaccio's collection of tales, *The Decameron*, greatly influenced the English poet Geoffrey Chaucer, who wrote *The Canterbury Tales*.

Dante's epic poem
Dante holds a copy of *The Divine Comedy*, which he wrote between 1307 and 1321. The poem describes a visionary journey through hell, purgatory (the "in-between" place where dead sinners try to make amends), and heaven.

"Abandon all hope, you who enter here."

Words written above the gate of hell in Dante's *The Divine Comedy*

Pilgrim stories
In *The Canterbury Tales*, Chaucer related the stories told by a group of pilgrims as he travelled with them to the shrine of Thomas Becket at Canterbury.

1360 · **1380** · **1400** ▶▶

1368

The brilliant Ming
Peasant-born general Zhu Yuanzhang overthrew the unpopular Mongol Yuan dynasty to proclaim himself emperor. He founded the Ming dynasty (1368–1644). Ming means "brilliant" in Chinese.

Palace of the Popes
In 1309 Pope Clement V, a Frenchman, moved the papal court from Rome to Avignon, southern France. Seven popes lived in the Palace of the Popes in Avignon until 1378.

Sultan Murad, who died at the Battle of Kosovo

1389

Battle of Kosovo
The Ottoman Turks defeated the Serbs at the Battle of Kosovo, although Sultan Murad I died in the fighting, as did the Serbian commander Prince Lazar. In less than a century, the Ottomans had expanded out of Anatolia to control most of the Balkans south of the River Danube.

Ottoman Empire See pages 142–143

Trapped in their heavy armour, the French knights flounder in the mud.

Battle of Agincourt

On 25 October 1415, during the Hundred Years' War, an English army led by King Henry V met a much larger French army outside the village of Agincourt in northern France. As the French knights charged, English and Welsh archers rained down arrows on them. The French knights fell on top of each other on the muddy ground and were slaughtered by the English. Following his great victory, Henry went on to conquer Normandy. In 1420 he married Catherine of Valois, the daughter of Charles VI of France, who named Henry as his heir. Henry died in 1422, leaving a baby son. The Hundred Years' War continued for another 20 years.

"The English... throwing down their bows, fought lustily with swords, hatchets, mallets, and bill-hooks, slaying all before them. "

French historian Enguerrand de Monstrelet's *Chronicle*, c 1450

1400 ▶ 1450

Zheng He's fleet contained 250 ships and 28,000 men.

One of Zheng He's ships

1370–1405   TIMUR THE LAME

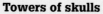

Timur (Tamerlane) was a war leader from Samarkand in central Asia. He spread terror far and wide in a 20-year career that included the conquest of Persia, the near-destruction of the Ottoman Empire, and the massacre of thousands of people in Delhi and Baghdad. He was heading for China when he died in 1405.

Towers of skulls
Timur is said to have made huge pyramids of the skulls of his victims, but despite his reputation for cruelty, he was a devout Muslim. He built many beautiful mosques and other buildings in his capital, Samarkand.

1422
Chinese explorer
Zheng He, a Chinese admiral, brought back giraffes from East Africa as a gift for the Ming emperor. Between 1405 and 1433 he made seven expeditions with his huge fleet of treasure ships and may have visited up to 30 countries.

1400   **1410**   **1420**

1406
The Forbidden City
The Yongle Ming emperor began building the Forbidden City in Beijing, a huge complex of nearly 1,000 buildings to house the imperial court. Enclosed by a moat and a high defensive wall, it was called the "Forbidden City" because only the emperor, his court, and servants were allowed to enter it without permission.

1410
Pitched battle
The Battle of Tannenberg was one of the largest cavalry battles of the Middle Ages. A huge army led by King Ladislaus Jagiello II of Poland and Lithuania defeated the Teutonic Knights, a religious order of knights that controlled the Baltic region.

1415–1453

By 1415 the war that England and France had been fighting on and off since 1337 had all but ceased. Then England's King Henry V decided to start it again. He invaded France and won a spectacular victory at the Battle of Agincourt.

War maker
King Henry V reasserted the English claim to the French crown.

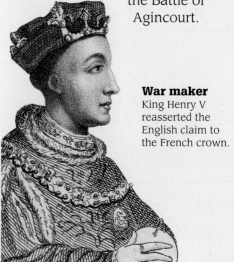

One of the Arrow Towers built at each corner of the Forbidden City

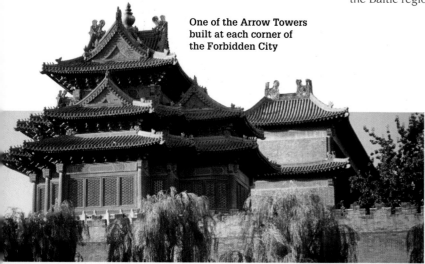

"I have been sent by God and his angels, and I shall drive you from our land of France."

Joan of Arc's challenge to the English

Age of Exploration
See pages 136–137

1431

French heroine
Joan of Arc, a young peasant girl, persuaded the dauphin (son of the French king) to fight back against the English. She was captured and tried for heresy for claiming the saints spoke to her. Found guilty, she was burned at the stake.

Joan in her battle armour

1434

African voyages
Sponsored by Prince Henry the Navigator, who set up a school of navigation, Portuguese sailor Gil Eanes rounded Cape Bojador, a dangerous reef off West Africa that had challenged sailors up till now. The Portuguese developed a sturdy type of vessel, the caravel, for long ocean voyages.

1430 ● ● ○ ● **1440** ○ ● **1450** ▶▶

1438

Inca ruler
High in the Andes of Peru, Pachacutec became ruler of the Incas. He set about creating a great military empire that stretched for 4,000 km (2,500 miles) from Ecuador to central Chile.

1446

Korean alphabet
Hangul, an alphabet with 14 basic consonants and 10 basic vowels, was introduced to Korea on the orders of King Sejong.

THE HUNDRED YEARS' WAR

The end of the war
Here the French army besiege English-held Cherbourg. After Henry V's death in 1422, an English army occupied northern France. Joan of Arc rallied French resistance, and the English were expelled in 1453.

Aztec knife
The warlike Aztecs had risen to power in central Mexico. They cut out the hearts of their sacrificial victims with knives like this one, made from obsidian, a very hard stone.

Aztecs and Incas
See pages 126–127

Aztecs and Incas

The Aztecs and Incas were the last great civilizations of ancient America. Settling in the Valley of Mexico, the Aztecs developed a vast empire by waging war on neighbouring lands. High in the Andes Mountains, the Incas forged their own empire, stretching from Ecuador to Chile. Both peoples were skilled and inventive, and both empires were overthrown by Spanish conquerors in the 1500s.

Tenochtitlán

The Aztec capital Tenochtitlán was built on an island in Lake Texcoco. At its centre was the Great Temple, surrounded by palaces, warrior schools, and shrines. Beyond the city were *chinampas* – little floating farms.

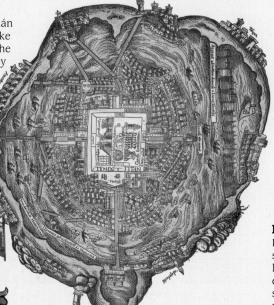

A 16th-century map of Tenochtitlán, which now lies beneath Mexico City

The bloodstained Aztec temple at Tenochtitlán

Sacred sacrifices

Human and animal sacrifice was a religious ritual for both the Aztecs and the Incas. Priests performed sacrificial ceremonies in temples or on mountaintops, during festivals or in times of trouble.

Eagle warrior

For the Aztecs, the eagle symbolized bravery. This life-size sculpture is of an elite eagle warrior. Aztec society depended on brave warriors serving the gods.

> **"We beheld... cities and towns on the water... it was like the things of enchantment."**
>
> Conquistador Bernal Díaz de Castillo describes entering the Aztec capital in 1519

Key events

1325

According to legend, the Aztecs founded Tenochtitlán at the spot where an eagle on a cactus was wrestling a snake in its beak.

1428

The Aztec Empire expanded during the 12-year reign of the fourth emperor, Itzcóatl. His nephew Moctezuma I took power on his death.

Aztec symbol for the Alligator day of the month

1438

Under Pachacutec, the ninth Inca leader of the kingdom of Cusco, the Inca Empire began to expand.

1470

The Inca ruler Tupac Inca Yupanqui conquered the great city-state of Chimú, now Trujillo, Peru.

The Inca Empire

🦙 The Inca Empire was linked by more than 20,000 km (12,500 miles) of road, much of it paved.

🦙 To cross steep mountain gorges, the Incas built suspension bridges of woven reeds.

🦙 Foot runners carried messages from place to place using *quipu* – bundles of dyed and knotted wool and cotton threads. The lengths of thread and the positions of the knots were used to record and pass on information.

🦙 The Incas did not have wheeled transport. They moved heavy goods on the backs of llamas and alpacas.

🦙 The Incas built rest houses at regular intervals, where travellers could spend the night and cook a meal.

Inca gold
Andean peoples were skilled metalworkers. They prized gold most, believing it to be the sweat of the gods. This golden mummy mask was made by a Chimú craftsman. After the fall of the Chimú Empire, the Incas took Chimú metalworkers back to their capital, Cusco.

Farming and food
Many foods enjoyed all over the world today were first cultivated by the ancestors of the Aztecs and the Incas in Central and South America:

★ **Corn (maize)**
★ **Potatoes**
★ **Tomatoes**
★ **Quinoa (a grain)**
★ **Cocoa / chocolate**
★ **Squashes**
★ **Chillies**

Ball games
Religion influenced every area of Aztec life, even sport. The Aztecs played a ball game in which the court symbolized the world and the ball was the Sun and Moon. Players hit the ball with their hips. Bets were placed on the game and some losing teams might have been sacrificed.

Inca ruins at Machu Picchu, Peru

1502

Moctezuma II, the last ruler of the Aztecs, began his reign. At this time, the Aztec Empire was at its most powerful.

Aztec symbol for the Rain day of the month

1519

Led by Hernán Cortés, the Spanish army landed on the east coast of Mexico. It defeated the Aztecs two years later.

1525

Civil war broke out for five years as brothers Huáscar and Atahualpa fought for the Inca Empire, which was left weakened.

1532

Spanish conquistador Francisco Pizarro invaded Peru with an army of 180 men. He captured and killed the Inca emperor, Atahualpa.

1450–1750
Exploring and reforming

From 1450 to 1750 the world became a smaller place as explorers opened up sea routes and mapped new lands. Wealth from the New World, coupled with the profitable trade in spices, made Europeans rich, but religious upheaval divided the continent. As empires grew, so did the conflicts between them. Powerful Muslim states emerged in Asia, but China remained the world's largest empire. The dawning of the Renaissance period in Europe brought education and art to the fore as established ideas were challenged.

1450 ▶ 1475

Constantinople falls to Mehmed II.

Ottoman Empire
See pages 142–143

1453
Fall of Constantinople
The 1,000-year-old Byzantine Empire, the Christian empire first established by the Romans, ended when the cannons of Sultan Mehmed II, the Ottoman ruler, blasted through the walls of the capital, Constantinople.

1456
Prince Dracula
Vlad III, known to history as "the Impaler", became prince of Wallachia (part of modern-day Romania). He owed his nickname to his habit of impaling his enemies on sharpened stakes – the origin of the legend of Dracula.

1450 • • • **1455** • **1460** • •

1450
City of Victory
Vijayanagara ("city of victory") was the capital of a Hindu kingdom that ruled all of south India. Its population of around 500,000 was double that of any European city at the time. A Persian visitor wrote "it had no equal in the world".

Virupaksha Temple, in the city of Vijayanagara, was dedicated to the Hindu god Shiva.

1455   THE PRINTING PRESS

German inventor Johannes Gutenberg printed the first book in Europe in 1455 on a press using moveable type (metal letters that could be used again and again). His invention opened up the world of learning as more people than ever before had access to books, many of them in local languages, as well as Latin and Greek.

Demonstrating the press
Although Gutenberg (above) was the first European to use moveable type, the Chinese had invented a similar process in the 11th century.

The Bible
The first book produced by Gutenberg was a Latin translation of the Bible. About 185 copies were printed. Before printing, books were copied by hand, which was costly and time-consuming.

1469 UNITED SPAIN

In 1469, Isabella, heir to the kingdom of Castile, married Ferdinand, heir to the kingdom of Aragon. They would rule their Spanish kingdoms as joint monarchs, bringing stability to both after years of civil war. Isabella died in 1504 and Ferdinand in 1516. Their marriage led to a united Spain from 1516 onwards.

Catholic monarchs
Both Isabella and Ferdinand were very devout Christians. The Pope gave Isabella and Ferdinand the title of "The Catholic Monarchs" in 1496.

Spanish kingdoms
Castile was the larger of the two realms, but Aragon had an extensive overseas empire. Their joint armies would take Granada, the last Muslim state, in 1492, and fully conquer Navarre in 1515.

NAVARRE · FRANCE · ARAGON · PORTUGAL · CASTILE · GRANADA

The long grip allowed the sword to be held by both hands.

Samurai sword
This Japanese *katana* sword dates from the 15th century. It is typical of those used in the 11-year Onin War, a dispute that began in 1467 over who would succeed Ashikaga Yoshimasa as shogun (military leader) of Japan.

The scabbard was worn outside the samurai's armour.

The blade was usually about 70 cm (27.5 in) long.

1465 · **1470** · **1475** ▶▶

1465 — African empire
Sunni Ali, ruler of Songhai in west Africa, set about creating the largest empire that Africa had ever seen. He raided deep into Mali and captured the city of Timbuktu to take control of trans-Saharan trade in gold and salt.

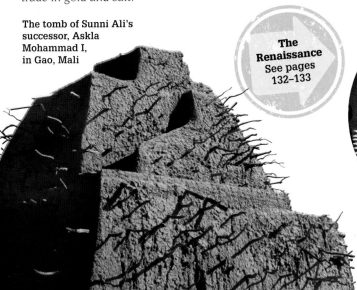

The tomb of Sunni Ali's successor, Askla Mohammad I, in Gao, Mali

1469 — Wealthy patron
Lorenzo de' Medici, known as the Magnificent, took charge of the Italian city of Florence. He used his vast wealth, gained through the Medici family's control of banking, to make Florence the undisputed capital of the Renaissance world.

The Renaissance See pages 132–133

1471 — Conquering Inca
Tupac Yupanqui became the tenth ruler of the Inca Empire. He conquered the Peruvian kingdom of Chimor, the largest remaining rival to Inca power, and deported its gold workers to the Inca capital of Cuzco.

Aztecs and Incas See pages 126–127

The Renaissance

In the early 1400s, artists and architects in Italy began working in styles that were inspired by those of the ancient Greeks and Romans. They were part of a cultural movement called the Renaissance, meaning "rebirth", that was influenced by the rediscovery of classical culture, and which sparked a new interest in politics, philosophy, and science.

Art out of stone

This masterpiece of sculpture, the *Pietà*, shows the body of Jesus being cradled by Mary, his mother. The sculptor, Michelangelo Buonarroti, once said that every block of stone has a statue in it, and it is the sculptor's task to discover it. Michelangelo designed much of St Peter's Basilica in Rome, where this statue stands today.

Michelangelo's *Pietà*

> **"The artist sees what others only catch a glimpse of."**
>
> Leonardo da Vinci

A page from one of da Vinci's notebooks

Renaissance man

Leonardo da Vinci, the most famous artist of the Renaissance, drew this self-portrait when he was about 60. He was also an inventor, scientist, and engineer. His notebooks – more than 13,000 pages in total – are full of studies of the human body and ideas for inventions. He wrote his most personal notes in mirror writing – reversed writing that appears the right way round when reflected in a mirror.

Key events

1415

Architect Filippo Brunelleschi discovered that drawing lines coming together at a single point (converging) creates linear perspective, making things look as if they are far away.

1486

Florentine artist Sandro Botticelli painted *The Birth of Venus* as a commission for the Medici family.

1498

Leonardo da Vinci painted the mural of *The Last Supper* for a convent in Milan.

1503

On becoming Pope, Julius II attracted artists like Michelangelo and Raphael to Rome.

Pope Julius II

Renaissance gallery

Cosimo de' Medici
Founder of the powerful Medici dynasty in Florence, Cosimo was a key figure in the early Renaissance through his support of artists such as Fra Angelico and Donatello.

Desiderius Erasmus
A Dutchman, Erasmus was an influential scholar and writer. His critical studies of Greek and Roman writers inspired the revival of learning in northern Europe.

Niccolò Machiavelli
The name of this Florentine diplomat has become a word, "machiavellian", to describe ruthless political cunning because of his book *The Prince*, a guide for Renaissance rulers.

Northern Renaissance
The Renaissance also flourished in northern Europe, and particularly the wealthy, wool-trading regions of Flanders and the Low Countries. *The Arnolfini Wedding* (above) by Belgian artist Jan van Eyck is a classic painting of the Northern Renaissance.

Archictectural revolution

The dome of the Florence Cathedral, designed by Filippo Brunelleschi and completed in 1436, dominates the city. Brunelleschi made use of various techniques, including a special pattern of bricks that spread the weight, to make the first self-supported dome built in western Europe since Roman times. It is a triumph of Renaissance engineering and remains the largest brick dome in the world.

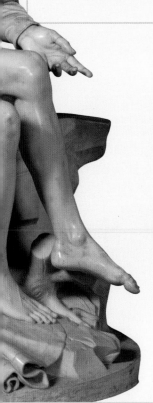

1504
Michelangelo's statue, *David*, was put on display outside the Palazzo Vecchio in Florence.

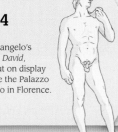

Michelangelo's *David*

1506
Leonardo da Vinci completed his most famous painting the *Mona Lisa*.

1509
The scholar Erasmus published *In Praise of Folly*, a work of satire that was his best-known book.

1543
Doctor Andreas Vesalius published the first textbook of the human body, a major work of human anatomy and scientific investigation.

1475 ▶ 1500

1480
Rise of Russia
Ivan III, Grand Duke of Muscovy, refused to pay the annual tribute demanded by the Khan of the Golden Horde – the descendants of the Mongols. His actions laid the foundations of the Russian state.

The furious Khan is dragged away as Ivan III tears up his demand.

1477
Land grab
The French crown seized hold of the duchy of Burgundy on the death of its last duke, Charles the Bold. Burgundy's rich possessions (modern-day Belgium and the Netherlands) passed by marriage to the Habsburg rulers of Austria.

> **"A horse, a horse, my kingdom for a horse."**
>
> **Richard III's dying words, according to Shakespeare**

1485
Tudors on top
Henry Tudor defeated and killed King Richard III of England to become King Henry VII, the first monarch of the Tudor dynasty. His victory marked the end of the War of the Roses, fought between rival groups of English nobles.

1475	1480	1485

1478–1492   CATHOLIC SPAIN

Ferdinand and Isabella set about unifying Spain by strengthening the power and position of the Catholic Church. In 1478, they introduced the Inquisition to root out heresy (ideas contrary to the Catholic faith). In 1492, their armies conquered Granada, the last Muslim kingdom in Spain. That same year, they ordered all Jews who refused to convert to Catholicism to leave Spain forever.

Burning of books
Tomás de Torquemada (right) was the infamous head of the Inquisition. He ordered the burning of books considered to be heretical, including the Jewish Talmud (sacred writings) and thousands of Arabic manuscripts.

The Inquisition
The Inquisition was a royal court tasked with discovering heretics, particularly Jews and Muslims who falsely claimed to be Christian *conversos* (converts). It relied on informers and used torture (such as the one above) to extract confessions.

BIRTH OF THE SIKH RELIGION

Guru Nanak (1469–1539), born in modern-day Pakistan, founded the Sikh religion after meeting and debating with religious leaders in India, Tibet, and Arabia. Sikhs believe in one God, and their religion blends elements of Hinduism and Islam.

Holy teachers
Sikhs believe Guru Nanak (right) was the first of eleven gurus, or teachers. The eleventh is the Sikh scriptures, known as Guru Granth Sahib, which were completed in 1604.

Black pepper was abundant in south India.

Nutmeg was traded in Indonesia.

Cloves came from Indonesia.

Golden Temple
The holy scriptures are housed in the Harmandir Sahib, more popularly known as the Golden Temple (left). It is the Sikhs' holy temple at Amritsar in the Indian state of Punjab.

1498
Spice route
Portuguese navigator Vasco da Gama used the winds of the south Atlantic Ocean to aid his journey from Europe into the Indian Ocean, and on to the riches and spices of Asia – the goal of European explorers.

1490 ● **1495** ● ● **1500** ▶▶

1492
Atlantic crossing
Christopher Columbus sailed west from Spain across the Atlantic, looking for a route to Asia. Instead, he landed in the Bahamas, a place he named San Salvador.

1494
Treaty of Tordesillas
Pope Alexander VI signed the Treaty of Tordesillas, which drew an imaginary line down the middle of the Atlantic Ocean and over modern-day Brazil. Land already or yet to be discovered to the west of the line belonged to Spain, and land to the east of it to Portugal.

1497
Religious tyrant
Italian monk Girolamo Savonarola thought the citizens of Florence had grown greedy and sinful. To seek God's forgiveness, he persuaded them to make a great pile of all their valuables in the city's main square and set fire to them – the event came to be known as the "Bonfire of the Vanities".

📢 **Columbus made 4 voyages to the Americas between 1492 and 1503**

1368–1644 THE GREAT WALL OF CHINA

The Great Wall of China, begun in 221 BCE, took on its present form under the Ming emperors, who ruled China from 1368 to 1644. They repaired and extended the fortifications to protect their northern border.

Age of Exploration

The European Age of Exploration began when Portuguese sailors started venturing out into the Atlantic and down the coast of Africa in the early 1400s, searching for a direct sea route to Asia – the source of spices and precious stones. Christopher Columbus was also looking for Asia when he sailed west across the Atlantic in 1492 and accidentally discovered the Americas, opening up new prospects for conquest, trade, and colonization.

Great explorers

Henry the Navigator
This royal prince spurred the discoveries by sending Portuguese ships to explore Africa's west coast.

Christopher Columbus
Although born in Italy, Columbus explored for Spain. He made four voyages to the Americas from 1492 to 1504.

Ferdinand Magellan
This Portuguese captain sailed from the Atlantic into the Pacific but died before completing the voyage around the world.

Jacques Cartier
This French navigator explored the St Lawrence River in Canada and claimed the country for France.

> **"I and my companions suffer from a disease of the heart which can be cured only by gold."**
>
> Hernán Cortés, 1519

Seeing the world

This map shows the sea routes taken by some of the early pioneers of exploration.

Christopher Columbus
Reached the Bahamas on the first of four expeditions.

Vasco da Gama
Da Gama was the first to round Africa en route to India.

John Cabot
Crossed the North Atlantic from Bristol, England, to Newfoundland.

Pedro Alvares Cabral
Discovered Brazil on his way to India and claimed it for Portugal.

Ferdinand Magellan and Juan del Cano
Magellan's circumnavigation was completed by Juan del Cano.

Jacques Cartier
Discovered the Gulf of St Lawrence on his first expedition.

The conquistadors
In the 50 years after Columbus's discovery of America, Spanish conquistadors (soldiers and adventurers) destroyed the civilizations of ancient America in their quest for gold and mission to make Christian converts. Seen here is Spanish conquistador Hernán Cortés greeting Moctezuma II, the Aztec ruler of Mexico whose lands he would seize and conquer.

Key events

1488
Portuguese navigator Bartolomeu Dias rounded the Cape of Good Hope in southern Africa into the Indian Ocean.

1492
Christopher Columbus sailed west from Spain and discovered the Americas.

One of Columbus's ships

1498
Vasco da Gama crossed the Indian Ocean to Calicut on the Malibar coast of India.

1500
Pedro Alvares Cabral discovered Brazil while sailing to India.

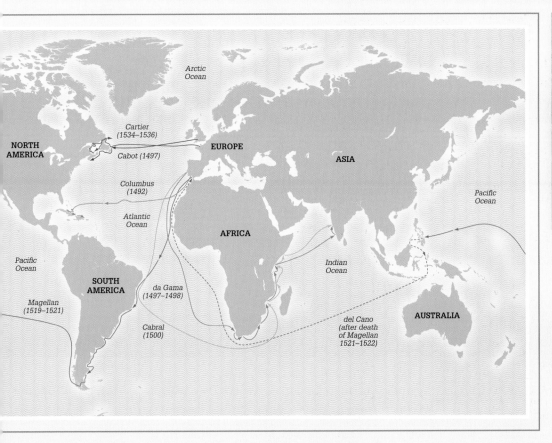

NORTH AMERICA

EUROPE

ASIA

Arctic Ocean

Cartier (1534–1536)

Cabot (1497)

Columbus (1492)

Atlantic Ocean

AFRICA

Pacific Ocean

Pacific Ocean

SOUTH AMERICA

da Gama (1497–1498)

Indian Ocean

Magellan (1519–1521)

Cabral (1500)

del Cano (after death of Magellan 1521–1522)

AUSTRALIA

Amerigo's land

The Italian navigator Amerigo Vespucci was Chief Royal Pilot of Spain. This meant all sea captains in Spanish service had to report to him with details of their journeys. Vespucci used the information to create maps of the New World and so sailors referred to the territory as "Amerigo's land", or America.

Give and take

The meeting between the Old World of Europe and the New World of the Americas changed both, with good and bad effects.

Taken to the New World

★ **Diseases** Smallpox, influenza, measles, chickenpox, typhus.

★ **African slaves** Up to 12 million slaves transported between 1500 and 1880.

★ **Technology** Wheeled transportation, weapons and tools of iron and steel, guns.

★ **Languages and religion** Spanish, Portuguese, French, and English; Christianity.

★ **Animals** Horses, cattle, sheep, pigs, chickens, brown rats.

★ **Food** Sugarcane, yams, bananas, and rice, wheat, oats, barley, onions.

Taken from the New World

★ **Gold and silver** Shipped back in vast quantities.

★ **Food** Maize, potatoes, sweet potatoes, squash, tomatoes, sweet and chilli peppers, pineapples, peanuts, chocolate.

★ **Animals** Turkeys, guinea pigs, Muscovy ducks.

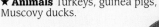

1507

The name America appeared for the first time on a world map made by German mapmaker Martin Waldseemüller.

1512

The Portuguese reached the Spice Islands (present-day Maluku Islands) of Indonesia.

1522

Magellan rounded Cape Horn to enter the Pacific Ocean from the Atlantic.

1535

Jacques Cartier sailed down the St Lawrence River as far as present-day Montreal.

1580

Francis Drake completed his three-year circumnavigation of the world.

1500 ▶ 1525

1500

Brazil on the map

Pedro Alvares Cabral, a Portuguese navigator, discovered the coast of Brazil by accident on his way to India. Sailing down the coast of Africa, he ventured out into the Atlantic to take advantage of favourable winds. Striking land, he claimed it for Portugal.

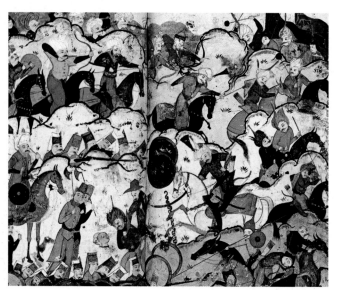

Cabral landing at Brazil's Bay of Porto Jeguro

The ceiling of the Sistine Chapel

The Renaissance
See pages 132–133

1508

Sistine Chapel

Italian artist Michelangelo began work on painting the ceiling of the Sistine Chapel in Rome (above) for Pope Julius II. It took him four years to complete the masterpiece of Renaissance art, which included more than 400 life-size figures.

1500 ● **1505** **1510**

1501

Rise of the Safavids

In Iran, Ismail I proclaimed himself Shah (king) and went on to conquer Iraq until halted by the Ottomans at the battle of Chaldiran in 1514. The Safavid dynasty he founded ruled Iran until 1722.

Ottoman and Safavid forces clash at Chaldiran.

1517–1529   THE REFORMATION

The Reformation was a religious revolt against the Catholic Church. It began in Germany when Martin Luther, a monk and university professor, demanded an end to corruption in the Church. As his ideas for reform spread, they were met with growing hostility from the Pope and the Holy Roman Emperor Charles V, a staunch Catholic. It led to a violent and lasting split in European Christianity between Protestants and Roman Catholics.

Public protest
In 1517, Luther nailed 95 Theses (statements) protesting against the Church to the door of a church in Wittenberg. In 1521, he appeared before Charles V at an imperial court (the Diet of Worms) and was found guilty of heresy, and excommunicated from the Church.

1519–1522   SAILING ROUND THE WORLD

In 1519, Ferdinand Magellan, a Portuguese captain sailing under the Spanish flag, set off to find a route to the Spice Islands in the Pacific by heading west. In November 1520, he sailed around the tip of South America and entered the Pacific Ocean.

Seaworthy ships
Magellan had a crew of 270. His flagship, the *Trinidad*, was a sturdily built caravel. The other four ships were large merchant ships, called carracks, which had space to carry provisions for a long voyage.

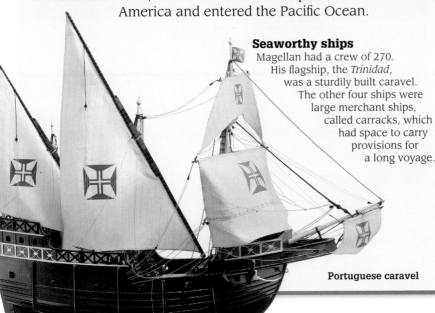

Portuguese caravel

Magellan's death
In April 1521, Magellan was killed in a fight with islanders in the Philippines. Sixteen months later, just one of his ships made it back to Spain. The 18 survivors on board had sailed right around the world.

1515   •   **1520**   **1525** ▸▸

1519
Holy Roman Emperor
On the death of his grandfather, Charles I of Spain was elected Holy Roman Emperor – ruler of an empire of states centred around modern-day Germany. He was just 19, and took the name Charles V.

1519
Spanish conquest
Hernán Cortés, a Spanish soldier, landed in Mexico with 600 men. They were welcomed into the capital Tenochtitlán, by the Aztec ruler Moctezuma II, but Cortés took him prisoner and in 1522 destroyed the city.

Moctezuma's feather headdress

Bible study
After the Diet of Worms, Luther went into hiding. He lived in secret for a year in the castle of Wartburg. Here he brought the Bible to many by translating the New Testament into German.

Luther's room in Wartburg castle

Reformation spreads
As the Reformation spread through northern Europe, it moved in new directions. Ulrich Zwingli (right) was an influential Swiss reformer who shared most, but not all, of Luther's beliefs. Zwingli was killed in battle by Swiss Catholics in 1531.

1525 ▶ 1550

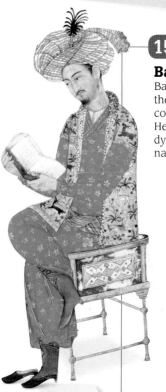

1526
Babur the Tiger
Babur, who claimed descent from the Mongol warlord Genghis Khan, conquered most of northern India. He was the founder of the Mughal dynasty of Indian emperors. His name means "tiger" in Arabic.

1527
The sack of Rome
The troops of the Holy Roman Emperor, Charles V, had not been paid for months. They went on the rampage in Rome, plundering its palaces and churches. The Pope was forced to flee the Vatican down a secret passage.

A Spanish army of 188 men led by Francisco Pizarro landed in Peru in 1532. It took them less than a year to conquer the Inca Empire of 5 million people. Stone weapons and padded cotton armour used by the Inca were no match for European guns and steel swords.

Francisco Pizarro
Spanish conquistador (soldier) Francisco Pizarro first set out find the Inca civilization in 1524. Afterwards, he returned to Spain to win the king's agreement to back a military expedition to Peru.

Spanish treachery
In 1533, Pizarro imprisoned Atahualpa, the last Inca king. Pizarro agreed to spare Atahualpa's life in return for a roomful of fabulous gold items, but he had the Incan king put to death before most of it had been paid.

Incan gold figurine

1525   **1530**   **1535**

1526
Victorious Suleiman
Suleiman the Magnificent, the greatest of the Sultans, extended Ottoman power deep into Europe when he defeated the king of Hungary at the Battle of Mohacs (below) and overran most of the country.

Ottoman Empire
See pages 142–143

1534
Royal divorce
The marriage of English king Henry VIII to Catherine of Aragon had produced no male heir. The king asked the Pope to grant him a divorce so he could marry Anne Boleyn, but the Pope refused. Henry broke with the Catholic Church and made himself head of the Church of England. He married Anne but later had her beheaded. He would go on to have four more wives.

Henry VIII and his six wives

Inca stronghold
About 1450, the Incas built the city of Machu Picchu, high on a ridge in the Andes. The site was so remote that it escaped discovery by the Spanish during their conquest of Peru.

Ottoman forces defeat the Hungarian army at the Battle of Mohacs.

Copernicus's view of the Earth's orbit, with the Sun at the centre

1545

Silver mountain

The Spanish discovered the world's biggest single source of silver at Potosí in present-day Bolivia. The huge quantities of silver shipped back from the New World paid for Spain's wars in Europe.

1545

Counter Reformation

Pope Paul III summoned the Council of Trent to discuss ways of challenging the Protestant Reformation. It met 25 times between 1545 and 1563, and launched the Counter Reformation, a movement to bring people back to the Catholic faith.

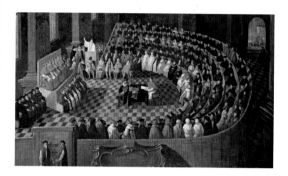

1543

Sun and Earth

Polish astronomer Nicholas Copernicus published a book that showed that the Earth and other planets orbit the Sun. This was against the Church's teaching that the Earth lay at the centre of the Universe. Copernicus's ideas began a revolution in the sciences.

1540   **1545**   **1550** ▶▶

1530–1584   IVAN IV

In 1547, Ivan IV, then a boy of 16, was crowned "Tsar of all the Russias". He was the first Russian ruler to use this title. The early part of his reign saw expansion and legal reform in Russia. But after the death of his wife in 1560, his character changed and he became suspicious and violent. He is known to history as Ivan the Terrible.

Reign of terror

The later years of Ivan IV's reign were marked by war, terror, and famine. He became convinced that the nobility were plotting against him, and created a private army, who became known as Ivan's dogs, to terrorize them.

St Basil's Cathedral

Moscow's most famous landmark, St Basil's Cathedral (above), was begun by Ivan IV in 1552 to commemorate his victory over the state of Kazan.

Ottoman Empire

The Ottoman dynasty took its name from Osman, a Turkish *ghazi* (Islamic warrior), who founded a small state in Anatolia (modern-day Turkey) in about 1300. In the 14th century, the Ottomans started to invade Europe. With the capture of Constantinople in 1453, the Ottoman state became an empire. Although the empire was at its peak in the 16th century, almost reaching Vienna in Austria in 1529, the Ottomans ruled until 1922.

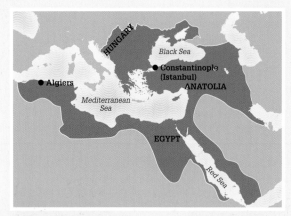

World conquerors

The Ottoman Empire was at its height in the 16th century, when it stretched from Hungary to the Arabian Gulf, and from the Crimea to Algiers. Its navy dominated the Black Sea, the eastern Mediterranean, and the Red Sea. Its continual drive for conquest threatened not only Eastern Europe but also the Safavid Empire, the rulers of Iran and their rivals for power in the Middle East.

Received at court

This painting by Italian artist Gentile Bellini shows Venetian ambassadors being received at the gates of the Ottoman court in Damascus, Syria. Bellini spent two years in Constantinople (since renamed Istanbul) as a cultural ambassador and visiting painter at the invitation of Sultan Mehmed II, who allowed Jews and Christians to settle in the city.

Key events

1300

Osman I, founder of the Ottoman dynasty, established a small independent state in Anatolia (Turkey) on the frontier of the Byzantine Empire – the eastern remnant of the Roman Empire.

1366

The Ottoman capital was established at Edirne in Europe, which was the former Byzantine city of Adrianople.

Selimiye Mosque in Edirne

1389

The Ottoman defeat of the Serbs at the Battle of Kosovo removed a major barrier to Ottoman expansion in the Balkans, and helped them reduce the Byzantine Empire to an area around Constantinople.

1453

Mehmed II conquered Constantinople (modern-day Istanbul) after a three-month siege, spelling the end of the Byzantine Empire.

Powerful sultans

Mehmed II "the Conqueror" (1444–1446 and 1451–1481)
A great military leader, Mehmed led more than 25 campaigns to conquer Constantinople, Greece, Albania, and the lands around the Black Sea.

Selim I "the Grim" (1512–1520)
Selim murdered all his male relatives to make sure he got the throne. He extended the empire into the Middle East and was made Caliph (ruler of Islam) in 1517.

Suleiman I "the Magnificent" (1520–1566)
The empire reached its fullest extent during Suleiman's reign. He spoke five languages, wrote poetry, and presided over the golden age of Ottoman culture.

> **"I who am the sultan of sultans, the sovereign of sovereigns, the shadow of God on Earth, sultan and emperor of the White Sea [Mediterranean] and the Black Sea..."**
>
> Sultan Suleiman I addresses King Francis I of France, 1526

Ottoman pottery
The arts flourished under the Ottomans. Iznik pottery, named after the town in western Anatolia where it was made, was decorated with arabesques (intertwined flowing lines) and stylized flowers in blues, greens, and reds. Huge quantities of tiles were produced to adorn the walls of the sultans' palaces and mosques.

Domes and minarets
The Blue Mosque in Istanbul, completed in 1616, is named for the blue Iznik tiles that decorate its interior. The dome imitates the great Byzantine church of Hagia Sophia (Holy Wisdom), built in 537 and turned into a mosque by Mehmed II, but its six minarets (slender towers) are Ottoman in style.

1514
Selim I defeated a Safavid army at the Battle of Chaldiran in northern Iran and went on to take control of the Middle East.

1529
In a show of might, Suleiman I led a huge army to besiege the Austrian capital of Vienna, but withdrew after a month.

1538
Under the command of Admiral Barbarossa, a former pirate of Greek origin, the Ottoman navy controlled the Mediterranean.

Admiral Barbarossa

1566
Suleiman I died in his tent at the age of 76 while leading a military campaign in Hungary. The Ottomans would progress no further into Europe.

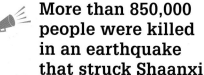

More than 850,000 people were killed in an earthquake that struck Shaanxi province in northwest China on 23 January 1555.

Fossil study
In 1565, Swiss naturalist Conrad Gessner published a book called, *"On things dug up from the Earth"*. The book included the first descriptions of fossils, such as ammonites (left), although he was not sure exactly what they were.

1558
Queen of England
Elizabeth I became queen on the death of her half-sister, Mary I, who was a devout Catholic. Elizabeth restored the Protestant faith to England. To preserve her independence, she refused to marry and deliberately created a powerful image of monarchy.

1555
Peace of Augsburg
An agreement was reached between the Catholic and Protestant princes of Germany that the ruler of each state could decide the religion of his subjects. Charles V, the Holy Roman Emperor, refused to attend the negotiations and handed control of the empire to his brother Ferdinand.

1550 | **1555** | **1560**

1542–1605   AKBAR THE GREAT

The grandson of Babur, Akbar was the third Mughal emperor of India. He succeeded his father Humayun – who had failed to preserve Babur's conquests – in 1556 at the age of 13. During his 50-year reign, Akbar created a mighty empire that stretched right across northern India.

Tolerant ruler
Akbar was a Muslim, but he allowed his Hindu subjects to worship freely and encouraged debates with members of other religions, including Hindus, Zoroastrians (the religion of Persia), and Christians.

Tiger hunt
This miniature painting shows Akbar on a tiger hunt – one of the favourite pastimes of the Mughal emperors. Akbar was a great patron of the arts, especially miniature painting, which flourished at the Mughal court.

1566 DUTCH REVOLT

Philip II of Spain was also the ruler of the Netherlands. When Dutch Calvinists (followers of French Protestant John Calvin) began sacking Catholic churches, he sent Spanish troops to restore order. Their brutality sparked a major Dutch revolt.

Dutch independence
By 1572, the rebellion had turned to open warfare, with William the Silent leading the Dutch resistance. Spain eventually recognized Dutch independence in 1648.

Catholic monarch
Philip II saw it as his divine mission to root out heresy, but his harsh policies and high taxes alienated his Dutch subjects. Wars had sapped Spain's economy, while the Dutch had become rich as a result of their Asian trade.

1572
Massacre in Paris
On 24 August, St Bartholomew's Day, 3,000 Huguenots (French Protestants) were massacred in the streets of Paris on the orders of King Charles IX and his mother, Catherine de' Medici. Thousands more were killed elsewhere in France.

St Bartholomew's Day massacre, Paris

1565   **1570**   **1575**

1568
Japanese overlord
Oda Nobunaga, leader of the Oda clan, seized the imperial capital of Kyoto and set about uniting Japan under his rule. His army was equipped with muskets, introduced into Japan by the Portuguese.

1570
Maps galore
Abraham Ortelius, a mapmaker from Antwerp in modern-day Belgium, published the first modern atlas, called the *Theatre of the World*. It contained 70 maps and was an instant success.

1571
Battle of Lepanto
A Christian fleet under the command of Don John of Austria defeated an Ottoman fleet at Lepanto off the west coast of Greece in the last major naval battle fought between galleys. The victory prevented the Ottomans from taking control of the Mediterranean Sea.

Oda Nobunaga

"Without destruction, there is no creation... there is no change."

Oda Nobunaga

The Battle of Lepanto

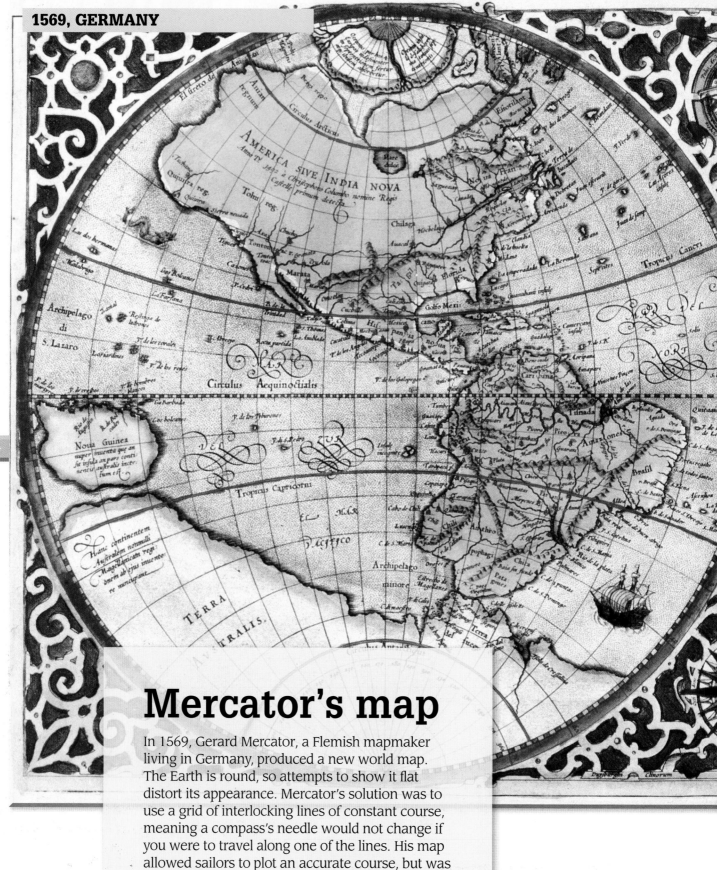

Mercator's map

In 1569, Gerard Mercator, a Flemish mapmaker living in Germany, produced a new world map. The Earth is round, so attempts to show it flat distort its appearance. Mercator's solution was to use a grid of interlocking lines of constant course, meaning a compass's needle would not change if you were to travel along one of the lines. His map allowed sailors to plot an accurate course, but was not commonly used for many years.

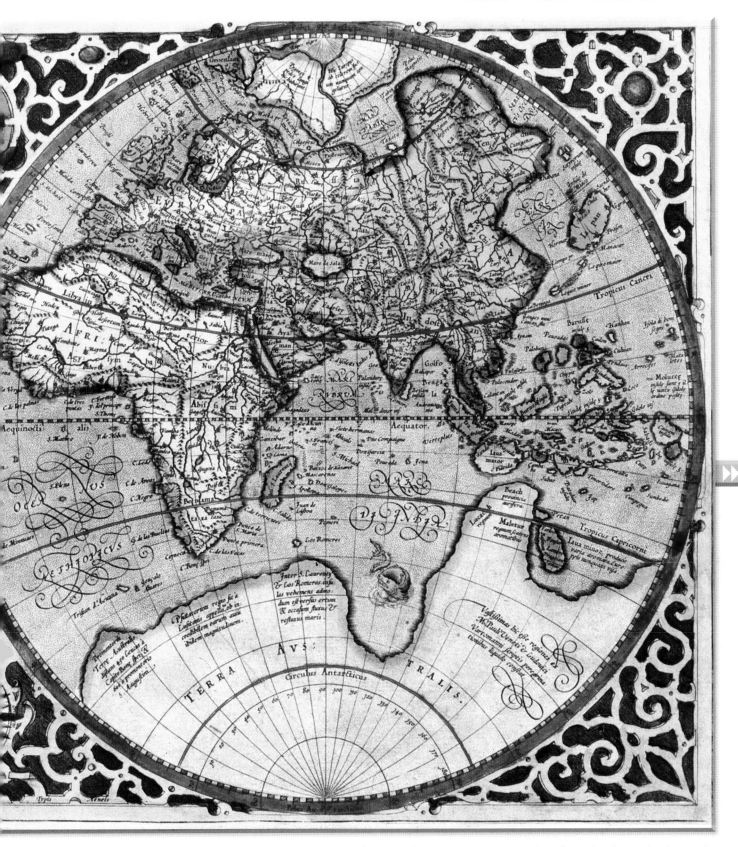

Mercator's map included an imaginary landmass in the south.

❝We have progressively increased the degrees of latitude towards each pole.❞

Gerard Mercator

Europe's Wars of Religion

The Reformation split the countries of Europe along a deep religious divide. The followers of Martin Luther and John Calvin became the main Protestant opposition to the Catholic Church. As people across Europe sought the freedom to practise their religion, the continent was shaken by a series of conflicts that spanned more than 150 years and are known as the Wars of Religion.

Catholic response

The Counter-Reformation, which sought to reorganize the Catholic Church, was launched by Pope Paul III. Meanwhile, Charles V, who ruled Spain and the Holy Roman Empire (which included land in Austria, Germany, and the Netherlands), pushed for a military victory against the Protestants.

Changing warfare

At the Battle of White Mountain of 1620 (below), the first major conflict of the Thirty Years' War, German Catholic forces defeated Protestant Bohemia (modern-day Czech Republic). The nature of warfare changed dramatically during this period. Armies grew in size, and were more professional and disciplined.

Religious wars

- **German Peasants' War (1524–1525)**
This was a social uprising sparked by the Reformation in Germany.

- **Schmalkaldic War (1546–1547)**
A war fought between an alliance of German Protestant princes and the imperial forces of Charles V.

- **French Wars of Religion (1562–1598)**
This bitter civil war between Protestants and Catholics in France ended when Henry IV, a Protestant, became a Catholic.

- **Dutch Revolt (1568–1648)**
The Protestant Dutch Republic fought an 80-year war to win its independence from Catholic Spain.

- **Thirty Years' War (1618–1648)**
This war between the Catholics and Protestants was fought mostly in Germany but involved most of the states of Europe.

Key events

1521
Emperor Charles V declared Martin Luther a heretic at the imperial Diet of Worms (assembly of the Holy Roman Empire), precipitating religious conflict.

Charles V

1534
Ignatius Loyola, a Spanish nobleman and former soldier, founded the Jesuit Order, a Catholic teaching order.

1545
Pope Paul III summoned the Council of Trent to bring about reforms within the Catholic Church.

1555
The Peace of Augsburg allowed German princes to decide the religion of their subjects, though the followers of French Protestant leader John Calvin were excluded.

This bronze cannon was used by the Swedish army when they entered the Thirty Years' War in 1630.

Thirty Years' War

This war between Protestants and Catholics in Germany escalated when other countries – Denmark, England, and Sweden – intervened to support the Protestant cause. Later, Catholic France led the fight against the Catholics in Germany. Religion had ceased to matter, and factors such as political and economic power became more important.

> **"War is one of the scourges with which it has pleased God to afflict men."**
>
> Cardinal Richelieu, chief minister of France, 1624–1642

Leading figures

Gustavus II Adolphus
Known as "the Lion of the North", the intervention of the Swedish king on the Protestant side in the Thirty Years' War widened the conflict.

Catherine de' Medici
The mother of three French kings, she had great influence and some believe her responsible for starting the French Wars of Religion.

Albrecht von Wallenstein
A Czech Protestant by birth, he was the military commander for the Holy Roman Empire and its allies in the Thirty Years' War.

Peace of Westphalia

The treaty that brought the Thirty Years' War to an end, known as the Peace of Westphalia, was signed by 109 delegates, representing the Holy Roman Emperor, the kings of France, Spain, and Sweden, the leaders of the Dutch Republic, and numerous German princes. It took four years to negotiate.

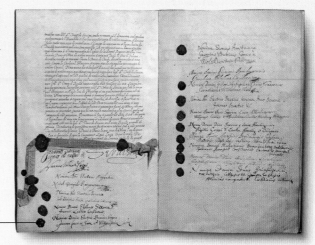

Seal of one of the 109 delegates

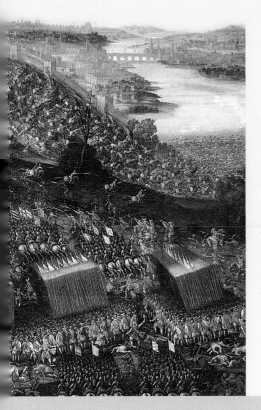

1576
Spanish troops slaughtered 7,000 people in Antwerp in one of the worst atrocities of the Dutch Revolt.

1618
Two Catholic officials were thrown out of a window by Protestants in Prague. This act led to the start of the Thirty Years' War.

Two men wrestle with one of the Catholic officials

1632
Gustavus II Adolphus of Sweden was killed at the battle of Lützen after intervening in the Thirty Years' War.

1648
Spain recognized Dutch independence as part of the Peace of Westphalia, ending the Thirty Years' War.

1575 ▶ 1600

 The world's first amusement park, Dyrehavsbakken in Denmark, opened in 1583 and is still open today.

1564–1616 WILLIAM SHAKESPEARE

William Shakespeare is regarded as the greatest writer in the English language. He wrote at least 37 plays, including *Hamlet*, *Romeo and Juliet*, and *Macbeth*, which have been translated into more than 80 languages.

The Globe Theatre
The London crowds flocked to see Shakespeare's plays performed at the Globe, an open-air theatre on the bank of the River Thames. A modern reconstruction of the theatre opened in 1997 (above).

Rare portrait
This portrait from the first printed edition of Shakespeare's plays is one of only two known portraits.

1587
Mary Queen of Scots
Mary Queen of Scots, the Catholic cousin of Queen Elizabeth I, was an exile in England. Elizabeth ordered her execution, fearing that Mary would become the centre of a plot to overthrow her and restore the Catholic Church in England.

1575 ▶▶   **1580**   **1585**

1580
Crisis in Portugal
When the king of Portugal died without an heir, Philip II of Spain – one of several claimants to the throne – sent an army to occupy Portugal and had himself crowned king. The enforced union between Spain and Portugal lasted until 1640. During this period Portugal's prosperity declined.

1582
The Pope's new calendar
Pope Gregory XIII introduced a more accurate calendar, which he named the Gregorian calendar after himself. At first, only Catholic countries used the Gregorian calendar, but it gradually won general acceptance and is used throughout the world today.

1585
First English settlement
English courtier and explorer Sir Walter Raleigh founded a colony at Roanoke (present-day North Carolina, USA). He named it Virginia for Elizabeth I, the Virgin Queen. By 1590 the colony was abandoned, possibly due to attacks from American Indians.

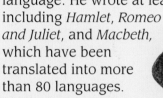
Chocolate delights
In 1585, cocoa beans, the source of chocolate, became commercially available for the first time in Europe. People had been using it in a drink for centuries in the New World.

Cocoa beans came from South America's tropical forests.

The arrival of English ships in Virginia

1588

Spanish Armada defeated

Philip II of Spain sent a large fleet (armada) of 130 ships from Spain with the twin aim of invading England and crushing the Dutch Revolt. His plan was a complete failure. The English fleet routed the Armada, inflicting heavy losses. Gales blew the surviving ships off course. Only 67 made it back to Spain.

English ships set off to attack the Spanish fleet.

1598

Edict of Nantes

King Henry IV of France signed the Edict of Nantes, which gave French Protestants freedom to practise their religion. Henry, formerly a Protestant himself, had become a Catholic in 1593 to secure his throne and bring an end to the French Wars of Religion.

1590

Japan united

General Toyotomi Hideyoshi brought an end to the wars that had divided Japan since the Onin Wars. He defeated the Hojo clan and united all of Japan under his rule, although he did not take the title of shogun (military leader).

Europe's Wars of Religion See pages 148–149

1590 **1595** **1600**

1598   NEW SAFAVID CAPITAL

Shah Abbas I, the greatest ruler of the Safavid dynasty of Iran, moved the capital to Isfahan. He transformed it into one of the most beautiful cities in the world, adorning it with mosques, colleges, baths, gardens, palaces, and a 5-km (3-mile) long bazaar. It became a centre for the arts, especially painting.

Imam mosque
One of three mosques built by the Shah Abbas around the *maidan* (central square) of Isfahan, the Imam mosque is said to contain 18 million bricks and 475,000 tiles.

Shah Abbas I
Abbas, who became Shah at the age of 16 in 1587, rescued the Safavid Empire from near extinction by recovering territories lost to the Ottomans and Uzbeks.

1600 ▶ 1625

Don Quixote
The first European novel, *Don Quixote*, was published in 1605. Written by Spaniard Miguel de Cervantes, the book follows the funny adventures of the knight Don Quixote and his squire, Sancho Panza.

Edo Japan
See pages 156–157

1600

Trading rivals
The English East India Company was set up to trade with Asia. Two years later, the Dutch established the Dutch East India Company. Future rivalry between the two would spur bitter trade wars.

1603

Shogun rule
Tokugawa Ieyasu became shogun (military leader) of Japan and moved the capital to Edo (Tokyo). The Tokugawa shogunate would rule Japan for the next 250 years.

1603

A united kingdom
King James VI of Scotland became James I of England. In 1605, a group of 13 Catholics conspired to blow up the English Houses of Parliament and murder the Protestant king. The plot was foiled in the nick of time. The most famous member of the group, Guy Fawkes, was in charge of the explosives.

1612

Slave trade grows
The number of slaves taken by Europeans from Africa to Brazil had risen to 10,000 a year. Slave traders in Brazil sold the majority on to the Spanish colonies to work in mines and on plantations, the proceeds of which went back to Europe.

1612

Up in smoke
Tobacco was first grown as a plantation crop in Virginia, USA. Not everyone welcomed it. King James I wrote a book denouncing the evils of smoking.

Guy Fawkes

▶▶ **1600**   **1605**   **1610**

1572–1610   GAZING AT THE UNIVERSE

Italian scientist Galileo Galilei's observations struck a blow to the belief that the Earth was the centre of the Solar System, around which the Sun and the planets orbited. Other scientists at this time also demonstrated that Copernicus's view of a Sun-centred Universe was right.

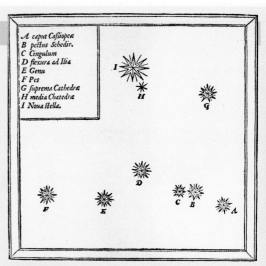

Galileo's telescope
Galileo built his own telescope (below), and used it to observe the effect of the Sun's light on the planets. In the telescope he saw three Moons of Jupiter that changed position over time, which proved that they did not orbit the Earth.

Planetary motion
German astronomer Johannes Kepler proved the Copernican system mathematically, demonstrating that the planets move around the Sun in elliptical paths, or orbits.

New star
In 1572, Danish astronomer Tycho Brahe identified a very bright star in the constellation of Cassiopeia as a "new star" (marked I on the map). It is now classified as a "supernova".

Tycho Brahe lost part of his nose in a duel over a mathematic formula in 1566. He wore a metal replacement for the rest of his life.

1614
Native wife
Pocahontas (above), an American Indian, married John Rolfe, a settler at Jamestown, Virginia. Pocahontas is said to have saved the life of John Smith, the colony's founder. She accompanied Rolfe to England, and died there in 1617.

1620 PILGRIMS ARRIVE IN AMERICA

The *Mayflower*, carrying about 102 Puritan Pilgrims from England, made landfall at Cape Cod, Massachusetts. They planned to found a colony in America where they would find religious freedom. They arrived in late November, and set about building a settlement. More than half of them died that winter.

Atlantic crossing
The *Mayflower* sailed from the port of Plymouth in Devon. It was packed with passengers and supplies for the new settlement, including farm animals. The stormy crossing took 66 days.

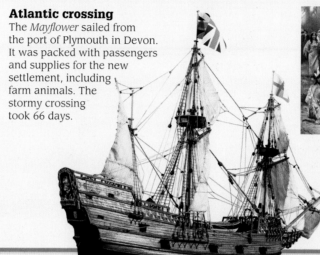

First Thanksgiving
The first spring, American Indians showed the colonists how to sow maize. Tradition says the pilgrims celebrated the first Thanksgiving after harvesting their crops.

1615 **1620** **1625** ▶▶

1618
Religious revolt
Ferdinand, king of Bohemia (modern-day Czech Republic) and future Holy Roman Emperor, tried to impose Catholicism on his Protestant citizens. They reacted with fury by throwing two of his officials out of the window of Prague Castle. The rebellion erupted into the Thirty Years' War, one of the most destructive episodes in European history.

Europe's Wars of Religion See pages 148–149

1613
First Romanov
Mikhail Romanov, a 16-year-old *boyar* (nobleman), was elected to the throne of Russia, ending a period of civil war, known as "The Time of Troubles". Mikhail was so afraid of the task ahead of him that he burst into tears, but Russia prospered under his rule. He was the first of the Romanov dynasty that ruled Russia until 1917.

This jewel-encrusted orb was used at Mikhail's coronation.

The officials are thrown out of the window of Prague Castle.

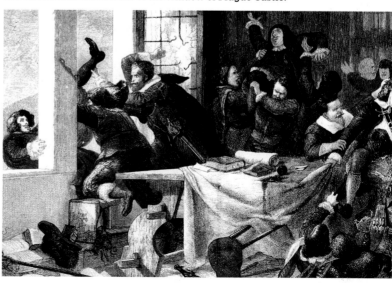

Galileo faces the court of the Roman Inquistion.

The trial of Galileo

In 1633, the Italian astronomer Galileo Galilei was tried before the court of the Inquisition in Rome. The charge against him was heresy – an offence against the teachings of the Church. Galileo supported the view that the Earth was not the centre of the Universe but, together with the other planets, orbited the Sun. Fearing torture and death, Galileo retracted his beliefs in court. But as he denied the Earth moved, it is said he muttered under his breath, "And yet it does move". He spent the rest of his life under house arrest.

> **"I do not feel obliged to believe that the same God who endowed us with sense, reason, and intellect had intended for us to forgo their use. "**
>
> Galileo, in a letter written in 1615

Edo Japan

In 1603, the first Tokugawa shogun, Ieyasu, moved the capital of Japan to Edo, the city that was to become Tokyo. This marked the beginning of more than 250 years of political and social stability, during which the shoguns kept the *daimyo* (feudal lords) under close control. The Edo period was a time of great cultural and artistic activity, but over time Japan cut itself off from the outside world.

Edo society

The feudal hierarchy of Edo society was very rigid, and it was impossible to move from one class to another. The emperor, supported by court nobles, was the head of state, but the real power lay with the shogun, who controlled the 200 *daimyo* and the rest of the population. Craftsmen and merchants lived in the cities, and peasants lived in the countryside. Entertainers, beggars, and undertakers were among the social outcasts.

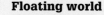

Emperor and court nobles

Shogun

Daimyo

Edo society was based on a strict class system.

Samurai	Peasants	Craftsmen	Merchants

Social outcasts

Floating world

The wealthy people living in the cities of the Edo period had a taste for refined culture and entertainment, and they referred to these urban pleasures as *ukiyo* ("floating world"). They were entertained by musicians, sumo wrestlers, actors, and geishas (professional female entertainers) such as the one portrayed here (right).

Samurai

The samurai, or warrior class, wore helmets like this and were the only people allowed to carry swords known as *daisho*. They owed total loyalty to their *daimyo* and lived by the code of honour called Bushido, or "the way of the warrior". During the Edo period, however, there were no wars, so most of the samurai became scholars and high-class administrators for their *daimyo*.

Bushido code
The samurai should:

★ Live simply
★ Behave honestly
★ Show respect and kindness to his parents
★ Be skilled with the sword and the bow
★ Keep physically fit
★ Give unquestioning loyalty to his *daimyo*
★ Be ready to commit *seppuku* (ritual suicide) rather than face the dishonour of fleeing the battlefield or being captured

Key events

1600
Tokugawa Ieyasu won the Battle of Sekigahara to take control of Japan. The battle ended 50 years of fighting, known as the Sengoku, or Warring States, period.

1603
The emperor granted Tokugawa Ieyasu the title of shogun. Ieyasu established his capital at Edo, then a small fishing village, which would later become Tokyo.

1609
The Dutch established a trading post at Hirado, Nagasaki, but they were not permitted to trade beyond the harbour.

1612
Ieyasu issued a ban on Christianity – Japanese Christians had to flee or faced death. The ban was relaxed in 1657.

1615
The Tokugawa army destroyed the Osaka stronghold of the Toyotomi clan – the last powerful opponents of the new regime.

Tokugawa Ieyasu
Born in 1543, Tokugawa Ieyasu rose to power as a *daimyo* during the clan wars of the 16th century. Over 43 years he fought up to 90 battles, culminating in the Battle of Sekigahara in 1600, which gave him control over Japan. He became shogun three years later.

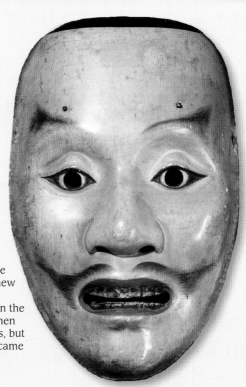

Noh mask representing a Samurai character

Theatre
Traditional Noh theatre, in which the actors wore elaborate masks, had been part of Japanese life since the 1300s. In the early 1600s a new style of comic dance-drama – Kabuki – became popular in the "floating world" of Edo. Women originally played all the roles, but – like Noh – Kabuki soon became an all-male profession.

> **"To come to know your enemy, first you must become his friend."**
>
> Tokugawa Ieyasu

Edo art
The coming of peace to war-torn Japan inspired a flowering of culture. Throughout the Edo period, poets, painters, and craftsmen created work of great beauty and delicacy that is now highly valued worldwide.

Imari
Exquisite porcelain, known as *Imari*, was made in Japan from the mid-1600s. It was vividly coloured and often adorned with gleaming gold.

Netsuke
Men carried personal items in small boxes attached to their sashes by *netsuke* – beautifully carved miniature sculptures such as these figures.

Inro
The containers slung from *netsuke* were called *inro*. Each is a finely carved stack of interlocking boxes held together by a pair of cords.

1635
The shogun put the *daimyo* under tight control by ordering them to spend several months each year living in Edo.

1637
More than 40,000 Christian peasants were killed by the shogun's forces during the suppression of the Shimabara uprising.

1639
All westerners except the Dutch were banned from entering Japan – and the Dutch were restricted to a single small island off Nagasaki.

1688
Beginning of the Genroku years – the "golden age" of Edo-period Japan, when urban entertainments and fine arts flourished.

Geisha

1868
Following the opening up of Japan to foreigners, the last Tokugawa shogun resigned. Power passed back to the emperor, ending the Edo period.

1625 ▶ 1650

Europe's Wars of Religion See pages 148–149

Tulip mania
Tulips, introduced from Asia, became the object of a buying frenzy in the Netherlands. The price of bulbs skyrocketed before collapsing overnight. Buyers who had mortgaged their houses to obtain a prize specimen lost everything.

📣 The top price paid for a single tulip bulb in 1637 was 5,500 Dutch guilders. A craftsman's annual earnings at that time was about 250 guilders.

1628
Heart of the matter
After years of research, English physician and anatomist William Harvey published a work that showed that the heart pumps blood around the body. It was a key breakthrough in the history of medicine.

1631
Swedish victory
Sweden's Lutheran king Gustavus II Adolphus intervened on the Protestant side in the Thirty Years' War. In 1631, he won a crushing victory over the imperial army at the Battle of Breitenfeld but was killed the next year at the Battle of Lützen.

1625 ● ● **1630** ● **1635** ●

1626
New Amsterdam
Dutch colonizer Peter Minuit purchased the island of Manhattan from local American Indians for 60 Dutch guilders ($24), and named it New Amsterdam. In 1664, the English took over and changed the name to New York.

1637
Great thinker
French philosopher René Descartes (1596–1650) published *Discourse on Method*, one of the most influential works in the history of philosophy. Descartes's starting point was to doubt everything, even his own existence, but because he was able to doubt, he reasoned that he must exist.

Minuit trades goods in exchange for Manhattan Island.

> **"I think, therefore I am."**
> René Descartes in *Discourse on Method*

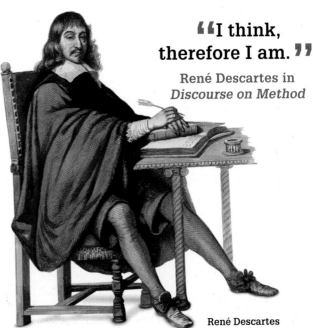
René Descartes

Edo Japan
See pages
156–157

1639

Japanese isolation

The Tokugawa shogunate of Japan was hostile to foreigners. It issued a series of edicts outlawing Christianity and limiting trade. In 1639, this led to a total ban on contact with the outside world, which lasted until 1853. The Japanese could not travel abroad and foreign ships could only visit a small island off Nagasaki.

1616–1642   THE DUTCH IN THE PACIFIC

In 1616, a Dutch expedition found a new route linking the Atlantic and the Pacific at the southern tip of South America. They named the island Cape Horn. The Dutch were also the first Europeans to explore the Pacific from their trading base at Batavia (modern Jakarta) in Java. They were hoping to find a southern continent full of untold riches.

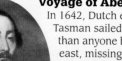

Voyage of Abel Tasman

In 1642, Dutch explorer Abel Tasman sailed further south than anyone before, then turned east, missing the south coast of Australia but discovering the island of Tasmania. Sailing on, he sighted the coast of New Zealand and named it after a province in the Netherlands.

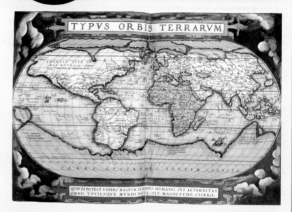

Terra Australis

European maps predicted that there would be a great southern continent, which they called "Terra Australis" (shown in green), in the Pacific Ocean. The Dutch were the first to find Australia in the early 17th century, but thought it was too barren to be Terra Australis, and called it New Holland.

1640   **1645**   **1650** ▶▶

1642

Civil war

When relations between King Charles I and Parliament broke down, England and Scotland were plunged into civil war. Following initial success, the royalists were defeated and in 1649 Charles was put on trial, found guilty of treason, and executed. A republic was set up under Oliver Cromwell.

1644

Ming collapse

The Ming dynasty came to an end as Manchu tribesmen from the north invaded China. They put in place the six-year-old Shunzhi emperor, who was the first emperor of the Qing dynasty.

Qing China
See pages
166–167

1648

Fighting is over

After four years of negotiation, the Treaty of Westphalia ended the Thirty Years' War. Up to one-third of the German population had died during the conflict, either as a result of fighting, or from disease.

The dome of St Peter's is 80.7 m (265 ft) high.

St Peter's

The great basilica of St Peter in Rome was completed in 1626, 120 years after building began in 1506. The piazza in front, a masterpiece of Baroque architecture, was finished in 1667.

King Charles was executed outside his Palace of Whitehall.

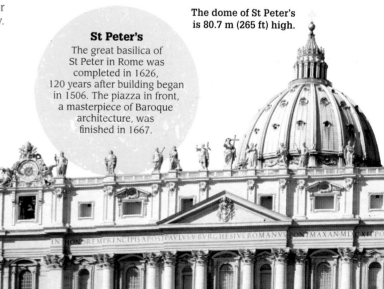

Mughal India

Founded by Babur, a Muslim descendant of the Mongol emperor Genghis Khan, the Mughal Empire saw the creation of some of India's greatest monuments. It lasted for more than three centuries, but peaked during the reigns of the emperors Akbar, Jahangir, Shah Jahan, and Aurangzeb, from 1556 to 1707. After the death of Aurangzeb, the empire went into steady decline, but it has left a glorious legacy of magnificent architecture and Islamic art.

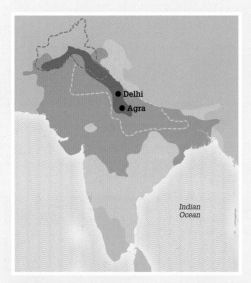

Indian Ocean

• Delhi
• Agra

Mughal expansion

When Babur founded the empire, it covered a small area of northern India. He conquered more land, but it was lost during the reign of his son, Humayun. Humayun's son Akbar inherited a small domain, but expanded it to cover a much larger area. The empire reached its greatest extent under Akbar's great-grandson Aurangzeb.

⌐ Babur's land
⌐ Babur's conquests
■ Akbar's land
■ Akbar's conquests
□ Aurangzeb's conquests

Taj Mahal

The Mughals borrowed ideas from Ottoman, Persian, Islamic, and Indian architectural styles to create their own. Perhaps the best example of the Mughal style is the magnificent Taj Mahal at Agra – built for Shah Jahan as a marble tomb for his wife Mumtaz Mahal, who died giving birth to their fourteenth child.

Taj Mahal facts

• Started in 1632, the building took more than 20 years to complete.

• More than 20,000 workmen were employed to build it.

• 1,000 elephants were used to haul building stone to the site.

• Its design is perfectly symmetrical.

• The marble is inlaid with precious and semi-precious stones, including jade, turquoise, and sapphire.

Key events

1526
Babur marched into northern India and defeated the Sultan of Delhi at the battle of Panipat to found the Mughal Empire.

1540
Babur's son Humayun was forced into exile for 17 years as power passed to a rival dynasty. He regained the throne in 1555, and passed it to his son Akbar.

1571
Akbar began building his new capital of Fatehpur Sikri near Agra in Uttar Pradesh. The empire was greatly expanded during his very successful reign.

A building in Fatehpur Sikri

1613
Emperor Jahangir allowed the British East India Company to establish a factory, or warehouse, at Surat on the west coast of India.

Mughal textiles
Mughal India was famous for its fine dyed and printed textiles, which became highly fashionable in Europe. Many Indian words for cloth and clothing entered the English language, including calico, chintz, and pyjamas.

Government and court
The Mughals were able to rule the Indian subcontinent because they gave previously independent princes a place in the Mughal system of government. At the centre, the court was very lavish, with the emperor sitting on the peacock throne, inlaid with precious stones.

Akbar sitting on the peacock throne

Mughal emperors

Babur
(1526–1530)
A lover of gardens and hunting, Babur founded the empire after defeating the ruler of northern India in 1526.

Jahangir
(1605–1627)
Jahangir was considered a great emperor, but his wife Nur Jahan was the real power behind the throne.

Shah Jahan
(1627–1658)
His passion for splendid buildings led to the creation of some of the finest monuments of the empire.

Elephant armour
The empire was created and extended by victories in battle, and the emperors often had to fight to retain power. Their armies used elephants that were trained to charge, trample, and terrify the opposing soldiers. The elephants were protected by armour that made it almost impossible to attack them, and some even wielded swords or metal clubs tied to the tips of their trunks.

1632
Shah Jahan began building the Taj Mahal at Agra as a memorial to his wife. This period marked the high point of the Mughal Empire.

Mumtaz Mahal, Shah Jahan's wife

1707
The last of the great Mughal emperors, Aurangzeb, died. The empire was plagued by rebellions, and began to decline rapidly.

1739
The Persian ruler Nadir Shah captured Delhi and removed the peacock throne. He agreed to withdraw, but the Mughal Empire's power had been destroyed.

1857
Bahadur Shah II, the last Mughal emperor, was deposed by the British as punishment for supporting the Indian rebellion.

Coffeehouses
Introduced to Europe through trade with the Ottoman Empire, coffee became all the rage in Paris and London. Coffeehouses acted as private clubs where men stayed all day discussing business and politics.

King Charles II

1654

The Swedish Empire
Queen Christina of Sweden abdicated to become a Roman Catholic. The Swedish Empire reached its greatest extent under her cousin and successor Charles X, after successful wars against Denmark and Poland-Lithuania.

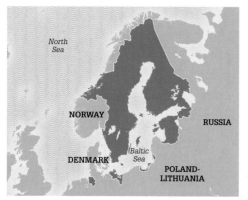

The Swedish Empire under Charles X

Coffee beans

1658

Mughal bloodbath
Aurangzeb, the last of the great Mughal rulers, proclaimed himself emperor after imprisoning his father Shah Jahan. He ruthlessly eliminated his three brothers, executing two and arranging the death of the third.

1660

Monarchy restored
When Oliver Cromwell died in 1658, he left England in disarray. In 1660, the exiled son of Charles I was welcomed back as King Charles II. One of his first acts was to execute the men who had signed his father's death warrant.

1650 ● **1655** ● **1660**

1652

Cape Town founded
A party of Dutch settlers arrived at the southern tip of Africa to establish a supply station for ships travelling to and from the Dutch East Indies. It would become the modern city of Cape Town. At that time, the area was inhabited by the indigenous Khoikhoi people, who were sheep and cattle farmers.

1638–1715   LOUIS XIV

Louis XIV became king of France in 1643, at the age of four. In 1661, on the death of his chief minister Cardinal Mazarin, he took sole charge of government. Louis increased French influence in Europe and the New World, reformed the French legal system, and was a great patron of the arts. His 72-year reign was one of the longest in European history.

The Sun King
Louis XIV gained the name of *le Roi Soleil* (the Sun King) after appearing as Apollo, the Greek god of the Sun, in a ballet as a teenager. Louis's numerous wars made France the leading nation in Europe.

The Palace of Versailles
Louis built a vast palace at Versailles, outside Paris. It was lavishly decorated throughout, and a Hall of Mirrors (above) served as a central gallery. Louis expected all his nobles to live at Versailles so he could keep an eye on them.

1665–1676   MICROSCOPIC LIFE

Scientists were experimenting with lenses at this time. In 1665, English scientist Robert Hooke published the amazing observations he made with his microscope in a book called *Micrographia*. Dutchman Antonie van Leeuwenhoek made powerful microscope lenses with a magnification of 250 times. He was the first person to see bacteria (which he called "animalcules") in saliva from his own mouth.

Compound microscope
Compound microscopes have more than one lens. Hooke improved their design by passing light from an oil lamp through a glass flask of water to illuminate the specimen.

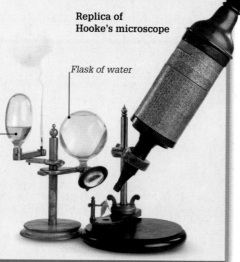

Replica of Hooke's microscope

Flask of water

Oil lamp

Larger than life
In *Micrographia* Hooke featured huge, detailed illustrations of the tiny objects he had seen under the microscope, including insects, such as the flea.

1674

Hindu king
In 1674, Shivaji, a warrior leader from Maharashtra in western India, was crowned with all the full ceremony and tradition of a Hindu king. He was the founder of the Maratha state that would go on to challenge the Mughals.

1665 ● **1670** ● **1675** »»

1666

London burns
For three days, a fire that had begun in a baker's shop swept through London, destroying most of the buildings within the old city walls. The devastation came a year after the city had been the centre of an outbreak of bubonic plague that had left 100,000 people dead.

1669

Fall of Crete
The Ottomans captured the city of Candia (modern Heraklion) on the island of Crete in the eastern Mediterranean from the Venetians. Their victory came after a 21-year-long siege, one of the longest in history.

 More than 88 churches, including St Paul's Cathedral, were destroyed in the fire of London.

From the safety of boats on the River Thames, crowds watch the Great Fire of London.

1675 ▶ 1700

> **"To every action there is always an equal and opposite reaction."**
>
> Isaac Newton

1642–1727   SIR ISAAC NEWTON

In 1687, English physicist Isaac Newton published the *Principia Mathematica* in which he outlined the law of universal gravitation. One of the most remarkable of all scientific discoveries, it explained that the Universe is held together by the force of gravity.

Man of ideas

Newton was a genius who established many laws of physics, and a new branch of maths called calculus. He also worked at the Royal Mint, where he introduced coins with milled (patterned) edges so they were harder to forge.

The science of light

This reflecting telescope is a replica of one made by Newton in 1670. It used concave mirrors, rather than lenses, to gather and focus light. His interest in light also led to his discovery that white light is made up of all the colours of the spectrum.

1675 ▶▶   **1680**   **1685**

1683   **1685**

Dead as a dodo

The dodo was a large flightless bird found only on the island of Mauritius. It was not accustomed to humans, and was so slow and easy to catch that it was hunted to extinction by about 1693 by visiting sailors.

Siege of Vienna

An Ottoman army laid siege to Vienna, but was driven off by a relieving army led by John Sobieski, king of Poland. The defeat marked the end of Ottoman expansion in Europe, and they were driven out of central Europe in 1697.

Flight of the Huguenots

After Louis XIV revoked the Edict of Nantes, ending religious toleration in France, thousands of Huguenots fled abroad to escape forced conversion. Many were skilled craftsmen who found refuge in England and the Netherlands.

Ottoman troops besiege Vienna.

1688

The Nine Years' War
Louis XIV's army crossed the River Rhine to invade the Rhineland-Palatinate region in western Germany, an act of aggression that led to the Nine Years' War. All the European powers, including Britain, united against France, forcing Louis to give up gains he had made earlier in eastern and northern France.

1688

Revolution in England
The pro-Catholic policies of King James II of England alienated his Protestant subjects, some of whom invited William III (right), Prince of Orange, married to James's daughter Mary, to invade England. James fled abroad and the Parliament offered the throne to William III and Mary II, who ruled as joint monarchs.

1694

Bank of England founded
The Bank of England was founded as a private venture and immediately loaned the government £1.2 million in return for the right to print bank notes. It meant that Britain was able to finance its part in the Nine Years' War.

1694

Number crunching
German mathematician Gottfried Wilhelm Leibniz built a digital mechanical calculator known as a Stepped Reckoner. It was the first calculator that could add, subtract, multiply, and divide. Only three examples are known to have been constructed.

Modern replica of the Stepped Reckoner

1690 · 1695 · 1700

1689

Treaty of Nerchinsk
By the 1650s, Russian expansion into East Asia had reached as far as the Amur River on China's northern border. In 1689, China signed its first treaty with a foreign power when it agreed upon its frontier with Russia. The treaty put an end to further Russian advances, though it gained the right to send trade caravans to Beijing.

The Elector Frederick William of Prussia encouraged 20,000 Huguenots to settle in Prussia by offering them special privileges.

1692

Salem witch trials
Mass hysteria spurred a witch-hunt in the small town of Salem, Massachusetts, USA, after a group of young girls claimed to be possessed by the devil. Three women were accused of practising witchcraft and hanged after a trial. By the time the witch trials ended in May 1693, 18 other women, and one man, had been put to death.

The first commercially successful steam engine

1698

Steaming ahead
Thomas Savery, a military engineer, patented a design for a steam engine. It was intended to pump water out of mines, but the risk of explosions made it too dangerous to use underground and it proved more useful in supplying water to towns.

Qing China

In 1644, the Chinese Ming dynasty was toppled by a revolution that led to an invasion from Manchuria in the far north. The Manchus brought their own language and culture to China, but worked with the native Han Chinese to create a stable empire. Under their rule, China trebled in size, and by the late 18th century it was the richest state in the world.

Three great emperors

The Qing dynasty survived until the early 20th century, but its golden era spanned the reign of three emperors, from 1661 to 1796.

Kangxi (1661–1722)

Kangxi became emperor at the age of just seven and went on to rule for 61 years. His reign was a time of territorial expansion and increasing prosperity.

Yongzheng (1722–1735)

On the death of Kangxi, his fourth son seized the throne. Yongzheng was a strong ruler who stamped out corruption and reformed government.

Qianlong (1735–1796)

An art lover, painter, and poet, Qianlong was also a military leader. He ruled for 63 years, giving up the throne three years before his death at 88.

The emperor

The Qing emperors took a very active interest in the economy and government of their empire. Unlike the Ming emperors they replaced, they made long tours through the Chinese provinces, spending a lot of time far from the palace of the Forbidden City in the heart of Beijing. Despite this, they kept close control over state affairs via the officials who travelled with them.

Carved jade

The prosperity of the empire encouraged the arts and crafts. New techniques, including glass-making and portrait painting, thrived alongside traditional arts such as the fine carving on this jade cup.

Key events

1616

Nurhaci, a clan leader, united the Manchu people of what is now Manchuria in northeast China, and founded the Qing dynasty.

1644

The Qing captured Beijing and replaced the Ming dynasty, which had ruled China since 1368.

1645

All Han Chinese men were ordered to wear their hair in a plait as a sign of submission to the Manchus.

1673

A rebellion led by three Ming generals broke out in southern China. The revolt lasted eight years.

Queue hairstyle

The imperial procession of Kangxi in the city of Kiang-Han in 1699

China and the silver trade

In the 18th-century, China was so big that it could produce everything it needed, except for the silver that it used to make coins. At that time, the Spanish colonies of Mexico and Peru were the biggest silver producers. Foreign merchants shipped it to the port of Canton (now Guangzhou) in southern China, where it was traded for silk, fine porcelain, and tea – all in high demand in Europe.

Canton harbour in imperial times

> **"Keep your hair and lose your head, or keep your head and cut your hair."**
>
> **Qing slogan about the shaving of hair**

Hair and feet

The Qing forced some of their own ideas on the Han Chinese population, but allowed other traditions to survive.

★ The Qing rulers made every Han Chinese man shave the front of his head and wear the hair at the back in a long plait, called a queue. Thousands of men were killed for resisting this order.

★ For centuries before the Qing dynasty, Chinese girls had their feet bound at an early age to stop them growing properly. The binding was painful and made walking difficult, but tiny feet were thought beautiful. The Qing emperors thought foot-binding was barbaric, but despite this they did not ban it.

Biggest book collection

Qianlong ordered the creation of the largest library of books in Chinese history.

★ Work on the books began in 1773 and ended in 1782, and involved 361 scholars and 3,825 copyists.

★ Each Chinese character had to be copied by hand.

★ The result was known as the *Siku Quanshu* ("The Emperor's Four Treasures").

★ 3,641 works were selected for inclusion. The books were bound in 36,381 volumes containing more than 79,000 chapters and 2.3 million pages.

Pair of shoes for bound feet from the late Qing dynasty

1683

Qing forces conquered the island of Taiwan, giving the emperor Kangxi control over all China.

1722

Yongzheng took over after a power struggle with his brothers following Kangxi's death.

1724

The Qing empire annexed part of Tibet, and Tibetan Buddhist culture was adopted at the Qing court.

A statue of Buddha

1757

Foreign traders were restricted to 13 trading posts, or "factories", in the port of Canton.

1796

Emperor Qianlong abdicated, and died soon after. After this the empire fell into a long decline.

1700 ▶ 1725

1710
Pretty porcelain
The Meissen factory near Dresden in Saxony began making fine porcelain wares (left). European pottery makers had long sought to discover the Chinese secret of making porcelain for themselves, and Meissen's finely modelled and painted products were an instant success.

1701
Sowing seeds
English farmer Jethro Tull invented a wooden seed-drill, a machine that sowed seed in straight rows. It wasted much less seed than the traditional method of scattering it by hand.

Jethro Tull's seed-drill

The slave trade
See pages 200–201

1709
Swedish defeat
Tsar Peter the Great's crushing defeat of a Swedish army at the Battle of Poltava ended Charles XII's over-ambitious plan to invade Russia. The victory confirmed Russia as a Baltic power.

1713
Britain's slave trade
As part of the treaty ending the War of the Spanish Succession, Britain won the right to supply African slaves to the Spanish colonies. The Triangle of Trade between British ports, Africa, and the Caribbean began.

1700	1705	1710	1715

1701
War of the Spanish Succession
Philip of Bourbon, son of Louis XIV of France, was named as heir to the Spanish throne in 1700. The following year, the rest of Europe, headed by Austria and Britain, went to war against France to prevent it. The war lasted until 1714.

The Battle of Blenheim (1704) was a major French defeat.

1716
Spanish in Texas
The Spanish intensified their efforts to establish a presence in east Texas, USA. Spain wanted to block French expansion west from Louisiana. At that time, the land was actively colonized by French settlers as part of New France, which extended from Hudson Bay to the mouth of the River Mississippi. The Spanish established a *presidio* (fortress garrison) at San Antonio.

1707
Death of Aurangzeb
Mughal emperor Aurangzeb died at the age of 88 after a reign of 49 years. A pious Muslim and a harsh ruler, he expanded the Mughal Empire far into south India, but, after his death, the dynasty began a long period of decline.

Mercury thermometer

German physicist Daniel Gabriel Fahrenheit invented the mercury thermometer with a standardized scale in 1714. This early mercury thermometer shows the scale from minus 13 to plus 217 degrees Fahrenheit.

1722

Easter Island

Dutch explorer Jacob Roggeveen chanced upon an island in the eastern Pacific Ocean. It was Easter Day, and so he called it Easter Island (modern-day Rapa Nui). He found the island completely stripped of trees and with only 2,000 inhabitants. Land erosion, warfare, and food shortages had almost wiped out the Polynesian population.

1720 **1725**

Making music

Between 1700 and 1725, Italian Antonio Stradivari created violins of amazing quality, famed for the beauty of their sound, which has never been matched. About 600 "Strads" still exist and are highly sought after.

1716–1726 AGE OF PIRACY

The presence of Spanish treasure ships in the Caribbean had long been a target for pirates. In the early 1700s, Spanish ports were poorly defended, and pirate activity intensified. There may have been as many as 2,400 pirates at this time, causing terror on the high seas as they plundered ships and seized the bounty.

Gold doubloons

Gold doubloons

The Spanish used gold and silver from the New World to mint gold doubloons and silver "pieces-of-eight" – the favourite booty of pirates. One doubloon was worth about seven weeks pay for a sailor. Pieces-of-eight were smaller change.

Blackbeard

English pirate Blackbeard (left) was said to have tied smoking fuses under his hat to frighten his enemies. He terrorized the Caribbean for two years before being killed in hand-to-hand fighting on the deck of his ship in 1718. His real name was Edward Teach.

Female pirates

Not all pirates were men. Irish-born Anne Bonny (right) joined the crew of pirate captain "Calico Jack" Rackham in 1718. She proved to be an excellent pirate, who was said to dress like a man, fight like a man, and swear like a man.

 Blackbeard captured 40 ships during his time as a pirate.

The rise of Russia

In the 17th century, Russian settlement began to spread eastwards from the Ural Mountains along the great rivers of Siberia. By 1639, Russians had reached the Pacific, and the trade in furs had become Russia's most valuable asset. Even so, Russia was weak and backward by comparison with the rest of Europe. The man who changed this and turned Russia into a modern state was Peter the Great, who became tsar in 1682.

The great modernizer
At first, Peter ruled jointly with his brother Ivan V. On becoming sole sovereign in 1696, he set out to modernize Russia. He toured Europe, visiting Prussia, the Netherlands, and Britain to learn about the latest technologies, especially shipbuilding. Back home, he created a strong navy and reorganized the army.

> **"I built St Petersburg as a window to let in the light of Europe."**
>
> Peter the Great

Children play on a street in St Petersburg in the late 1700s.

St Petersburg
Though he was born in Moscow, the capital of Russia, Peter had always disliked the city and longed to build his own capital from scratch. Victories against the Swedes provided him with land to the north of Moscow on the Baltic Sea, and in 1703, he founded the city of St Petersburg. An intense period of building began, but in 1712 he was finally able to move the capital from Moscow to St Petersburg.

The Peter and Paul Cathedral in St Petersburg

Key events

1632
Russian fur traders founded a fort at Yakutsk in Siberia, 4,870 km (3,000 miles) east of Moscow.

1670
Stenka Razin led a Cossack and peasant rebellion in southern Russia.

Stenka Razin

1696
Peter the Great became sole tsar on the death of his sickly half-brother Ivan V.

1696
Peter the Great captured the fortress of Azov from the Ottomans, but lost it again in 1711.

1703
Peter the Great founded St Petersburg on the Gulf of Finland, an outlet to the Baltic Sea.

Russian empresses

Quite unusually for the times, Russia had four women rulers in the period following Peter's death in 1725.

Catherine I (1725–1727)

The second wife and widow of Peter the Great, Catherine I rose from the peasantry in Lithuania to become the leader of Russia.

Anna (1730–1740)

The niece of Peter the Great, Anna spent most of her time fighting the Ottomans.

Elizabeth (1741–1762)

The daughter of Peter the Great, Elizabeth is remembered for building the beautiful Winter Palace in St Petersburg.

Catherine II (the Great) (1762–1796)

Catherine II was a German princess who became one of Russia's greatest rulers. Russia truly became a great European power during her long reign.

Russian icon

This Russian icon (holy picture) shows the Virgin and Child, and dates from the reign of Catherine the Great. The subjects depicted on icons remained much the same over the centuries, and the icons were highly revered. Under the reforms of Peter the Great, the Russian Orthodox Church became a department of state.

Off with their beards!

The *boyars*, Russia's hereditary nobles, were extremely proud of their long beards. Peter the Great made them wear European clothes and shave off their beards (or pay a beard tax) in an effort to modernize them.

Peter cutting a *boyar's* beard

Cossacks

The Cossacks were warriors and adventurers who played an important role in Russian history.

- Warrior bands of Cossacks originally formed in Ukraine and southern Russia to fight the Tatars.

- Cossacks were fiercely independent. Each group had its own elected *ataman*, or headman.

- In 1670–1671, Cossack leader Stenka Razin led a band of 20,000 rebels against the Russians. He was captured and executed. His exploits made him a popular folk hero.

- The Cossacks were later recruited as soldiers to guard the borders of the Russian Empire.

1709
Peter the Great defeated the army of Charles XII of Sweden at the Battle of Poltava.

1718
Alexei, the son of Peter the Great, was charged with treachery and murdered on his father's orders.

1721
The Treaty of Nystad, which ended the Great Northern War with Sweden, gave Russia land on the Baltic.

1722
Peter the Great abolished the rank of *boyar* and based promotion in the army and civil service on merit.

1783
Catherine the Great annexed the Crimean region to the southwest and built a port on the Black Sea.

1725 ▶ 1750

Bering's ship was wrecked on his second expedition to Alaska in 1741.

1728
Alaskan explorer
Sailing under the Russian flag, Danish-born explorer Vitus Bering entered the narrow strait that separates Siberia from Alaska. It is now named the Bering Strait after him. In 1741, he made a landing on several of the islands off Alaska. He claimed the whole area for Russia.

1739
Looting of Delhi
Nader Shah, a military leader who had overthrown the last Safavid shah of Persia in 1736, invaded the Mughal Empire and looted Delhi in India. He carried off the Peacock Throne of the Mughals and many other treasures, including the Koh-i-Noor diamond, which is now part of the Queen of the United Kingdom's crown.

1725 ▶ **1730** ▶ **1735** ▶ **1740** ▶

1733
Flying shuttle
British inventor John Kay patented the flying shuttle, an improvement to wool looms that enabled weavers to work faster. Kay's inventions led to protests from textile workers, who feared that he was depriving them of their livelihood.

1736
Discovery of rubber
French explorer Charles de la Condamine travelled to the Amazon and sent back samples of rubber obtained from the latex (milky fluid) of a rainforest tree, *Hevea brasiliensis*. The substance proved useful for rubbing out pencil marks, giving it the English name of rubber.

1735
Emperor Qianlong
Qianlong became the sixth emperor of China. Although he appreciated the West's technical abilities, he thought it had nothing to offer China. His reign lasted for 60 years – the longest in Chinese history.

1735
Classifying nature
Swedish botanist Carl Linnaeus published *Systema Naturae* (System of Nature), the first of three influential works, in which he devised a method of describing plants and animals by genus and species.

172 Classification of fish in *Systema Naturae*

Russia owned Alaska until 1867, when it was sold to the United States for $7.2 million.

Best breeding

English Leicester sheep (below) were bred by English agriculturalist Robert Bakewell. He improved sheep and cattle herds by selectively breeding them in order to produce more meat.

1745 ● **1750**

1746

Last battle in Britain

Prince Charles Edward Stuart (also known as Bonnie Prince Charlie), the grandson of the deposed King James II, landed in Scotland to reclaim the British throne. His army of Scottish Highlanders was destroyed at the Battle of Culloden (below), the last pitched battle fought in Britain.

1712–1786   FREDERICK THE GREAT

In 1740, Frederick II became king of Prussia after his father died. Shortly after taking the throne, Frederick II invaded and seized the Austrian province of Silesia (parts of present-day Poland, Germany, and the Czech Republic). Frederick the Great, as he is known, turned the small German kingdom of Prussia into a major European power.

Complex character

Frederick ruled Prussia for 46 years. A military genius, he loved literature, poetry, and philosophy, composed music for the flute, and corresponded with the French philosopher Voltaire. Despite introducing liberal reforms, he ruled as an absolute monarch.

Frederick the Great in battle

Battles won and lost

Frederick's invasion of Silesia in 1740 was the trigger for a European-wide war known as the War of the Austrian Succession, ended by the Treaty of Aix-la-Chapelle (1748). Frederick did not allow Europe to remain at peace for long. In 1756 he invaded Saxony, an act that led to the Seven Years' War (1756–1763), when Prussia, Great Britain, and Hanover fought an alliance of European states headed by Austria, France, and Russia. In the course of the war, Frederick successfully averted several attempts to conquer Prussia.

Frederick's gains

Brandenburg and East Prussia were the main Prussian territories when Frederick became king. Aside from adding Silesia and East Frisia, Frederick's largest territorial gain came about, not through war, but as a result of the First Partition of Poland (1772), when Prussia acquired West Prussia on the break-up of the state of Poland-Lithuania.

EAST FRISIA

Baltic Sea

EAST PRUSSIA

WEST PRUSSIA

BRANDENBURG

POLAND

SILESIA

☐ Prussia before Frederick
☐ Frederick's conquests

"The boldest and biggest enterprise that any prince of my house has ever undertaken."

Frederick the Great on the seizure of Silesia

173

Life at sea

From the early days of sailing ships, up until the 19th century, a boy as young as eight could seek his fortune at sea as a cabin boy. Cabin boys usually came from poor families, and were tempted by possible treasure or the excitement of exploring. Two boys were with Christopher Columbus on his first voyage to the New World. Generally, though, they did the most lowly jobs on board, but if a boy worked hard, he could learn the trade of seaman, and even become an officer.

All hands on deck
As a French man-of-war prepares for battle, every man attends to his duties. A barefoot boy is shown running with a cannonball – in reality a heavy load for a grown man.

Sunk by a whale
In 1820, the whale ship Essex *was sunk by a sperm whale. Thomas Nickerson, the 14-year-old cabin boy, was one of eight who survived 90 days adrift in a boat.*

Powder monkey

On a warship, the nimblest and shortest boys might become "powder monkeys". In battle, their job was to rush gunpowder and cartridges to the gun crews from the ammunition store, which lay deep inside the ship away from dangerous sparks. A short boy would be hidden by the sides of the ship and stood less chance of being picked out by enemy guns.

Midshipmen

Only the sons of wealthy or aristocratic families, aged between 12 and 14, could join the Navy as midshipmen to train as officers. The ship's schoolmaster taught them to read and the mathematics necessary for navigational calculations. They also learned about knots and the points of a ship, and carried out simple duties.

Harsh discipline

For all ranks, discipline was strict. It had to be, both for safety at sea and to keep the rough, restless crew under control in the cramped conditions on board. As punishment for a minor offence, a young sailor might be "masted" – sent up to sit near the top of the mast for a few hours, usually missing a meal. For a major crime, offenders were beaten or flogged.

Rising through the ranks

Despite the danger and harsh conditions of a career at sea, it offered many boys opportunities they would never have had on land, and several rose through the ranks. John Paul Jones, naval hero of the American Revolution, started as a ship's boy at the age of 13. The cabin boy on board Captain Cook's first voyage to Australia, Isaac Manley, ended his career an admiral.

Cat-o-nine tails
Victims of flogging often had to make their own whip, called a cat-o'-nine-tails, by unravelling a short length of rope to give nine threads and a handle.

Ship's biscuits
Instead of bread, the crew ate hard biscuits made of flour and water. The arrow on this biscuit meant that it was government property.

> **One morning after breakfast, all the midshipmen were sent for... and four of us were tied up one after the other to the breech of one of the guns, and flogged upon our bare bottoms with a cat-o'-nine-tails... Some received six lashes, some seven, and myself three.**

Jeffrey Baron de Raigersfeld,
Life of a Sea Officer, c. 1830

"I had made a confidant of a boy... who, like myself, considered his daily life on board the *Condor*, to be only a species of slavery."

Daniel Weston Hull,
Arctic Rovings: Adventures of a New Bedford Boy, 1861

Cabin boy
The duties of a cabin boy included waiting on the captain and crew, mopping the decks, and cleaning out the ship's pigsties and hen coops. This cabin boy is better dressed than most – bare feet and a plain shirt and trousers would have been more usual.

1750–1850
Time for change

From 1750 to 1850, the world was radically transformed. Populations moved from the fields into the factories, where new technology was powering the Industrial Revolution. People dared to think differently and increasingly explained the world using science and reason rather than superstition and religion. These new ideas influenced political revolutions that toppled oppressive governments, threw off foreign powers, and hailed a new era, in which people began to choose who would govern them.

A massive tsunami followed the Lisbon earthquake.

1752

Lightning power
American politician and scientist Benjamin Franklin experimented with the power of lightning. He flew a kite with a metal key attached to it in a storm. Sparks from the key proved that lightning is a form of electricity.

Franklin flies his kite in a storm.

1755

Lisbon earthquake
On the morning of 1 November, the people of Lisbon were preparing for All Saints' Day when an earthquake measuring about 8.5 in magnitude struck the city. Many grand buildings were destroyed as fires broke out and smoke filled the air. The city was left in ruins, with almost 40,000 dead.

> " I assure you this once opulent city is nothing but ruins... "
> Reverend Charles Davy, eyewitness to the Lisbon earthquake

1750 • • • • • • • • • • **1760**

1752

Gregorian calendar
Following other European countries, Britain finally adopted the Gregorian calendar. It was first introduced by Pope Gregory XIII in 1582. Based on a cycle of 400 years comprising 146,097 days, it makes one year 365.2425 days. This links to the tropical year – the time it takes for Earth to orbit the Sun.

1754

A new gas
Scottish chemist and physicist Joseph Black proved that a gas previously known as "fixed air" occurred in the atmosphere and also formed the breath exhaled by humans. It was made up of one part carbon and two parts oxygen, and became known as carbon dioxide.

1758

Halley's Comet returns
Astronomer Edmond Halley wanted to show that comets were part of the solar system and orbited the Sun in a similar way to the planets. He predicted the return of a particular comet in 1758, and was proved correct. The comet now bears his name and it comes back every 76 years.

Dilute acid passes from funnel into a round flask containing limestone

Apparatus used in chemistry to separate gases

Acid reacts with limestone to produce carbon dioxide gas

Carbon dioxide gas builds up at top of receiving jar

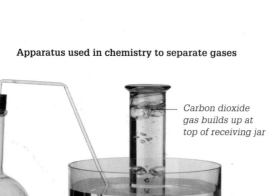

1756–1763   THE SEVEN YEARS WAR

The first large-scale global conflict, the Seven Years War (also called the French and Indian War) began in Europe where the Prussians were fighting the Austrians and Russians over territory. Britain agreed to support Prussia, while France backed Austria. But as both Britain and France had colonies overseas, and wanted to seize each other's territories, the fighting spilled over into North America and India.

Frederick the Great of Prussia

King Frederick II was a strong but ruthless military commander who wanted Prussia to become a wealthy European superpower. Despite battles won and lost, and the death of almost one-third of his army, Prussia held on to its territories.

War in India

War broke out in India in 1756 when a French ally, the Nawab of Bengal, captured a British trading base at Calcutta (now Kolkata). He is said to have held 145 prisoners overnight in a small cell where almost all of them died of heat and suffocation. The famous incident became known as "the Black Hole of Calcutta".

British prisoners in "the Black Hole of Calcutta"

King Frederick II on his horse Conde

Battle of Quebec

In North America most of the fighting took place in New France, now Canada. During the first years of the war, the French had the upper hand. That all changed in 1759 when British General James Wolfe sailed his army up the St Lawrence River (below), taking the French by surprise and capturing the French fortress of Quebec from General Montcalm. Both Wolfe and Montcalm died from battle wounds.

British Empire

The war finally ended with the Treaty of Paris (1763) when France was forced to hand over its lands in North America and forts in parts of the Caribbean, while Spain agreed to cede its Florida territory. Britain was now the world's leading colonial empire and much of America remained British.

Signatures on the Treaty of Paris

1760 ▶ 1770

Qing Dynasty
With the invasion of the Manchus, tribes from northeast Asia, the Qing dynasty began. Qing emperors used military forces to extend the empire, conquering Mongolia, Tibet, Taiwan, and much of the land in western Asia that was inhabited by nomads.

Warrior on horseback

Mozart as a boy playing the piano

1764
Mozart the child star
From an early age, it was clear that the Austrian Wolfgang Amadeus Mozart was a musical genius. In 1764, at the age of eight, he composed his first symphony. When he died, aged 35, he left a legacy of more than 600 works.

Philip Astley's amphitheatre in London

1768
Modern circus
Englishman Philip Astley was a gifted horserider who had fought in the Seven Years War. On his return, he opened a riding school called Halfpenny Hatch in London where he performed tricks on horseback in a ring. It was so successful that he added extra acts, including jugglers, acrobats, and muscians, thus creating the first true circus.

1760

1762
Catherine the Great
In Russia, Emperor Peter III was assassinated and his wife Catherine seized power. As Catherine II, ruler of Russia, she expanded its borders and also introduced reforms in agriculture and education.

Portrait of Catherine the Great

1764
Sugar Act
Keen to increase revenue from its American colonies, Britain introduced the Sugar Act, which taxed imported sugar. In 1765 it was followed by the equally unpopular Stamp Acts, which charged taxes on most printed papers, from newspapers to playing cards. This increased hostility to British rule.

American Revolution
See pages 188–188

Sugar was formed into cones for exportation.

1767
Soda water
English chemist Joseph Priestley, co-discoverer of oxygen, invented the first carbonated (soda) water after watching the reaction of gas from the brewery next to his home.

In 1762, John Montagu, the fourth Earl of Sandwich, created the now popular snack of two slices of bread with a filling in between them.

1728–1779 CAPTAIN COOK

Navigator James Cook was a farmer's son, born in Yorkshire, England, who developed his sailing skills through the ranks of the Royal Navy. In 1768, Cook was secretly ordered by the British government to find the fabled southern continent, *Terra Australis Incognita*. So, Cook led a scientific voyage to the Pacific aboard his ship *Endeavour*. He was the first European to map out Hawaii, the eastern coastline of Australia, and the coastline of New Zealand.

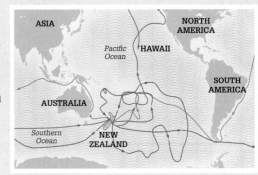

Three voyages

Cook undertook three major expeditions to the Pacific Ocean. He made his first voyage in 1768 (red), the second in 1772 (blue), and the third in 1776 (green).

Replica model of Captain Cook's ship *Endeavour*

The Industrial Revolution See pages 182–183

The Industrial Revolution See pages 182–183

1770

1769

Industrial inventions

James Watt's improved steam engine and condenser were patented and manufactured. This was a key development in the Industrial Revolution starting up in Britain. New machines and the use of steam power dramatically increased production levels.

Endeavour

The first ship, *Endeavour*, was chosen by Captain Cook because of its strong construction. The ship set sail with 96 men on board, including renowned botanist Joseph Banks. *Endeavour* narrowly avoided disaster after running aground near the Great Barrier Reef and had to undergo substantial repairs.

Natural world

While repairs were made to the ship, botanists searched for new species of plant and animal life. In Australia Joseph Banks recorded tropical birds, flying fish, and the most stunning butterflies and plants.

Specimens discovered and recorded on the *Endeavour* voyage: hibiscus leaves and flowers, and one of the many butterflies collected

KEY DATES

1763 *Cook sails to Newfoundland and makes surveys of the coast.*

1768 *First voyage: Cook takes Australia in the name of Great Britain.*

1772 *Second voyage: Cook becomes the first person to cross the Antarctic Circle.*

1776 *Third voyage: Cook sets sail in search of the Northwest Passage.*

The Industrial Revolution

Until the mid-18th century most people worked on the land, just as their ancestors had done for centuries. But this was about to change with new technologies that would create a different type of economy, based on manufacturing rather than farming. This Industrial Revolution started in Britain in about 1750, changing society as people moved to towns to work in the new factories, and soon spread to continental Europe and the USA.

Britain's Coalbrookdale ironworks

Home of industry
The Industrial Revolution depended on a supply of raw materials such as water, iron, and coal – all readily available in Britain. The country also had a huge market for manufactured goods, as well as ships to transport them worldwide. There were plenty of wealthy people keen to invest money in enterprises that might make big profits.

Britain's products:
Mass production in the factories of industrialized Britain flooded world markets with a wide variety of machine-made goods. These included:

- Textiles
- Ceramics
- Metal tools
- Machinery
- Soap
- Cement

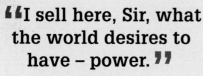
Wedgwood plate

"I sell here, Sir, what the world desires to have – power. "

Matthew Boulton,
British engineer, 1776

New factories at
Le Creusot, France,
in the mid-19th century

Changing landscape
As more and more factories were built in Europe, the landscape changed dramatically. Big towns sprang up around the factories to house the workers, and the air was filled with smoke from the factory chimneys. Many people lived – and died – in dirty, overcrowded conditions.

Key events

1709
Coke was used for the first time to produce iron at Coalbrookdale in northern England.

1712
Thomas Newcomen built the first steam engine capable of pumping water.

1764
James Hargreaves invented the spinning jenny, the first multi-spindle yarn spinner.

1771
Arkwright's cotton mill used mass-production manufacture for the first time.

1802
The first Factory Act was passed in Britain to regulate factory working conditions.

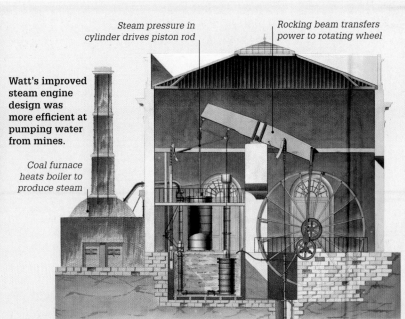

Watt's improved steam engine design was more efficient at pumping water from mines.

Steam pressure in cylinder drives piston rod

Rocking beam transfers power to rotating wheel

Coal furnace heats boiler to produce steam

Down the mine

By 1800, industry relied on coal to power steam engines and to produce iron. The coal had to be mined from deep below ground, which was hard and dangerous work. Men, women, and children worked long hours down the mines. Ponies lived underground, transporting the coal through the shaft.

Who's who

Isambard Kingdom Brunel

English engineer Brunel built the first high-speed railway, reaching speeds of more than 96 km/h (60 mph) in the 1840s. He also built bridges and steamships.

Abraham Darby

In 1709 Darby perfected a way of using coke (processed coal) instead of charcoal for producing iron. This made iron much cheaper and more plentiful.

James Brindley

One of the most important engineers of the 18th century, Brindley created the Bridgewater Canal, which became the prototype for future canals.

Isambard Kingdom Brunel
(1806–1859)

Full steam ahead

The first practical steam engine was invented in 1712, but it was slow and jerky, and only good for pumping water out of mines. In 1776 Scottish engineer James Watt perfected an engine with a fast, smooth action that could drive machinery. This became the basis of the engines used in the first steamships and railway locomotives.

Timely travel

The first public railway opened in England in 1825, and the network soon covered most of Britain. This radically speeded up long-distance travel, taking hours instead of days. In 1819 the American ship *Savannah* made a partly steam-powered crossing of the Atlantic, showing how steam could transform international travel as well. This marked the beginning of a brand new era of travel.

1804

English mine engineer Richard Trevithick exhibited the first steam railway engine.

1807

American engineer Robert Fulton built the world's first commercial steamboat.

American steam-powered ship *Savannah*

1825

The Stockton and Darlington railway ran the world's first passenger train (above).

"Well, there was some little bitty children to grown old people worked in the mill, doing different things... from the cards onto the spinning and then to the weave room."

Letha Ann Sloan Osteen, former child mill worker, South Carolina, USA

CHILD OF THE TIME

Working at the cotton mill

Children's lives during the Industrial Revolution, in Europe and the United States, were very different from today. Education was not compulsory and cost money, and many families could not afford to send children to school. Instead, they worked alongside their parents. Cotton mills, in particular, employed many children, who were perfect for wriggling under the machines. Their small hands were also nimble with the threads, and they were cheaper to hire than adults.

Spinner girls

The cotton mill had a large spinning room with long rows of machines. This was where cotton was pulled into thread and wound onto spools. Girls often started out as spinners because they were considered to be more patient than boys.

Doffer boys

Young boys worked in the cotton mills as doffers. Their job was to replace full spools of thread with empty ones. While the spools were filling up they could run off and play for short bursts. Boys could start off as doffers aged seven, and the shortest boys often had to climb up onto the working machines to reach the spools.

Dangerous equipment

The mill was a tough environment for child workers. Accidents were common because the children were inexperienced and easily distracted. Equipment was heavy and fast-moving, so in a split-second a worker's clothing, hair, or finger could get caught.

Hot work

The oppressive heat generated by all the machinery in use proved a challenge for children. Some managers at the mills let employees open the windows a little, but children would all end the day exhausted and leave in sweat-drenched clothes.

"We'd ride the elevator rope up to the pulley and slide back down. I was riding one day and was looking round over the spinning room and my hand got caught under the wheel... that thing was mashed into jelly. "

James Pharis, who began working in the Spray Cotton Mill, North Carolina, USA, aged eight

Break time
This girl is taking a break from her work in the spinning room of Globe Cotton Mill, Georgia, USA. Children could take breaks and less strict supervisors gave permission for them to go outside to play.

Family business
Mrs Young's husband died leaving her with 11 children. Two left to get married. Except for the youngest children, all the others worked at the Tifton Cotton Mill, Georgia, USA.

"If a child becomes sleepy, the overlooker touches the child on the shoulder and says "Come here". In the corner of the room there is an iron cistern filled with water. He takes the boy by the legs and dips him in the cistern, and then sends him back to work. "

Jonathan Downe, English cotton mill worker, 1832

Sweeper
These boys are working at Elk Cotton Mills in Tennessee, USA. When they were not on doffer duty, they worked as sweepers, clearing the floors of stray cotton and lint.

Flying shuttle
This invention allowed wide measures of cloth to be woven on machine looms.

1770 ▶ 1780

Arkwright's first water mill at Cromford in Derbyshire, England

A huge crowd watches as 342 chests of tea are thrown into Boston harbour.

1771
Arkwright's mill
When English inventor Richard Arkwright discovered he could harness the power of free-flowing water, he set up the first water-powered textile mill. Production increased so rapidly he was able to open many more mills in England and Scotland.

1773
Boston Tea Party
In protest at new laws imposed on tea imports by the British government, a group of American colonists boarded cargo ships in Boston harbour and dumped their entire load of tea into the water. The event became known as the Boston Tea Party.

1775
Revolution in America
Following years of tension, the American revolutionary war began in 1775, when colonists united against British rule. The first shots were heard at the battles of Concord and Lexington, where the colonists were victorious.

1770

1776
Steaming ahead
Scottish engineer James Watt, a pioneer of steam power, improved steam engine design with a separate condensing chamber that prevented loss of steam and increased efficiency. The new engine would be used to power factories and mines.

When Marie Antoinette first became queen, she was admired for her beauty and charm.

18th-century replica of James Watt's steam engine

1770
French connection
Aged 15, the French king's eldest son, Louis-Auguste, entered an arranged marriage with 14-year-old Austrian archduchess Marie Antoinette. In 1775, he was crowned King Louis XVI and inherited a country in grave financial trouble.

Separate cistern containing condenser and air pump

In 1770, English chemist Joseph Priestley discovered how effective rubber is for erasing pencil marks.

American Revolution
See pages 188–189

1779

Murder in Hawaii

During his third voyage, English explorer James Cook made the fatal decision to return to Hawaii. A fight broke out over alleged thefts by the local inhabitants, and Cook and some of his men were killed in the skirmish.

1780

The *Turtle*

Built in 1776, *Turtle* was the world's first submarine. It was used in the American War of Independence, when the operator attached a mine to an enemy ship, but the attack failed due to technical problems.

THE ENLIGHTENMENT

During the 18th century, people began to cast aside their old beliefs based on religion and superstition, and started to reason for themselves. Scientists and philosophers across Europe dared to think differently and their new ideas influenced politics, economics, and science. This exciting movement became known as The Enlightenment, or The Age of Reason.

Challenging ideas

A key figure of The Enlightenment was the French writer, historian, and philosopher Voltaire. He championed ideas, seen as very dangerous at the time, such as freedom of religion, freedom of expression, and the separation of the church and state.

Hummingbird hawk moth (*Macroglossum stellatarum*)

Wide-mouthed purpura shells (*Purpura patula*)

> **"Science is organized knowledge. Wisdom is organized life."**
>
> Immanuel Kant, German philosopher

A scientific approach

The Swedish botanist Carl Linnaeus developed a universal system for describing plants and animals, using Latin names for their genus (sub-family) and species. This binominal (two-name) system is still used today.

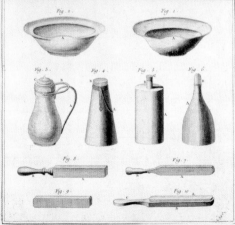

A page on the tools and craft of a wigmaker

The first encyclopedia

In 1751 French philosopher and writer Denis Diderot published the first volume of his encyclopedia, or "dictionary of science, arts, and crafts". The work aimed to cover everything, including the ideas of The Enlightenment and information about all trades. It took more than 20 years to complete.

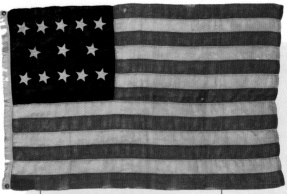

American Revolution

During the 1760s the provinces on the east coast of North America were British colonies. But the colonists had no representation in the British parliament, so when it was decided to make them pay taxes, they refused. Fighting broke out and the Americans declared their independence. The war ended with British defeat in 1781, and the birth of a new nation – the United States of America.

Thirteen colonies

The Americans who rebelled against British rule lived in 13 colonies founded on the east coast between 1607 and 1732. The 13 stars of this American flag represent the colonies, and it dates from about 1860.

* Delaware
* Pennsylvania
* New Jersey
* Georgia
* Connecticut
* Massachusetts Bay
* Maryland
* South Carolina
* New Hampshire
* Virginia
* New York
* North Carolina
* Rhode Island

"We hold these truths to be self-evident, that all men are created equal..."

US Declaration of Independence, 1776

Declaration of Independence

After the first big battle of the war at Bunker Hill in June 1775, the English king, George III, denounced the colonists as rebels against British rule. The Americans responded with a Declaration of Independence, which was signed on 4 July 1776. The first draft was written by lawyer Thomas Jefferson, who would go on to become the third president of the newly created United States of America.

Key events

1764
The Sugar Act, and later the Stamp Act, were taxes imposed by the British on the American colonies against their will.

1770
Five colonists were killed by British soldiers during an anti-British rally in Boston – an event known as the Boston Massacre.

1773
At the Boston Tea Party, colonists dumped valuable chests of tea into Boston Harbour as a protest against taxation.

1775
The war began when the colonists defeated the British at the Battle of Concord, and then lost at Bunker Hill.

Redcoats   Loyalists

Who's who
The early battles of the war were fought between the British soldiers, known as redcoats, and part-time colonial militias, known as riflemen or minutemen (because they were ready to fight at a few minutes' notice). Some colonists sided with the British, and were known as loyalists. In June 1775 the new Continental Congress appointed George Washington commander of a properly trained Continental Army, but it took time to set up.

Riflemen   Minutemen   Continental Army

Musket

Heroes and villains

Paul Revere
American revolutionary hero Paul Revere (1734–1818) was best known for his "midnight ride" from Charlestown to Lexington in April 1775 to alert patriots to an impending British attack.

John Paul Jones
Scotsman John Paul Jones (1747–1792) was a naval captain who settled in America and fought for the Revolution. He is famous for engaging the British Navy in his ship *Bonhomme Richard*.

Benedict Arnold
As an American commander, Benedict Arnold (1741–1801) was highly effective, but he changed sides after losing faith in the war. His secret negotiations with the British made him a traitor.

Battles with the British
The first shots were fired at Lexington on 19 April 1775, leading to a British defeat at nearby Concord. A few weeks later the British won a costly battle at Bunker Hill, but as the war continued, the Americans became better organized under the command of George Washington. After a British defeat at Saratoga in 1777, the French entered the war on the American side. The alliance was too much for the British, who finally surrendered after an 18-day siege at Yorktown, Virginia, in 1781.

This painting shows General Cornwallis surrendering his sword to Washington – in reality, Cornwallis refused to meet him.

1776
The Declaration of Independence was signed on 4 July.

1777
American forces under General Gates captured a demoralized British army at Saratoga in New York State.

1778
France entered the war on the American side, and was soon followed by Spain. Both began fighting the British on land and sea.

1781
The British under General Cornwallis surrendered to American and French forces at the Battle of Yorktown.

1783
Britain acknowledged the United States to be a free, sovereign, and independent nation at the Treaty of Paris.

1780 ▶ 1790

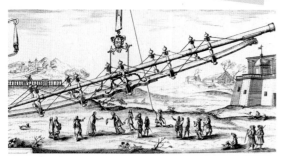

William Herschel's giant telescope

US Constitution

After the War of Independence, leaders from the 13 US states met to make rules about how the country should be run. This became known as the Constitution. Part of this decreed that there should be an elected president.

1781

A new planet

British astronomer William Herschel discovered Uranus, the first new planet since ancient times. Herschel built his own telescopes and constructed more than 400 in his lifetime, including one that was 12 m (40 ft) long.

1783

Balloon brothers

In June, French brothers Joseph and Étienne Montgolfier gave the first public demonstration of a hot air balloon. On this occasion, the balloon was tethered to the ground, but in November, an improved design made the first manned free flight.

Straw and wool were burned to fill the Montgolfier balloons with hot air.

1785

Power loom

English clergyman Edmund Cartwright patented his steam-powered, mechanically operated loom for weaving cloth. It went on to revolutionize the textile industry.

1780

1782

A new Thai dynasty

Siam, now Thailand, had been ruled by King Taksin for 15 years. After a power struggle following his death in 1782, a new dynasty was established by the Chakri. This dynasty still rules today.

1783

Laki volcano

Clouds of poisonous gases from the dramatic eruption of Laki volcano destroyed crops and livestock and caused terrible famine in Iceland. There was also a global drop in temperature, and crop failure in Europe.

1784

East India Company

In 1600, British merchants established the East India Company to trade with India. Over the years, it formed its own military and administrative departments and made increasing demands for money on the British Government. In 1784, Prime Minister William Pitt passed the India Act, which set up a new Board of Control to better oversee the company's affairs.

1786

Scaling Mont Blanc

The highest mountain in Europe, Mont Blanc in the Alps, was conquered for the first time by two Frenchmen, Dr Jacques Balmat and Michel-Gabriel Paccard. They climbed without ropes or ice axes.

Laki volcano in Iceland today

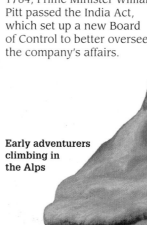

Early adventurers climbing in the Alps

In 1887 a settlement was established in Sierra Leone, West Africa, for freed slaves from British colonies.

1788 THE COLONIZATION OF AUSTRALIA

In 1788, 11 ships of the British First Fleet arrived at Botany Bay in Australia. About 778 of the passengers were convicts sent by the government to ease prison overcrowding. The fleet moved on in search of fresh water and landed in Sydney Cove, where a British flag was raised and the first European colony settled.

First Australians
The original inhabitants of Australia arrived more than 40,000 years before Europeans. They lived by hunting and gathering, and believed that their land went back to the Dreamtime – the ancient era of creation. When European settlement began, at least 300,000 Aboriginals lived in Australia. Relations between the two races deteriorated quickly as settlers spread across their land.

Boomerangs were used for hunting by the Aboriginal people.

NEW HOLLAND (AUSTRALIA)
Sydney Cove
Botany Bay
Indian Ocean

New Holland
The large landmass of Australia lies in the Indian Ocean. When Dutch explorer Abel Tasman first sailed around the land in 1642, he named it New Holland.

Sydney Cove
The colonists chose Sydney Cove in Port Jackson as their new site. This had everything the new settlers needed. It had deep water close to the shore, shelter, and fresh water. Captain Phillip named the site Sydney Cove, after the British Home Secretary, and today it is the city of Sydney. Within 60 years, there were 60,000 settlers in Australia.

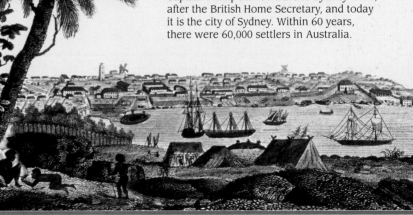

1789
First US President
General George Washington, commander-in-chief of the Army and the Navy, was elected the first US President. He took the oath of office in New York City, the capital at the time. He led a new government, shaping its institutions, offices, and political practices.

1790

The French Revolution
See pages 192–193

1789
Storming of the Bastille
In Paris, an angry mob of French citizens stormed the Bastille prison, a symbol of the monarchy, to release prisoners and seize ammunition.

Frog's legs
In the 1780s, Italian biologist Luigi Galvani discovered that the muscles of a dead frog's legs twitched when struck by an electric spark. His experiments would go on to reveal the electrical nature of the nervous system.

The French Revolution

In 1788, France was ruled by a king, queen, aristocracy, and clergy who lived in luxury, while many of their subjects starved. Just five years later, the king and queen were dead, along with thousands of others, and the country was controlled by radical revolutionaries who abolished the monarchy and nobility, and attacked Christianity. Centuries of tradition and privilege were swept away, but the chaos cleared the way for a new era of political freedom and democracy.

Tennis Court Oath

When Louis XVI became king in 1774, France was bankrupt. His attempts at reform were blocked, and by 1789 bread shortages were causing riots. In a bid to raise taxes, Louis called a meeting of the Estates General parliament. It was the first meet since 1614. But the representatives of the common people, the Third Estate, declared that they alone had the right to be the "National Assembly". Meeting in an indoor tennis court in June (above), they swore an oath to create a new constitution for France.

> **"Liberty, equality, fraternity! "**
>
> **Rallying cry of the French Revolution**

Storming of the Bastille

On 14 July 1789, a rumour that the king was going to shut down the National Assembly caused a riot in Paris. Some 600 rioters attacked the Bastille prison, a symbol of the absolute power of the king. They freed the seven prisoners held inside and proceeded to destroy the fortress. The Revolution had begun.

Key events

1789

The National Assembly was established and the Bastille was stormed. Later there was the Versailles protest and the bread riots.

1790

The National Assembly abolished the nobility.

1791

The king and queen tried to flee France but were captured and kept under guard.

1792

The guillotine was used to execute prisoners for the first time.

1793

King Louis XVI was sent to the guillotine and the "Reign of Terror" began.

March on Versailles

By September, the National Assembly was in virtual control of the government, but there were still bread shortages. On October 5, about 7,000 armed market women marched on the royal palace of Versailles, demanding bread for their hungry families and calling for the king to move from Versailles to Paris. He was forced to agree.

Armed female protestors head for Versailles.

Reign of Terror

After the death of the king, the radicals, led by Maximilien Robespierre, began a ruthless campaign against aristocrats and other "enemies of the Revolution." Between 18,000 and 40,000 people were condemned and killed, mostly by public execution under the guillotine. The period was known as the "Reign of Terror."

Who's who

The French Revolution was driven by the anger of poor, hungry people ruled by rich aristocrats. They were encouraged by radical politicians who wanted to destroy the political power of the aristocracy and the Catholic Church. Some revolutionaries went by curious names:

Sans-culottes
The name means "no shorts," since the workers could not afford short silk *culottes*.

Les tricoteuses
The women who knitted as they watched the daily executions became known as "Les Tricoteuses" (knitters).

Jacobins
Radical activists called Jacobins took over the government and began the Reign of Terror.

Power shift

In 1791, Louis XVI and Queen Marie Antoinette tried to escape France in disguise. They were caught and sent back to Paris under armed guard, and all political power passed to parliament. In January 1793, Louis was executed, and Marie Antoinette followed nine months later.

The royal coach is captured.

Execution machine

In late 1789, a member of the National Assembly and medical doctor named Joseph-Ignace Guillotin called for all executions to be as quick and painless as possible. His motive was humane, but his name was soon given to the machine that sliced off the heads of thousands during the Reign of Terror.

1794
Maximilien Robespierre is arrested and sent to the guillotine.

1795
Heir to the throne Louis Charles dies in prison. The Jacobins are replaced by a less radical government called the Directory.

A blue-and-red cockade showed that a person was a revolutionary.

1799
The Directory is overthrown by Napoleon Bonaparte, who takes power as First Consul.

1804
Napoleon Bonaparte crowns himself Emperor of France.

1790 ▶ 1800

Engraving of L'Ouverture revolting against the French

Volta battery
After years of experimenting, Italian inventor Alessandro Volta built the voltaic pile, or battery. This was the first practical method of generating electricity. Volta published his findings in 1800, and the unit "volt" is named after him.

1796
First vaccination
English doctor Edward Jenner carried out the first vaccination—giving a patient a mild or reduced-strength injection of something in order to prevent a more serious disease.

Early vaccination kit

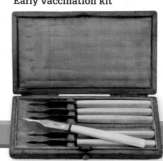

Voltaic pile

1791
Haitian slave revolt
Inspired by the revolution in France, slaves working on plantations in the colony of Haiti seized the opportunity to revolt. Toussaint L'Ouverture emerged as the leader of the revolution, helping Haiti to became the first black-ruled state.

1790

1792
Women's rights
Writer, philosopher, and feminist Mary Wollstonecraft published *A Vindication of the Rights of Woman*. Her radical book argued that women only appeared inferior to men because girls never had an equal right to education.

1793
Death of Louis XVI
The French king was charged with treason, found guilty, and condemned to death. On January 21, he was guillotined.

1793
Fruity cure
When it was discovered that the disease scurvy was caused by a lack of vitamin C, the British admiralty began supplying citrus fruit to its sailors on board ships.

1799
Rosetta Stone
French soldiers in Egypt unearthed a stone inscribed with three versions of the same passage, two written in Egyptian scripts (hieroglyphic and Demotic) and one in ancient Greek. Known today as the Rosetta Stone, it enabled experts to decipher hieroglyphs for the first time.

Ancient Egyptian hieroglyphic

Demotic

Ancient Greek

Mary Wollstonecraft
(1759–1797)

Lemons, used to prevent scurvy

1769–1821   NAPOLEON BONAPARTE

A driven and fearless soldier, Napoleon Bonaparte came to power at the end of the French Revolution. His military genius brought him many victories and resulted in much of Europe coming under French control. He also introduced a system of law, the *Code Napoléon*, that gave poor people in France new rights. However, his ambition was his undoing and he ended his life in exile.

Napoleon's throne

Empire of France
Napoleon was crowned emperor in 1804 at the Notre Dame Cathedral in Paris, thus ending the Republic. His reorganization of the territories he conquered, in Italy and parts of Germany, had a profound impact, including the ending of the Holy Roman Empire.

Military hero
Napoleon headed a series of successful battles and expanded his empire across western and central Europe. He also led the French army to a successful invasion of Egypt. However, the invasion of Spain and a disastrous invasion of Russia led to his exile.

KEY DATES

1769 *Born in Corsica*

1796 *Made commander of the French army in Italy*

1798 *Conquers Ottoman-ruled Egypt*

1799 *Appoints himself first consul after a coup*

1804 *Made emperor*

1805 *Victory at Austerlitz*

1812 *Failed invasion of Russia*

1813 *Defeat at Leipzig*

1814 *Forced into exile*

1815 *Escapes to France before Battle of Waterloo*

1821 *Dies after six years imprisoned on St. Helena*

1800

> " **Death is nothing, but to live defeated and inglorious is to die daily.** "
> Napoleon Bonaparte, 1814

Battle of Waterloo
Napoleon escaped to France and continued to wage war. The Battle of Waterloo, near Brussels, in 1815, was the last military engagement of the Napoleonic Wars. It was fought between Napoleon's army and coalition forces, led by the Duke of Wellington from Britain and General Blucher from Prussia. The outcome of this closely fought battle saw the end of 26 years of fighting between European powers and France.

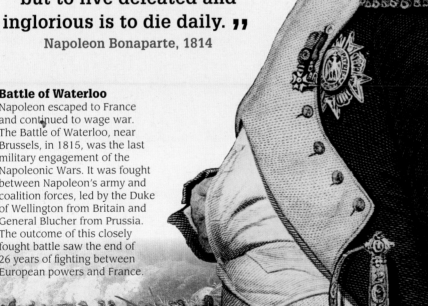

"It is with regret that I pronounce the fatal truth: Louis ought to perish rather than a hundred thousand virtuous citizens; Louis must die that the country may live."

Maximilien Robespierre,
at the trial of Louis XVI

Louis XVI was executed in the Place de la Révolution.

Execution of Louis XVI

On a bleak winter's morning in January 1793, a green coach trundled through the streets of Paris on its way to the Place de la Révolution. Inside was Louis XVI, king of France, guilty of high treason and sentenced to death. After more than 1,000 years of monarchy, France had become a republic in 1792 and was now ready to execute its former king. The blade fell at 10:22 a.m., watched by 20,000 people. One of the assistants showed the king's head to the crowds, and their cheers and artillery fire rang out to celebrate a new era.

1800 ▶ 1810

1804

Steam locomotives

English engineer Richard Trevithick invented a steam engine on wheels, called a locomotive. It was much more efficient than horses at pulling heavy loads and was designed to travel on roads.

1801

Act of Union

Negotiated by Prime Minister William Pitt, the Act of Union was passed by the Irish and British parliaments despite much opposition. It created the United Kingdom, abolished the Irish parliament, and united the Church of Ireland and England.

 Present-day Mexico, Central America, and the western United States were under Spanish control in this decade.

One of Trevithick's first steam engine locomotives

Union flag—the flag of the United Kingdom

1800

1803 LOUISIANA PURCHASE

With France's finances in trouble, Napoleon decided to raise funds by selling the Louisiana Territory to US president Thomas Jefferson. This transaction doubled the size of the United States and gave it control of the Mississippi River and the port of New Orleans.

LOUISIANA TERRITORY

Louisiana Territory

Louisiana was a large territory that covered what is now Oklahoma, Nebraska, Kansas, Missouri, and Iowa, plus parts of nine other states.

Pocket compass used during the Lewis and Clark expedition

Lewis and Clark

Facing unknown dangers, Meriwether Lewis and William Clark set out on a two-year trek across the Louisiana Territory to find and explore the best trade route through the area by water. They confronted American Indian tribes and saw wild animals that had never been described before, including new species of beaver.

This engraving shows one of Lewis and Clark's team hiding in a tree, taking shot at a bear.

THE ROMANTIC MOVEMENT

The Romantic Movement was a reaction to the industrial world of the time, influencing art, literature, philosophy, and music. Artists wanted to convey emotion and imagination, often setting them within the natural world. This was a direct challenge to the scientific reasoning of the Enlightenment. It was most active in western Europe, especially England and Germany.

Wanderer above the Sea of Fog (1818)

German landscapes
Caspar David Friedrich was a German Romantic artist whose work emphasized the beauty of nature. When people appeared in his paintings, they were shown in silhouette.

Beethoven's music
German composer Ludwig van Beethoven (1770–1827) wrote some of the most famous symphonies and sonatas for the piano at this time. Although he gradually lost his hearing, Beethoven continued composing.

1806

Empire's end
The Holy Roman Empire—a Central European empire ruled by emperors appointed by the pope—was an unusual union of territories that had existed since 962 CE. It was finally ended when the last emperor, Francis II, abdicated.

1810

1805

Battle of Trafalgar
For five hours, the Battle of Trafalgar raged at sea, pitting the navies of France and Spain against Great Britain. It ended with a clear victory for the British, although Lord Horatio Nelson died from his battle wounds.

Warring ships at the Battle of Trafalgar

The slave trade
See pages 200–201

1807

Abolition of slave trade
During the 18th century, Britain had one of the largest fleets of slave ships. But in 1807, the slave trade was brought to an end by William Wilberforce, a member of the British parliament who fought tirelessly for the abolition of all forms of slavery.

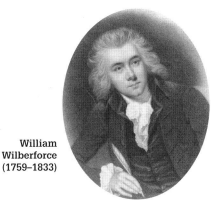

William Wilberforce (1759–1833)

1808

Peninsular War
This six-year war was fought for control of the Iberian Peninsula with Spanish, Portuguese, and British forces pitted against the French under Napoleon. Defeat at the Battle of Vitoria in 1813 contributed to Napoleon's demise and established the British Duke of Wellington's reputation.

> **" You may choose to look the other way but you can never say again that you did not know. "**
> William Wilberforce, discussing slavery in 1789

The slave trade

Since the beginning of history, there have been people forced to work as slaves, with no reward and no liberty. In ancient times, many slaves were prisoners of war or criminals. But in the 16th century, slavery became a profitable trade that stole the lives of more than 12 million Africans. They were kidnapped, sold to traders, then shipped to the Americas in such appalling conditions that many died on the way.

Forced labor

The Atlantic slave trade exploited the labor of African men, women, and children who were forced to work in the colonies of Brazil, the Caribbean islands, and mainland North America (now the United States). They worked as farm laborers on the plantations, as miners, and as servants. They had no rights, and most were granted only the most basic necessities and brutally punished for any disobedience.

> **❝I should have quitted it sooner, had I considered it, as I do now, to be unlawful and wrong. But I never had a scruple on this head at the time.❞**
>
> John Newton, former slave trader turned abolitionist, from *Thoughts Upon the African Slave Trade*, 1788

Slaves were transported in chains.

Slave auctions

By the 1780s, between 80,000 and 100,000 enslaved Africans were being forcibly transported to the Americas every year. Those who survived the voyage were sold at auction, and became the legal property of their buyers. The strongest and fittest slaves brought the highest prices. Families might be split up, never to see each other again.

Key events

1510
The first African slaves to cross the Atlantic are shipped to South America by Spanish traders.

1672
The Royal African Company is set up in London to trade goods with Africa and buy slaves.

1780
The Atlantic slave trade reaches its peak. Most of the slave traders are British-born.

1787
A campaign for the abolition of the slave trade is launched in Britain by William Wilberforce.

1803
Denmark becomes the first European country to abolish slavery and the slave trade.

Trading system
Slave ships set sail from ports around Europe, loaded with iron, guns, wine, and textiles. They headed to West Africa where the goods were exchanged for slaves. The slaves were shipped across the Atlantic to sell to land owners in the Caribbean and North America. The ships returned to Europe laden with sugar, coffee, and tobacco.

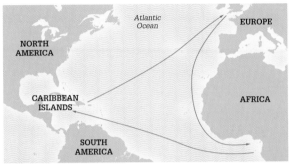

Triangular trade
The route taken by the slave ships from Europe to Africa to the Americas and back again was known as the triangle of trade.

Slaves were bought in West Africa, where they boarded slave ships.

Cotton plantation on the Mississippi

Plantations
Slaves in America and the Caribbean were made to work on plantations—big estates where crops were grown. Slave labor reduced costs, so owners made huge profits.

Plantation goods included:
- Sugar
- Cocoa
- Coffee
- Cotton
- Tobacco
- Rice

Inside a cocoa bean

Coffee beans

Abolition of slavery
After 20 years of campaigning, activists such as British politician William Wilberforce succeeded in getting Britain to outlaw the Atlantic slave trade in 1807. Slavery throughout the British Empire was abolished in 1834, as commemorated by this coin. In the United States, it continued until the end of the Civil War in 1865. Slavery was outlawed in Brazil in 1888, finally ending it entirely in the Western Hemisphere.

Slave ships
The slaves were crammed so tightly below the decks that they could barely move during a voyage lasting up to ten weeks. During the 1700s, up to 10,000 slaves were dying on board the ships every year.

A model of the slave ship *Brookes* showing how the slaves were packed close together on board

1807–1808
Britain declares the abolition of the slave trade, but not the institution of slavery itself, as does the US in 1808.

1825–1850
Almost 70,000 slaves are shipped from Africa each year in defiance of the slave-trade ban.

1833
The American Anti-Slavery Society is founded by abolitionists in the United States.

1860
There are 4 million slaves in North America and their value is estimated at $4 billion.

1865
Slavery is abolished in the United States under the presidency of Abraham Lincoln.

1810 ▶ 1820

Mural showing Miguel Hidalgo

1810
Call to arms
In Mexico, Priest Miguel Hidalgo called people to join him in a revolt against the government. His rallying speech became known as *Grito de Dolores*, or Cry of Pain, and led to the Mexican War of Independence.

1811
Luddites
Skilled workers, later known as Luddites, wrecked looms in textile mills to protest against the new machinery that was making their jobs redundant.

1812
War of 1812
America declared war on Great Britain as a result of numerous disputes. The main reasons cited were the British navy forcing American sailors to join its warships and British ships blockading US ports. The war ended with the Treaty of Ghent in 1814.

1812
Grimm's Fairy Tales
German brothers Jacob and Wilhelm Grimm published the first volume of folk tales. The 86 stories included the tales of Snow White, Hansel and Gretel, and Rapunzel.

Snow White and Rose Red, one of the stories in *Grimm's Fairy Tales*

1814
Congress of Vienna
Following the fall of Napoleon's army, a congress of the great powers of Europe met in Vienna, Austria, to settle the future boundaries of the whole continent. This resulted in the restructuring of Europe, which stood until World War I in 1914.

1810

1810
Tin can
British merchant Peter Durand patented his idea for preserving food in tin cans. The first cans had to be hammered open.

1811–1825   INDEPENDENCE IN SOUTH AMERICA

For most of South America, independence from Spain and Portugal came between 1811 and 1825. In Colombia, Venezuela, and Ecuador, Simón Bolívar led the way. In the south, Jose de San Martin and Bernardo O'Higgins liberated Argentina and Chile. Brazil declared itself independent of Portugal in 1822.

Miranda and Bolívar sign the Declaration of Independence.

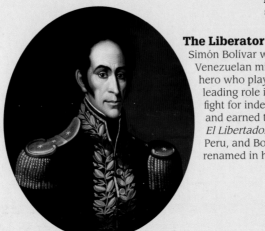

The Liberator
Simón Bolívar was a Venezuelan military hero who played a leading role in the fight for independence and earned the nickname *El Libertador*. He freed Peru, and Bolivia was renamed in his honor.

Venezuela
In 1811, Venezuela became the first part of Spain's empire to break away. Francisco de Miranda and Simón Bolívar led the campaign.

Civil war
Argentina gained independence in 1816, but a civil war followed between city dwellers and ranchers of the provinces. Argentine ranchers, called gauchos, were opposed to government.

1817

Basic bicycle

German Baron von Drais introduced a new machine to the public in Paris. It had two wheels connected by a wooden frame. The rider sat astride and pushed it along with his feet while steering the front wheel.

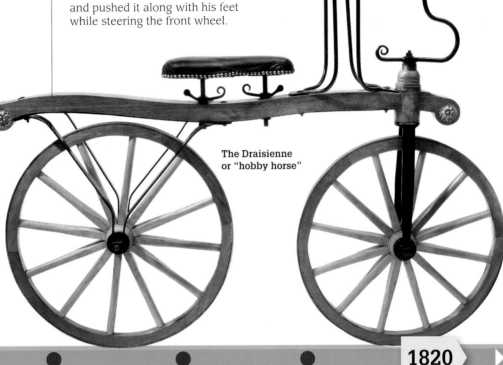

The Draisienne or "hobby horse"

Sir Humphry Davy testing his lamp

1815

Safety lamp

Miners' lives were made safer when English chemist Sir Humphry Davy invented a special lamp for use in gas-filled coal mines. This replaced earlier lamps, which could spark off a fire.

  1820 »

1816

First stethoscope

French physician René Laennec invented the first stethoscope using a rolled paper tube to funnel the sound. In addition to magnifying the heartbeat, it also helped doctors understand how blood moves through the heart. The tube design was later adapted to have two earpieces.

Argentine gauchos

Laennec's single-tubed stethoscope enabled him to listen to a patient's heartbeat.

1818

Science fiction

Considered one of the earliest examples of science fiction, English novelist Mary Shelley wrote *Frankenstein* during a trip to Switzerland. In the book, Victor Frankenstein, an arrogant Swiss chemist, conducts an experiment to create life. Instead, he creates a monster who will haunt him forever.

1819

Singapore

Sir Thomas Stamford Raffles, an agent of the British East India Company, arrived in Singapore in search of a suitable trading port. After signing a treaty with the Temenggong—the local Malay chief—and Sultan Hussein, he established the free port of Singapore, and the Union Jack flag was officially raised.

 The year 1816 was known as "the year without a summer" as clouds of gas and dust from the volcanic eruption of Indonesia's Mount Tambora circled the world, causing heavy rain and snowfall.

1820▶1830

Present-day Antarctica

1820

A new continent
Although others had sailed close, Russian explorer Thaddeus von Bellingshausen was the first person to see the ice shelf that edges the continent of Antarctica. The sound of penguins convinced him that land was nearby.

▶▶ 1820

1822

Florida handover
Florida was ruled by Spain until, in 1819, Spain handed over the territory to the US and it was admitted to the Union in 1922. This was part of a deal to cancel $5 million in debts owed by the Spanish. In 1845, Florida officially became the 27th state.

1822

Independent Brazil
When the Portuguese royal family fled their country in 1808 as Napoleon invaded, they sailed to their colony in Brazil. Although King Jao VI returned to Portugal in 1821, his son Pedro remained in Brazil and became Emperor Pedro I. He declared Brazil's independence the following year.

ELECTRICITY

The energy of electricity had always fascinated scientists and, during the first half of the 1800s, the understanding of its true potential advanced rapidly. In 1821, following Danish physicist Hans Christian Oersted's discovery of electromagnetism, Michael Faraday demonstrated how to make electricity from magnetism.

Michael Faraday (1791–1867)

Michael Faraday
The son of a poor blacksmith from the north of England, Michael Faraday received very little formal education. However, he had an intuitive understanding of physics and became one of the most influential scientists of his time.

> **" Nothing is too wonderful to be true if it be consistent with the laws of nature. "**
>
> Michael Faraday, from his diary, March 19, 1849

Electric motor
In 1821, Faraday started his most important work on electricity and magnetism. He demonstrated that an electric current could be produced in a coil of wire when a magnet was moved through the coil. He had invented the world's first electric motor.

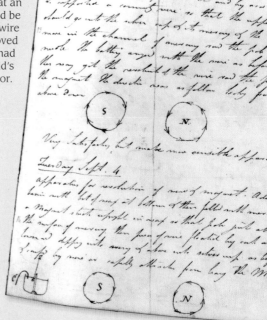

Details of Faraday's electric motor were recorded in his laboratory notebook.

 In 1824, *Australia* is finally adopted as the name of the country once known as New Holland.

View from the Window at Le Gras,
the world's first photograph

1829
Rocket winner
The first steam locomotive engine was George Stephenson's *Rocket*. It came to fame when it won the Rainhill Trials, a competition to find the best locomotives. Thousands of people turned up to watch the *Rocket* reach a speed of 36 mph (58 km/h) and take the 500 pound prize.

Stephenson's *Rocket*

1826
First photograph
Frenchman Joseph Niépce took the world's first photograph. It captured farm buildings and the sky, and the exposure time was eight hours. Niépce called his work a "heliograph" as a tribute to the power of the Sun.

1830

1825
Steam railroad
Britain's Stockton and Darlington Railway became the world's first permanent steam locomotive railroad. The line, which was 26 miles (40 km) long, was built to take coal to Stockton, where it was loaded onto cargo boats.

Morton's seed drill ensured an even sowing rate compared to sowing by hand.

1828
Sowing sensation
Following the invention of Jethro Tull's seed drill in 1701, S. Morton improved the design to create a drill that farmers could adjust to suit different crops and conditions.

1825
New waterway
Begun in 1817, the Erie Canal finally opened eight years later. It was 363 miles (584 km) in length and provided a navigable water route between the Great Lakes and the Atlantic Ocean.

Tom Smith, a
London bobby

1829
Books for the blind
Frenchman Louis Braille invented a system of reading for blind people. Blinded himself in a childhood accident, Braille's alphabet was made up of raised dots arranged in patterns that could be read by touch. In 1829, he published his first book to explain how his system worked.

1829
Bobbies on the beat
Robert Peel was a British politician, later Prime Minister, who introduced important reforms of criminal law. He also created the Metropolitan Police Force at Scotland Yard. The term *bobby*, meaning policeman, comes from his name.

Medical science

For centuries, most medicine was based on traditional remedies that were often useless, and when they did work no one knew why. Pioneers such as Galen, who lived in the Roman era, had a more systematic approach, but medical science really began in the 16th century with the work of doctors who studied the body by dissecting it. Breakthrough medical inventions and safer hospitals had transformed health care by the 19th century.

> **"The doctor of the future will give no medicine, but will interest his patients in the care of the human frame, in diet, and in the cause and prevention of disease. "**
>
> Thomas Edison, American inventor

Medical inventions

Early 19th-century doctors and surgeons carried a basic tool kit of scalpels, forceps, probes, and small saws. But medical technology progressed quickly, and earlier versions of much of the equipment used today were developed during the 1800s.

False teeth, 1860
This spring-loaded set of porcelain and ivory "teeth" is mounted on metal.

Dentist's drill, 1864
A wind-up clockwork motor drove this early dental drill for about two minutes.

Candle

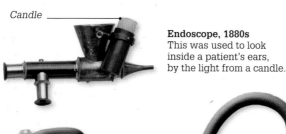

Endoscope, 1880s
This was used to look inside a patient's ears, by the light from a candle.

Thermometers, 1865
The straight version was used in the mouth, and the angled one in the armpit.

Syringes, late 1800s
Invented centuries earlier, hypodermic syringes were perfected in the 1800s.

Ether inhaler, 1847
The glass jar contained sponge soaked in ether, an early general anesthetic.

Blood pressure meter, 1880s
The pressure needed to stop blood flow in an artery was shown on the dial.

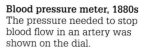

Key events

1796
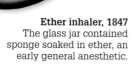
Edward Jenner develops a vaccine for smallpox, derived from a similar but far less dangerous cattle disease known as cowpox. This is the world's first safe vaccine.

1800
The Royal College of Surgeons receives a royal charter. As an association dedicated to promoting the highest standards of surgical care, it has helped make surgery much safer.

1810
German physician Samuel Hahnemann (1755–1843) produces his first major work on homeopathy—an alternative to the medical techniques of his era. His theories are never proven.

1816
Frenchman René Laennec invents the stethoscope, allowing doctors to hear the heart and lungs, and check for sounds that indicate disease.

An English hospital
in the early 1900s

Who's who

Edward Jenner
In 1796, British scientist Jenner (1749–1823) developed a safe vaccine to prevent the deadly disease smallpox. It was the first vaccine created, leading to the global eradication of smallpox in 1979.

Florence Nightingale
As a volunteer nurse caring for casualties of the Crimean War, Nightingale (1820–1910) reorganized the hospital and cut patient death rates. Her work established nursing as a new profession.

Joseph Lister
British surgeon Lister (1827–1912) pioneered the use of chemical antiseptics and sterile equipment in surgery, making operations much safer.

Louis Pasteur
Experiments with the contamination of milk and other liquids convinced French scientist Pasteur (1822–1895) that diseases were caused by the transmission of microscopic germs. He went on to develop the first vaccines against the deadly diseases anthrax and rabies.

New hospitals
Hospitals in the past had treated specific problems, such as military casualties or those suffering from leprosy, but by the 19th century they became treatment centers for all kinds of injury and disease. The techniques were primitive at first, but over time a better understanding of hygiene and infection made medical care far safer and more effective.

British-made microscope, from 1826

Under the microscope
First used for medicine in 1830, the microscope was to become a crucial tool for understanding disease. Doctors were able to check tissues for cancer by close examination of their cell structures, and positively identify bacteria and other microscopic organisms as causes of infection.

Louis Pasteur in his laboratory

Thirty seconds was all it took for surgeon Robert Liston to amputate a human leg—without anesthetic.

1817
The disease cholera spreads west from the Indian subcontinent through the crowded cities of industrial Europe. The pandemic lasts until 1824, killing hundreds of thousands of people.

1818
British doctor James Blundell performs the first successful blood transfusion from one human to another. He uses a syringe to transfer blood from donor to patient.

1822
The French chemist Louis Pasteur is born. He goes on to develop the theory of disease transmission by microscopic germs. This paves the way for antiseptics and antibiotics.

1846
US dentist Henry Morgan holds a public demonstration of the use of ether as a general anesthetic. Long, complex operations become possible without the patient feeling pain.

1830 ▶ 1840

Flag of Greece

AMERICAN INDIANS

When European settlers arrived in America, the land had already been occupied for more than 11,000 years by native peoples. It is believed that they first arrived by traveling across a land bridge from Siberia to Alaska before making their homes in what is now the United States and Canada.

Way of life
The American Indians were grouped into tribes, or nations, usually based on where they lived and their culture, such as customs and language. They generally led a nomadic existence. Many, especially those on the Great Plains, hunted buffalo, but they treated the land with respect.

American Indian hunting buffalo

Ceremonial mask of the Kwakiutl tribe of British Columbia

Buffalo parts
Every part of the buffalo was used by the American Indians. The hide became clothing and teepees, the bones were crafted into tools, and teeth were used for ceremonial masks and rattles.

Trail of Tears
To facilitate the movement of settlers to the West, the US government passed the Indian Removal Act in 1830. This forced native tribes to move to reservation lands, though most did not want to leave their spiritual homes. The Cherokee were made to trek almost 1,250 miles (2,000 km) in what became known as the Trail of Tears.

1831
Independent Belgium
In 1814, the Congress of Vienna had joined Belgium with Holland to form the Kingdom of the Netherlands. In 1830, inspired by the July Revolution in France, discontented Belgians rioted in Brussels. By 1831, Belgium was declared an independent country.

1832
Greek getaway
A desire to break away from the Ottoman Empire was finally realized after the Greek War of Independence, which established Greece as an independent kingdom.

1832
Great Reform Act
Serious riots across England forced Parliament to pass new laws, which made the way people voted for Members of Parliament (MPs) more fair and less open to bribery and corruption.

1830

1833
Factory Act
To improve appalling conditions for children working in factories, the British government passed a Factory Act. The act ruled that there should be no child workers under nine years old.

1830
King of France
Charles X was forced to abdicate during the July Revolution. Louis Philippe, Duke of Orléans, was crowned King of France. During his reign, Louis improved France's position in Europe and introduced new democratic reforms. He would be the last king of France.

Louis Philippe I

Illustration from Hans Christian Andersen's book

1837
Photo finish
French artist Louis Daguerre refined Joseph Niépce's earlier work when he created a photographic image that did not fade over time.

1837
Queen Victoria
Heir to the British throne, Princess Victoria became queen on the death of her uncle William IV, who was childless. She was 18 years old. A year later in 1838, she was crowned queen at London's Westminster Abbey.

Victoria's coronation

1835
First fairytales
Danish poet and storyteller Hans Christian Andersen published his first collection of *Fairy Tales Told For Children*. The book included stories such as *The Princess and the Pea* and *Thumbelina*.

VOORTREKKERS

From 1835 onwards, Dutch settlers or their descendants left British Cape Colony in southern Africa to escape hardship and seek new land. Called Voortrekkers, they made the Great Trek into the fertile heart of what is now South Africa.

Wagons roll
The trekkers crossed the country in ox wagons that carried household goods, clothes, bedding, furniture, and agricultural tools. They established two states – the Orange Free State, between the Orange and the Vaal rivers, and the Transvaal.

1840

1836
Battle of the Alamo
US settlers in Texas had rebelled against the governing Mexican authorities in 1835, launching the Texas War of Independence. In 1836, about 200 Texans held the fort of the Alamo against the Mexican army. The siege ended with the Alamo captured and the death of the defenders. Texas became fully independent later this year, but a new war began with Mexico in 1846, ending two years later with the United States annexing California, Arizona, Utah, Nevada, and New Mexico.

1838
Great Western
The first steam ship built for trade across the rough Atlantic Ocean was the *Great Western*. This oak-hulled ship was designed by British engineer Isambard Kingdom Brunel. In April 1838, the vessel sailed from Bristol, UK, to New York, USA, in 15 days and 12 hours.

1839
Opium Wars
Frustrated by Britain's refusal to stop importing the drug opium into China from India, a Chinese commissioner ordered a British warehouse and ships in Canton to be destroyed. This triggered the First Opium War between Britain and China.

Opium poppy

In 1830, the first American-built steam locomotive, *Tom Thumb*, was raced against a horse. The locomotive led until a technical fault caused the engine to lose power.

209

"The most deeply affecting invention... in terms both of people's lives and of the development of the American economy was surely Cyrus McCormick's reaper. "

Carroll W Pursell,
from his book *Invention in America*

McCormick's reaper at work in the American midwest in 1870

Revolutionary reaper

The mechanical reaper was one of the major inventions that would revolutionize agriculture in the 19th century. Created by American Cyrus McCormick (1809–1883), the reaper enabled farmers to harvest grain quicker than ever before. The horsedrawn machine had a rotating wheel to pull crop stalks against its cutting bar before dropping the cut ears onto a platform. Farmhands raked them up ready for gathering. The reaper made McCormick one of the USA's richest men.

1840 ▶ 1850

Young miner

The Industrial Revolution
See pages 182–183

1842

Mines Act

In reponse to growing concern about women and children working in coal mines for up to 12 hours a day, the Mines Act came into force in Britain. It ruled that no females of any age or boys under 10 years were to work underground.

1844

Morse code

American inventor Samuel Morse proved that signals could be transmitted down a wire by tapping out a code of dots and dashes. The words of the first message between the Washington and Baltimore telegraph line were "What hath God wrought?". Samuel Morse had sent the first electrically coded message.

Machine for key-tapping Morse code

1840

Penny post

In Britain, Rowland Hill introduced the first prepaid postage stamp. This cheap new stamp was called the Penny Black. Until that point, the cost of postage was paid for by the receiver, so letters were often delivered but not paid for.

 1840

1842

Treaty of Nanking

When China lost the Opium War in 1842 they also lost part of their country. The Treaty stated that Hong Kong be given to Britain on a 99-year lease and that the Chinese ports of Canton, Amoy, Foochow, Ningpo, and Shanghai open to British trade.

Agreement in English (left) and Chinese (below)

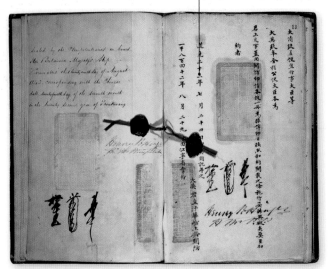

The Treaty of Nanking gave Britain control of Hong Kong.

Oregon Trail

During the 1840s, hopeful families drove from Missouri, America, across dangerous territory to find new homes in the west. This route was called the Oregon Trail. Most pioneers travelled in farm wagons with covers stretched over hooped frames.

A typical horse and wagon used by pioneering families to travel across America

Irish families crowded onto paddle steamers to Liverpool to escape the famine.

Flag of Liberia – the white star represents freedom

Sound of the sax
Belgian manufacturer Adolphe Sax patented his new instrument – the saxophone – in 1846, having exhibited it to the world at the 1841 Brussels exhibition.

1845
Irish Potato Famine
For many years, Ireland's population had depended on potatoes for basic food. In September 1845, a disease called potato blight devastated the crop. England did little to help, and between 500,000 and 1.5 million Irish people died from famine while millions of others fled the country.

1847
Independence of Liberia
Freed slaves from America had been settled in Liberia (meaning "land of the free") since 1822. Under pressure from Britain, America granted the country independence, making the West African nation the first democratic republic in African history.

1848
Revolution in Europe
Towards the end of the decade, revolutions swept through Europe, fired by the desire for political and social change. The rebellions began in France, forcing the French king to abdicate, and soon spread to Germany, Austria, and beyond.

1850 ▶▶

1846
Mormon settlement
When the religious group known as Mormons were driven from their community in Illinois, USA, they needed to find somewhere free from persecution. A small group, led by missionary Brigham Young, found the perfect place in Salt Lake City. During the first four years of settlement, almost 12,000 Mormons joined the community.

Mormon leader Brigham Young

" It's enough. This is the right place. Drive on. "

Brigham Young, on finding Salt Lake City, 24 July 1846

Panning and mining for gold in California

1848
Gold rush!
When James Marshall's work crew started building a sawmill for Swiss immigrant John Sutter on a river in California, they found a few tiny nuggets of gold. Further discoveries followed, and news of the find travelled fast. Before long 500,000 people from around the world arrived in the hope of getting rich quickly.

Promised land
Pioneers were lured west by posters promising cheap land. Between 1839 and 1850, about 55,000 people had travelled west.

CHILD OF THE TIME

Heading west

In the middle of the 19th century, thousands of families living in the east of America packed all their belongings into wagons and headed west. Before them lay a journey of 3,200 km (2,000 miles) and the promise of land for farming, or even gold! Most pioneers travelled in large groups of families and friends, with often more children than adults. A strict routine was needed to keep them all in order, but every day on the trail was an adventure.

An early start
The days began at 4 o'clock, when a guard on the night shift fired a rifle to wake the camp. From wagons and tents sleepy pioneers emerged to start their fires. The men and older boys would round up the cattle and horses and bring them back to camp, while the women and children made breakfast. Then everything had to be stowed in the wagons.

Wagons ho!
At 7 o'clock, the cry went out "Wagons ho!", and the procession set off down the trail. Most wagons were pulled by oxen, which were strong but slow, with a speed of about 3 km/h (2 mph). Only the youngest children, or the sick, rode. The rest walked, so as not to add to the weight of the wagon.

Nooning time
There would be a short stop around noon, then the walking continued. The pace was slower now, and tired children often walked in silence. Towards the end of the afternoon, a scout went ahead to find a campsite. He marked out a circle in the dust, and led the wagons in to form a barricade.

Camp life
The children had lots of chores, including sewing, milking the cows, fetching water, and collecting buffalo chips (dried dung) for the fire. But there was also time to play tag with friends, or with hoops, dolls, and skipping ropes. Young people gathered to chat, sing, play the fiddle, and dance. About 8 o'clock the pioneers settled down for the night, to sleep and dream of their futures. Most of them ended up settling on farms in California or Oregon, where they built new lives for their families.

> **"The road was lined with the skeletons of the poor beasts who had died in the struggle… Sometimes we found the bones of men bleaching beside their broken-down and abandoned wagons."**
>
> Luzena Stanley Wilson, gold rush entrepreneur, describing the deserts on her family's travels west in 1849

River crossing
The journey held many dangers and one of the greatest was getting the animals and heavy wagons across the rivers along their path.

> **"When we stopped, the boys' faces were a sight; they were covered with all the dust that could stick on. One could just see the apertures where eyes, nose and mouth were through the dust; their appearance was frightful."**
>
> Sarah Raymond, from her diary of her journey in 1865

Family portrait
This photograph shows a mother, her young children, and dog outside their wagon on the long journey west.

"So Pa sold the little house. He sold the cow and calf. He made hickory bows and fastened them upright to the wagon box. Ma helped him stretch white canvas over them."

Laura Ingalls Wilder, the American author of a series of books based on her childhood in a pioneer family.

1850–1945
Empires and World Wars

Between 1850 and 1945, the world was brought together as never before. The development of the telephone, radio, television, trains, cars, and aeroplanes got the whole world talking and on the move. But as nations became more influential and powerful, they also came into conflict with each other. Vast areas of the planet were taken over by Europe's empire builders. Increasing international rivalries exploded in two global wars and resulted in the death of millions.

1850 ▶ 1860

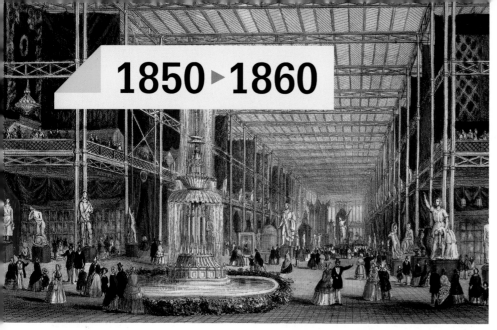

The Great Exhibition attracted more than six million visitors – a record for the time.

Japan opens up

Since the 1600s, the Japanese rulers, the Tokugawa Shogunate, refused to engage with the outside world. In 1853, US Commodore Matthew Perry sailed four warships to Japan, determined to open up trade between America and Japan. After a brief standoff, the Japanese agreed, and the following year, the two nations signed the Kanagawa Treaty, permitting the USA to create a base and conduct trade in Japan.

The Crystal Palace was made of 293,655 panes of glass.

1851

Great Exhibition

More than 14,000 exhibitors from around the world showed off the latest technological wonders at Britain's Great Exhibition. The venue was the Crystal Palace – a giant, temporary glasshouse built in London's Hyde Park.

1850

1850

Taiping rebellion

This was a period of unrest in China, in which people turned to outside ideas as a protest against the unpopular Manchu rulers. In an act of rebellion, Christian convert Hong Xiuquan formed the breakaway Taiping Heavenly Kingdom. This led to a civil war lasting 14 years and killing 20 million people before the government regained control.

1853–1856   THE CRIMEAN WAR

The two sides in the Crimean War were Russia against an alliance made up of the Ottoman Empire, Sardinia, Britain, and France. After three years of fighting, mostly in Crimea (modern Ukraine), the Russians were defeated. This was the first conflict to be reported and photographed in newspapers.

Crimean War medal

Charge of the Light Brigade

A misunderstood order spurred a brigade of British cavalry to attack a battery of Russian cannons. When the pointless charge was over, more than 150 British soldiers lay dead.

Florence Nightingale

The British death toll was kept to a minimum by the work of the nurse Florence Nightingale. Known as the "lady with the lamp", she improved the hygiene of the soldiers' hospital, which greatly reduced the disease and infection rate. In 1907, she became the first woman to be given the Order of Merit, an award for her services during the war.

Casualties fall during the charge.

Commodore Matthew Perry arrives in Japan to build relations.

1809–1882 CHARLES DARWIN

British naturalist Charles Darwin is regarded as one of the world's greatest scientists thanks to his groundbreaking theories of evolution. After travelling in South America, he developed his theories for 20 years before publishing his celebrated book, *On the Origin of Species*.

Scientific voyage

Born to a large family in England, Charles Darwin studied at school and university until he joined a scientific voyage to South America's Galápagos Islands. In 1831 he set sail on board the ship HMS *Beagle* and spent five years studying the animal and plant life he encountered on the islands.

A variety of finch beaks

Natural selection

In the Galápagos, Darwin noticed each island had similar species that were slightly different. He realized that animals with the best characteristics for the environment survived, for example, birds with the best beak for finding food available on the island. Animals then passed on these characteristics to their young, and so the species gradually evolved by a process he called natural selection.

1860

1857

Indian rebellion

Resentment at the British presence in India was building. The native armies of the East India Company – the British business that ruled India at the time – finally revolted (left) following the introduction of a new rifle. Its cartridges were rumoured to be greased in pork and beef fat, sparking outrage among Muslims and Hindus because these animal products were against their religions. The rebellion lasted a year, after which Britain took direct control of India as the British Raj.

Laying cables under the Atlantic Ocean

American inventor Elisha Otis designed and installed the world's first lift in New York, USA.

1858

Mexico's War of the Reform

During the 1850s, there were two main political groups in Mexico. The conservatives wanted the government controlled by the military and the Catholic Church, while the liberals wanted power to be spread among the people. The liberals introduced laws reducing the power of the Church and military. The conservatives staged a rebellion, but were defeated by the liberals.

1858

Transatlantic communication

The first telegraph cable was laid across the Atlantic Ocean, signalling a new age of inter-continental communication. However, the first cable worked for only a few weeks before breaking down. A reliable replacement would not be in place until the middle of the next decade, laid by the SS *Great Eastern*.

1860 ▶ 1870

1861
American Civil War
In the USA, the northern and southern states went to war over slavery and states' rights. After four years of fighting and millions of casualties, the North proved victorious and slavery was officially abolished.

London's Baker Street Station in 1863

Infantry drum used during the American Civil War

American Civil War
See pages 222–223

1863
Underground travel
The world's first underground railway, the Metropolitan railway, opened in London, with 30,000 passengers travelling on the first day. The wooden carriages were pulled by steam locomotives belching thick clouds of smoke.

1860　　　　**1862**　　　　**1864**

1861
Freeing the serfs
In the 19th century, 23 million Russians were serfs – slaves who farmed the fields for rich land owners. In an effort to radically reform his country, Tsar Alexander II gave the serfs their freedom.

Tsar Alexander II

1863
Second Mexican Empire
After gaining independence in 1821, Mexico briefly had a monarchy (1821–1823) – this was the First Mexican Empire. By the 1860s, conservative supporters of the monarchy, backed by France, overthrew the liberal government and made Austrian Duke Maximilian I the new emperor of Mexico. With support from the USA, the liberal forces rebelled. France withdrew in 1866, the liberal government was reinstalled, and Emperor Maximilian was executed.

Paraguayan troops charge into battle, suffering huge loss of life

1865
War of the Triple Alliance
In South America, Paraguay entered into a disastrous war with its three neighbours, Uruguay, Brazil, and Argentina. The country was devastated, experiencing some of its worst losses in conflict, with the population reduced by more than half.

Karl Marx

1868 MEIJI RESTORATION

The military rulers of Japan – the Tokugawa Shogunate – still distrusted other nations and tried to limit their access to the country. Japan finally opened up to the outside world when the Tokugawa Shogunate was overthrown in 1868 and replaced by 15-year-old Emperor Meiji.

Emperor Meiji on horseback

Emperor Meiji
Japan emerged as a major world power under Emperor Meiji (1852–1912) who introduced radical political, social, and economic change. His policy was to modernize Japan by taking the best from other nations, while keeping the distinctive Japanese culture.

Golden vase from the Meiji period

Meiji art
During the Meiji (meaning "enlightened rule") period, Japan experienced rapid change. The economy was modernized and international trade began. Art was now supported by the Japanese government and Meiji artefacts grew popular in Europe and the USA.

1867

Das Kapital published
The German philosopher and socialist writer Karl Marx published the first volume of his book, *Das Kapital*, a criticism of capitalism. His theories would become a major influence on the communist regimes of the 20th century.

1866 | **1868** | **1870**

1866

German unification
Prussia and Austria went to war to see which country would dominate the German-speaking world in the years ahead. Prussia was victorious. Over the next few years, several German states joined forces with Prussia, resulting in the proclamation of a united German Empire in 1871.

Unification of Germany
See pages 226–227

1867

Founding of Canada
The North American provinces of Canada, Nova Scotia, and New Brunswick were brought together to found Canada – a dominion of the British Empire. Ottawa was chosen as the capital of the new country, which was home at the time to more than three million people.

Crowds gathered to watch the canal's opening.

1869

Transcontinental railway
The USA's Atlantic and Pacific coasts were linked together for the first time with the construction of the 2,860-km- (1,777-mile-) long First Transcontinental Railroad. A golden spike was driven into the last section of track to signal the route's completion.

1869

Suez Canal
Egypt's Suez Canal opened in 1869. It speeded up the sea trade between East and West, as ships no longer had to undertake the hazardous journey all the way around the bottom of Africa – a trip of several thousand kilometres. Instead, ships could take a shortcut through the new 164-km (102-mile) waterway between the Red Sea and the Mediterranean.

 Swedish scientist Alfred Nobel patented his invention – explosive dynamite – in 1867.

American Civil War

In the 1860s, the USA went to war over slavery and states' rights. The northern states, where slavery was already illegal, wanted it abolished throughout the country. However, the southern states wanted to keep slavery, as they relied on African slaves to farm their main crops of cotton and tobacco. It was a bloody battle that tore the country apart before slavery was finally abolished.

Battle of Gettysburg
Union and Confederate troops clashed thousands of times over the course of the war. A major turning point came in July 1863, when the Union troops halted the South's advance (below) at Gettysburg, Pennsylvania. About 51,000 soldiers, on both sides, were killed.

Union versus Confederate

The American Civil War resulted in the greatest loss of US life. About 620,000 Americans died, more than in any other conflict, including both world wars combined. The two sides were the Union (northern states) and the Confederacy (southern states).

UNION

Flag of the northern states, or Union

- 23 states remained loyal to the Union at the start of the war. Another two, Nevada and West Virginia, joined during the conflict, making 25.

- Population: 22 million

- Soldiers: 2.1 million

- No. of deaths: 360,000

- Cost of war: $6.2 billion

- Soldier's monthly pay: $13

Union uniform

CONFEDERATE

Flag of the southern states, or Confederacy

- 7 southern states broke away from the Union at the start of the war. These were later joined by another 4 states, making 11.

- Population: 9 million

- Soldiers: 1.1 million

- No. of deaths: 260,000

- Cost of war: $4 billion

- Soldier's monthly pay: $11

Confederate uniform

Key events

1860
In November, Abraham Lincoln was voted the 16th President of the USA. In this decade, the country went to war over slavery, as the north wanted it abolished and the south wanted to keep it.

1860
In December, South Carolina was the first state to withdraw from the Union. By February 1861, six more states joined, forming the Confederacy.

1861
The opening shots were fired at Fort Sumter, South Carolina, when southern forces opened fire on Union troops.

1861
The First Battle of Bull Run ended in victory for the Confederacy, as did the Second Battle of Bull Run a year later.

1862
The Battle of Antietam stopped General Lee's march north and saw the greatest number of Americans killed or wounded in a day.

The dragoon pistol was a heavy single-shot weapon.

New warfare
Many new technologies were used during the war, most of which benefited the more industrially advanced Union in the north. Railroads allowed troops to move around quickly, while telegraph lines ensured that orders were delivered immediately. The invention of new weapons resulted in a high number of casualties.

African American soldiers
About 180,000 African Americans served in the Union army, making up approximately 10 per cent of the total force (about 40,000 of whom died). Towards the end of the war, the South even mooted the possibility of forming African American battalions, although these never materialized.

Sword bayonets could be attached to a rifle or used independently.

The 1861 Springfield rifle musket was used throughout the war.

Battlefield medicine
The war saw medical as well as military advances. With the men off fighting, women worked as nurses for the first time. They worked in portable field hospitals, such as this one in Virginia, USA, set up to care for wounded soldiers.

Who's who

UNION CONFEDERATE

Abraham Lincoln
The election of the slavery abolitionist Lincoln as US President in 1860 kick-started the Civil War. He led the North to victory and signed the law freeing the slaves.

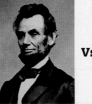

Vs

Jefferson Davis
President of the Confederacy, Davis was a less effective leader than Lincoln. He failed to get support from foreign countries or devise a strategy to stop the North's advance.

Ulysses S Grant
He led the Union army from 1862 onwards. Grant masterminded a series of victories over the Confederates. He served two terms as US President after the war.

Vs

Robert E Lee
Lee was such a hugely respected professional soldier that he was even asked to be commander of the Union army. But he remained loyal to the South.

1862
At the naval Battle of Hampton Roads, the Confederates failed to break the North's blockade.

1863
The Emancipation Proclamation was issued by Lincoln on 1 January, declaring all slaves in the Confederacy to be freed.

1863
A month after the Battle of Gettysburg, Lincoln made his famous "Gettysburg Address", vowing to continue the fight.

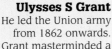

Grenade found at Gettysburg

1864
The Union army marched through Confederate territory from Atlanta to the sea at Savannah, destroying towns, railroads, and supplies.

1865
The Union captured the Confederate capital of Richmond, Virginia, and Lee surrendered to Grant. The Civil War was over.

King Victor
Emmanuel II
on horseback

1871
Unified Italy
The French occupation
of Rome began in 1849,
when French troops
overthrew the revolutionary
Roman Republic. It ended in
1870, allowing the city to
become part of Italy. Under
King Victor Emmanuel II,
Rome became the capital
of a newly unified Italy
the following year.

1874
British Gold Coast
The Asante people were rulers of a large
stretch of West Africa. They saw off the
British in the First and Second Anglo-Asante
Wars of the 1820s and 1860s, but were less
fortunate in the Third Anglo-Asante War,
when the British took control of most of
their territory. It became the British Empire
territory of the Gold Coast (now Ghana).

1870 **1872** **1874**

1870
Franco-Prussian War
Having defeated Austria a few years earlier,
the Prussians, under Otto von Bismarck,
provoked France, under Napoleon III, into
war. The Prussians easily steamrollered the
French in a series of battles, toppled Napoleon,
and marched into Paris as victors in 1871.

**Unification
of Germany**
See pages
226–227

Prussian soldiers
on horseback
attack the
French army.

First Wimbledon
In the early 1870s, a new racket game, "Sphairistike," grew in popularity in the UK. Renamed tennis, the sport's first official championship was held at the All England Lawn Tennis and Croquet Club in Wimbledon in 1877.

In 1872, America's Yellowstone National Park became the world's first national park.

A wooden frame and thick strings were typical of the 19th-century tennis racket.

The Battle of Little Bighorn left hundreds dead, including Colonel Custer.

1876
Battle of Little Bighorn
Sioux and Cheyenne Indians joined forces to attack American troops under the command of Colonel George Armstrong Custer. It was a rare reversal for the US government in the ongoing American Indian Wars, which forced many American Indians from their lands.

1878
Second Afghan War
Britain invaded Afghanistan to prevent Russia from gaining influence there. This was part of the so-called "Great Game," in which the two powers competed for supremacy in Central Asia. Following its defeat in 1880, Afghanistan was forced to give up control of its foreign policy to Britain.

1876 — **1878** — **1880** ▶▶

1876
The Porfiriato Era
Former Mexican soldier Porfirio Díaz overthrew the president of Mexico, and went on to rule the country as a dictator until 1911—a period known as the *Porfiriato*. He oversaw tremendous economic growth and industrial modernization, but he also grew increasingly unpopular, and was eventually overthrown after more than 30 years in power.

1878
Treaty of San Stefano
Following the Russo-Turkish War of 1877–1878, the weakening Ottoman Empire lost control of a number of Balkan countries, which it had ruled for centuries. The Treaty of San Stefano in 1878 ended the war and granted Serbia, Romania, and Montenegro their freedom. Bulgaria received limited independence.

Lieutenant Melvill, on horseback, attempts to cut through Zulu lines.

1879
Anglo-Zulu War
At the Battle of Rorke's Drift in Zululand, South Africa, 130 British troops repelled an attack by more than 4,000 Zulu warriors. The battle was part of the Anglo-Zulu War, in which Britain extended its colonial interests in South Africa through the conquest of Zulu territory.

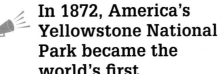

Invention of the telephone
Scottish-born inventor Alexander Graham Bell patented his telephone design on the same day in 1876 that American Elisha Gray tried to patent his version. But Gray got there too late. Bell's patent became the most valuable ever granted.

One of Bell's early model phones, known as a box telephone, had a trumpetlike mouthpiece.

Unification of Germany and Italy

The map of Europe was constantly being redrawn during the 19th century as old empires crumbled and new powers emerged. In 1850, the countries of Germany and Italy didn't exist. Instead, there were many different German-speaking and Italian-speaking states, each with their own leaders, which formed part of several different unions, kingdoms, and empires. But in the 1860s and 1870s, ambitious politicians brought these states together, through a combination of warfare and political agreements, to create the countries of Germany and Italy.

> **"The main thing is to make history, not to write it."**
>
> Otto von Bismarck (1815–1898)

Rival forces

Otto von Bismarck
Bismarck, prime minister of Prussia, was a crafty politician who provoked the wars and arranged the deals that resulted in a united Germany with him as the chancellor (political ruler).

Napoleon III
The emperor of France was the big loser of German unification. Following his army's defeat in the Franco-Prussian war, he was forced into exile in Britain.

The German states
In 1866, the armies of Prussia (a north-central European industrial power including what is now northern Germany and Poland) easily defeated those of the traditionally dominant German power of Austria. This allowed Prussia to unite several German states into the North German Confederation under its command.

- Prussian territory
- Other North German States
- South German States
- Border of the North German Confederation, 1867
- Border of the German Empire, 1871

Germania
This image shows Germania, the symbol of a united Germany. Germania is usually depicted as a woman carrying the *Reichsschwert* (imperial sword) and a shield bearing a black eagle. Following unification, Germany would become a major power by the late 19th century.

War and peace
In the Franco-Prussian War of 1870–1871, German states led by Prussia defeated France. This victory meant that France's domination in Europe was over. As part of the peace deal, France gave up two of its German-speaking provinces, Alsace and Lorraine. A new unified German Empire was proclaimed on January 18, 1871.

Key events

1864
Prussia and Austria united for a short war during which they captured the provinces of Schleswig and Holstein from Denmark.

1866
Prussia and Austria went to war, with Prussia emerging victorious and taking control of a number of German states.

1870
Bismarck dragged France into the Franco-Prussian War by publishing an edited telegram (left) that made it look like the Prussian king had insulted the French ambassador.

1871
Wilhelm I of Prussia was crowned emperor of the German Empire. The ceremony was held in Paris, further rubbing salt in France's wounds.

Italian divide

In the mid-19th century, Italy was split between a number of rulers, including Austria, which controlled the north; the Spanish branch of the Bourbons, who controlled the south; and the Pope, who controlled Rome. Between 1859 and 1870, Italy was unified into a single state.

Italy's territories in 1815, with red line to show the country's unified borders in 1870

Kingdom of Sardinia	Parma
Kingdom of Lombardy-Venetia	Tuscany
Modena	Rome
Papal States	Lucca
Kingdom of the Two Sicilies	Italian borders, 1870

Swiss businessman Henri Dunant founded the Red Cross because he was shocked by the slaughter at one of the battles for unification in 1859.

Influential Italians

Count Camillo di Cavour

The prime minister of the Kingdom of Sardinia provided the political leadership for the unification movement. He became Italy's first prime minister in 1861.

Giuseppe Garibaldi

If Cavour was the cool, calculating politician, then Garibaldi was the fiery, headstrong revolutionary who led a campaign of conquest through Sicily and southern Italy.

Crowning glory

Like the German Empire, the new united Italy was headed by a king. Victor Emmanuel II had been ruler of the Kingdom of Sardinia, the Italian state that led the unification process, before he was crowned king.

Crown worn by the Italian king until the fall of the monarchy in 1946

Waging war

In the north, the Italian Kingdom of Sardinia made an alliance with the French to force out the Austrians in conflicts such as the Battle of Magenta in 1859, shown here. The Battle of Solferino resulted in a French victory, but it was so bloody that it forced Napoleon III to consider the price of victory.

Key events

1852
Count Camillo di Cavour became prime minister of the Kingdom of Sardinia, later becoming one of the leading figures of unification.

1859
Piedmontese and French forces combined to force the Austrians out of most of northern Italy.

1860
Garibaldi led a popular uprising in Sicily and southern Italy, after which these states voted to become part of a united Italy.

1861
A united Kingdom of Italy was declared, but Rome, protected by the French, stayed separate.

Traditional Venetian gondola

1866
The separate state of Venetia (including Venice) joined the new united Italy.

1870
After Rome's French protectors abandoned the city to fight in the Franco-Prussian War, Rome finally became part of a united Italy.

1880 ▶ 1890

 One of the world's first electric street lights was installed in Indiana in 1880.

The first automobile
Though many other inventors were working on creating an automobile powered by gasoline, it was German engineer Karl Benz who got there first in 1885. He was awarded a patent the next year.

Bertha Benz, wife of Karl, took his car on the first known road trip in an automobile.

1881
Alexander's assassination
The Czar of Russia, Alexander II, was assassinated by the terrorist organization Narodnaya Volya ("People's Will"). Russia's Jewish population was falsely accused of the crime, causing antisemitic hostility (violence against the Jews). Thousands of Jews emigrated to Europe, the US, and Palestine.

1882
Anglo-Egyptian War
Following a short war, Britain made Egypt a territory of its empire. Britain also faced a revolt in Sudan led by Muhammad Ahmad, who claimed to be the Mahdi— a great ruler prophesied in Islamic teaching. Sudan finally fell to the British in 1898.

1884
Scramble for Africa
The major European powers met at the Berlin Conference to discuss dividing up Africa between them. No African leaders were invited or even consulted. The so-called "Scramble for Africa" was underway.

Scramble for Africa
See pages 230–231

1847–1931 THOMAS EDISON

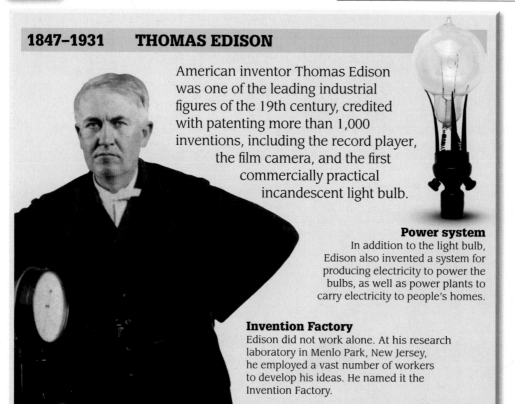

American inventor Thomas Edison was one of the leading industrial figures of the 19th century, credited with patenting more than 1,000 inventions, including the record player, the film camera, and the first commercially practical incandescent light bulb.

Power system
In addition to the light bulb, Edison also invented a system for producing electricity to power the bulbs, as well as power plants to carry electricity to people's homes.

Invention Factory
Edison did not work alone. At his research laboratory in Menlo Park, New Jersey, he employed a vast number of workers to develop his ideas. He named it the Invention Factory.

1883
Eruption of Krakatoa
In what is believed to be the loudest eruption in recorded history, the Indonesian volcano Krakatoa blew its top in 1883. At least 35,000 people were killed. The explosion was heard more than 3,000 miles (5,000 km) away.

An early leather soccer ball

1888

First soccer league

The world's first soccer league competition took place in England between autumn 1888 and spring 1889. Twelve teams took part, and after 22 games, Preston North End were the champions. Soccer league competitions soon caught on all over the world.

1890

1888

Commercial camera

Invented by American entrepreneur George Eastman, the Kodak was the first camera to use photographic film. It came loaded with enough film for 100 photographs, but had to be sent back to the factory for the pictures to be developed. As Eastman put it in his advertisements, "You press the button, we do the rest."

Eastman named his camera *Kodak* because he liked the letter *k*.

1887–1889   EIFFEL TOWER

France celebrated the centennial of the French Revolution with an international exhibition in Paris. The main attraction was a giant iron tower named after its creator, Gustave Eiffel. The iconic structure became one of the world's most recognizable buildings.

In 1889, the Eiffel Tower was by far the world's tallest structure.

Under construction

Designed by the same man responsible for building the iron supports of the Statue of Liberty, the tower was a marvel of engineering. Made of 18,000 separate parts, it weighs 10,000 tons and stands 1,050 ft (320 m) tall. It took 300 workers just under two years to build.

Tourist attraction

Not everyone liked the tower. After its construction, a group of Parisian artists signed a petition demanding its destruction, calling it an "atrocity." But as visitor numbers grew, so did public appreciation of the landmark building. Today, about seven million people visit the tower every year.

The Scramble for Africa

Europeans had been involved in Africa since the days of the slave trade, but had acquired little territory. However, the speed and scale of their colonization of Africa during the 1880s and 1890s was unprecedented. In 1870, just 10 percent of the continent was controlled by Europeans. By 1900, Europeans ruled 90 percent of the continent, or one-fifth of the globe's landmass. Only Liberia and Ethiopia remained free.

British takeover

The major winner in the scramble was Britain. By 1900, the country was in control of 30 percent of the African population. Britain took over territory stretching from Egypt in the north and Gambia in the west to Kenya in the east and South Africa.

Colonizing countries in Africa, 1914

Atlantic Ocean

Indian Ocean

- France
- Spain
- Germany
- Italy
- Portugal
- Belgium
- England
- Uncolonized

Berlin Conference

In 1884–1885, the Berlin Conference on the future of Africa started the empire-building scramble. The European countries claimed that they wanted to help Africa stamp out slavery. But in reality, they decided to carve up the continent between them in order to exploit its resources. No African leader was invited to the conference.

Key events

1881

Tunisia became a French protectorate. The following year, Egypt became part of the British Empire.

1884

American-born Hiram Maxim invented the first self-powered machine gun, giving the British a military advantage in Africa.

Maxim's machine gun

1884–1885

The Berlin Conference gave the green light to European powers to begin the "Scramble for Africa."

1885

Germany acquired new territories, including what is now Namibia, while Britain acquired what is now Botswana.

1889

The Southern Ivory Coast became a French protectorate, while the Northern Ivory Coast followed two years later.

Looting of Africa

The Europeans paid little attention to the rights of native Africans. Treasures were stolen, such as this bronze carving from Nigeria, looted by the British in 1897. In Central Africa, King Leopold II of Belgium established a personal colony—the Congo Free State—employing a private army to force the local people to harvest rubber.

Key figures

David Livingstone
The first European to see Victoria Falls in southern Africa, Livingstone crossed Africa to convert people to Christianity.

Cecil Rhodes
One of the most ruthless colonizers of southern Africa, Cecil Rhodes had Rhodesia (now Zimbabwe) named after him.

King Leopold II
The Belgian king's brutal exploitation of his African colony triggered outrage and the intervention of the Belgian government.

Henry Morton Stanley
This Welsh-born American journalist helped King Leopold II establish his African colony in the Congo.

Reasons for the scramble

★ **To end the slave trade**
This was given as one of the official reasons for colonization. However, the colonial powers did exploit and mistreat the African people.

★ **Religion**
Many European missionaries went to Africa to convert people to Christianity.

★ **Exploration**
The African adventures of European explorers, such as Livingstone and Stanley, had helped map the continent. This raised interest in the riches to be found there.

★ **Exploitation**
Africa had vast mineral deposits and other resources that could be exploited.

★ **Medicine**
The discovery of quinine as a cure for malaria meant that more Europeans were prepared to settle in Africa.

★ **Power and prestige**
The great European powers—particularly Britain, France, and, after unification, Germany and Italy—competed with each other to build bigger empires.

★ **Military superiority**
The development of superior weapons, such as rifles and machine guns, gave the Europeans a military advantage over the Africans.

★ **Racism**
Some believed white people were superior to blacks, and had the right to take over their land to "civilize" them.

British soldiers gathered at the Sphinx in 1882, the year Egypt became part of the British Empire.

African resistance

The colonization of Africa was often a hard fought, bloody affair. The Asante people of West Africa, the Edo people of Benin City, Nigeria, and the Zulus of South Africa (right) all fought fiercely to defend their land. However, the superiority of European weapons was usually the deciding factor.

Zulu spear

1890
Britain acquired the island of Zanzibar and the city of Pemba from the Germans in return for the North Sea island of Heligoland.

1892
Britain seized Yorubaland (now part of Nigeria), while France gained control of much of Senegal.

1893
France took over Dahomey (now Benin).

1896
Italy tried to conquer Ethiopia, but was defeated at the Battle of Adowa.

1899–1901
The Second Boer War resulted in Britain taking over the whole of South Africa.

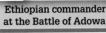

Ethiopian commander at the Battle of Adowa

CHILDREN IN HISTORY

Children of Ellis Island

In the late 19th and early 20th centuries, hundreds of thousands of children traveled from Europe to the United States to start new lives. Some came with their families, while others made the trip alone, usually because their parents had gone ahead to find work. After a long, miserable sea journey, they would land at Ellis Island in New York Harbor, where they were checked before they could begin new lives in America.

Welcome to America
Most families traveling to the United States were escaping poverty or religious persecution back home. Many cheered and wept with joy as their steamships passed the Statue of Liberty in New York Harbor. They had endured storms and seasickness, but the long journey was finally over.

First impressions
The Immigration Station was busy and noisy with crowds of new arrivals waiting to be seen by the authorities. Different languages were heard as people talked excitedly to each other. Nurses were on hand to welcome and talk to the children. They reassured the youngsters, holding their hands and giving them milk to drink. Doctors and inspectors wore uniforms, which was intimidating for many of the immigrant children.

Entry tests
Families were put through a series of entry tests. The most important was the medical test. Anyone with an infectious disease was not allowed into the country. In the mental test, immigrants were asked a few arithmetic questions. Children gave their names to inspectors for the official documents, while parents had to prove they had money (usually about $25) to support the family. Those who were ill but could be treated at Ellis Island Hospital were detained. Children traveling alone were kept until relatives came, or until money or a prepaid ticket was sent for them.

A new life
Once all the tests were over, the new arrivals could live in the United States—the land of freedom and opportunity. On the first floor of the Ellis Island Immigration Station, family and friends waited in anticipation for loved ones to arrive after months or even years apart. This area of the building became known as "the kissing post," since reunited relatives kissed and hugged each other there. About one-third of the immigrants stayed in New York, where many worked in industries such as textile and clothing production. Thousands of children were employed as cigarette rollers, bobbin doffers in mills, and general helpers on production lines.

Island of Hope
New York's Ellis Island Immigration Station opened in 1892 to process the vast numbers of people arriving from Europe—about one million a year.

"So when I came to Ellis Island, my gosh, there was something I'll never forget. The first impression—all kinds of nationalities. And the first meal we got... I said, 'My God, we're going to have a good time here. We're going to have plenty to eat.'"

Marta Forman, Czechoslovakian immigrant, at Ellis Island in 1922

Milk service
There were hundreds of employees on Ellis Island. This worker pours milk for waiting women and children.

Loaded with luggage
This child has arrived at Ellis Island with his family. Families brought everything they could carry with them, ready to start their new lives in the United States.

Open wide
Doctors carefully examined every child as soon as they arrived at the island to make sure they were not bringing any diseases into the country.

1890 ▶ 1900

Poster advertising the Trans-Siberian Railway

 Italian baker Raffaele Esposito created the classic Margherita pizza in 1899 as a treat for the visit of Queen Margherita.

1890

Ellis Island opens
In New York Harbor, work began on the construction of Ellis Island Immigration Station. Work was completed two years later in 1892. When the station closed in 1954, more than 12 million people had passed through. Today, at least 40 percent of the US population has an ancestor who entered the country in this way.

Children of Ellis Island See pages 232-233

1891

Russian railroad
Construction of the world's longest railroad began in Russia. It took more than a decade to build, and eventually the Trans-Siberian Railway linked the capital, Moscow, with the port of Vladivostok on the Pacific coast, 5,785 miles (9,310 km) to the east.

1893

Votes for women
New Zealand became the first self-governing country in the world to give women the right to vote. This was the result of a series of petitions to Parliament organized by the British-born women's rights campaigner Kate Sheppard.

1890

1890

Battle of Wounded Knee
American Indians lost their battle with the US Army at Wounded Knee Creek in South Dakota. In the massacre, 150 American Indians and 25 army troops were killed. It was triggered by the American government's attempt to ban the Ghost Dance—a new religious ceremony that American Indians believed would stop US expansion into their land.

Club used in the Ghost Dance by the Arapaho, a tribe of American Indians

1894

First Sino-Japanese War
When China and Japan sent troops to calm an uprising in Korea, the two nations ended up at war. The Chinese were defeated and forced to give up the island of Formosa (now Taiwan) to the Japanese. Japan became a new power, and Korea gained independence from China.

The Chinese and Japanese navies battle at the mouth of the Yalu River dividing Korea and China.

1895 A YEAR OF INVENTION

This groundbreaking year saw three dramatic technological breakthroughs, which would have long-lasting effects: Italian Guglielmo Marconi invented the wireless telegraph, German physicist Wilhelm Röntgen discovered X-rays, and the French Lumière brothers premiered the world's first moving picture film.

Moving pictures
Viewers of the first motion picture film, presented by Auguste and Louis Lumière in Paris using a projector, were shown a 50-second scene of workers leaving a factory.

Film projector belonging to the Lumière brothers

Wireless telegraph
This is a replica of Marconi's wireless telegraph, which used radio waves to transmit Morse code signals. The invention paved the way for the development of broadcast radio in the 20th century.

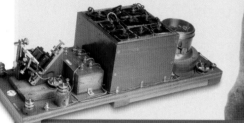

X-rays
With the discovery of X-rays, it was finally possible for doctors to see inside the human body. The world's first X-ray showed the hand and wedding ring of Wilhelm Röntgen's wife. He was awarded the first Nobel Prize for Physics in 1901.

1899
Second Boer War
In South Africa, war broke out between the Boer settlers and the British imperial forces. After bitter fighting, the Boers were defeated in 1902, but the British were criticized for their brutal tactics—sending civilians to concentration camps (where 25,000 died) and trying to starve the Boers into submission.

1900

1896
Olympic Games
Believing that sports could be used to promote peace between nations, French aristocrat Pierre de Coubertin organized the first modern revival of the Olympic Games in Athens, Greece. About 300 athletes competed in various competitions, including swimming, cycling, weightlifting, wrestling, and track and field.

Medal given to all participating athletes at the 1896 Olympic Games

1898
Spanish-American War
In the Cuban War of Independence, the United States came to assist Cuba against the Spanish. Spain was defeated and forced to give its remaining colonies—the Philippines, Guam, and Puerto Rico—to the US. Although Cuba was supposed to have achieved independence, the United States continued to occupy the island for years to come.

1896
Battle of Adowa
At this time, all of Africa except for Liberia and Ethiopia was under European control. Italy hoped to add Ethiopia to its empire, but was defeated at the Battle of Adowa in the First Italo-Ethiopian War. But Italy would try again in 1935 and win the Second Italo-Ethiopian War.

Future US president Theodore Roosevelt and his troops plant the American flag to celebrate victory in the Spanish-American War.

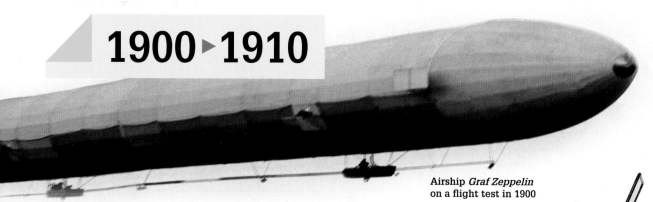

1900 ▸ 1910

Airship *Graf Zeppelin* on a flight test in 1900

The Model T paved the way for the mass ownership of automobiles.

1900
High flier
Air travel got off to a flying start in the 20th century with the first flight of a new type of airship. Known as the zeppelin, it was named after its German inventor, Ferdinand von Zeppelin. Commercial flights began in 1910, and the craft was used for bombing missions during World War I.

1902
Riyadh captured
A member of the exiled ruling family of Riyadh in Arabia, Ibn Saud returned in 1902 to capture the city of his birth. For the next two decades, he took control of the rest of central Arabia, founding the Kingdom of Saudi Arabia in 1932, which he ruled as King Abdulaziz.

1900

1900
Boxer Rebellion
In China, a nationalist group, the Righteous and Harmonious Fists (nicknamed "Boxers"), led an uprising against foreigners. It was eventually stopped by an international force including British, American, Russian, and Japanese troops.

Learning to fly
See pages 238–239

1903
First flight
American brothers Wilbur and Orville Wright invented the first powered flying machine, named *Flyer*. The maiden flight took place at Kill Devil Hills, North Carolina, and lasted just 12 seconds.

1904
Russo-Japanese War
In the Boxer Rebellion of 1901, Russia occupied the region of Manchuria in northeast China. This caused hostility between Russia and Japan. When talks failed, Japan declared war. Japan drove the Russians out of Manchuria and emerged from the conflict as a world power.

1901
Australian Commonwealth
Although still part of the British Empire, six Australian colonies joined together to form the federal Australian state, which would control its own domestic and foreign policy. A new capital, Canberra, was built a decade later.

Depiction of the Russo-Japanese War

1879–1955   ALBERT EINSTEIN

In 1905, German scientist Albert Einstein published a revolutionary paper that explained many of the mysteries of the Universe. Einstein worked in an office in Switzerland and had developed his "Special Theory of Relativity" in his spare time.

Scientific genius
Born in Germany to a Jewish family, Einstein moved to Switzerland to study, and then to the United States in 1933, where he lived until he died. After his paper was published, he became the world's most famous scientist and was awarded the Nobel Prize for Physics in 1921.

German stamp celebrating the centennial of Einstein's theories in 2005

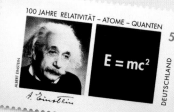

100 JAHRE RELATIVITÄT – ATOME – QUANTEN

ALBERT EINSTEIN

$E = mc^2$

55

DEUTSCHLAND

Special Theory of Relativity
Einstein suggested that mass and energy are versions of the same thing, which he expressed in his famous equation: $E=mc^2$. His later work explained how space and time form an interconnected whole called "space-time."

Model T
Before the Model T, cars had been handmade and expensive. In 1908, American businessman Henry Ford revolutionized the industry by building his vehicles on factory assembly lines and selling them cheaply. By 1927, about 15 million had been built.

1910

1905
Russian revolt
Already unpopular with most of the nation, Czar Nicholas II faced mass protests following Russia's defeat by Japan. To avoid being overthrown, the Czar was forced to introduce a new elected parliament, called the Duma, in 1905.

1906
San Francisco earthquake
An enormous earthquake hit San Francisco early in the morning of April 18, destroying most of the city's buildings and killing more than 3,000 people. The damage took years to repair.

1909
Young Turk movement
The Ottoman Empire in Turkey was taken over by the Young Turk movement, which forced the sultan to grant a constitution and allow democratic elections. The Young Turks also advocated for legal reforms and more rights for women.

The two US baseball leagues—the American League and the National League—competed in an end-of-the-year championship for the first time in 1903. It is now the World Series.

Crumbling buildings lined the streets after the earthquake.

Wilbur Wright watches his brother Orville take off from Kill Devil Hills, North Carolina.

❝We could not understand that there was anything about a bird that would enable it to fly that could not be built on a larger scale.❞

Orville Wright

Learning to fly

On a blustery morning in 1903, two American brothers—bicycle-makers by trade—proved that powered flight was possible. In an aircraft of their own design equipped with a small engine, Orville Wright nervously took the controls while his brother walked alongside. The first flight lasted just 12 seconds and covered only 120 ft (37 m), but it launched the age of aviation. That morning, four flights were made in all, two by each brother. The final one, piloted by Wilbur, lasted 59 seconds and traveled a distance of 852 ft (260 m)—the world's first air pilots had shown that the sky was now the limit.

1910▸1915

On April 14, 1912, the British liner *Titanic* hit an iceberg and sank in the Atlantic Ocean. More than 1,500 passengers and crew died.

1911
Chinese Revolution
More than 2,000 years of imperial rule in China ended with a rebellion against the unpopular Manchu Dynasty. Puyi, the six-year-old emperor, was forced to abdicate, and the country was declared a republic.

1910
Mexican Revolution
After more than four decades as Mexico's dictator, Porfirio Díaz was finally forced from power by an uprising demanding greater freedoms for the people. However, fighting between liberal and conservative forces continued for another decade.

1911 — THE RACE FOR THE SOUTH POLE

In 1911, two men competed to be first to reach the world's last unexplored territory, the South Pole, in Antarctica. Robert Scott, a British navy officer, got there on January 17, 1912, only to discover that the Norwegian explorer Roald Amundsen had beaten him to it.

Norwegian victory
Captain Amundsen and his four companions arrived at the South Pole on December 14, 1911, where they planted the Norwegian flag. The trip had been meticulously planned and all the explorers made it home safely.

1910

1867–1934 — MARIE CURIE

In an age when most scientists were men, Marie Curie was a notable exception. Born Marie Sklodowska in Poland, she studied in Paris, France, where she met and married Pierre Curie, a physics professor. Together, they investigated the recently discovered phenomena of radiation and X-rays, winning the Nobel Prize for Physics in 1903.

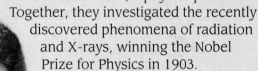

Nobel Prize
Pierre was killed in a car accident in 1906, but Marie continued her work and was awarded a second Nobel Prize for Chemistry in 1911. She also pioneered the use of X-rays in surgery during World War I.

Nobel Prize medal

1912
First Balkan War
The Balkan League—an alliance between Bulgaria, Greece, Montenegro, and Serbia—declared war on the Ottoman Empire to free Macedonia from Turkish rule. The Ottomans were defeated the following year and lost Albania and Macedonia, which represented almost all of its remaining European territory.

1911
New Delhi is born
In 1911, George V was crowned king of England. During his coronation celebrations in India, the king declared New Delhi to be India's new capital, replacing the old capital of Calcutta.

Crowds gather at a *durbar* (assembly) held to celebrate the king's coronation.

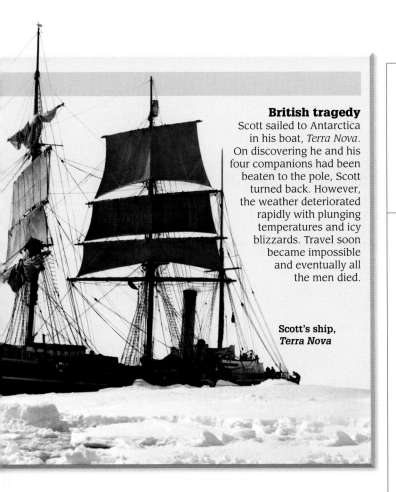

British tragedy
Scott sailed to Antarctica in his boat, *Terra Nova*. On discovering he and his four companions had been beaten to the pole, Scott turned back. However, the weather deteriorated rapidly with plunging temperatures and icy blizzards. Travel soon became impossible and eventually all the men died.

Scott's ship,
Terra Nova

1914
World War I begins
The assassination of Archduke Franz Ferdinand, heir to the throne of Austria-Hungary, in Sarajevo in late July, prompted the first truly global conflict. Austrian emperor Franz Joseph declared war against Serbia and World War I started. The network of alliances between the major European powers drew the continent into all-out war.

1914
First Battle of the Marne
September saw Germany sweep through Belgium into France, winning a series of quick battles and reaching the outskirts of Paris. However, the German advance was stopped by a French counter-offensive at the Marne River, forcing the German army into retreat.

World War I
See pages 242–243

1915
Second Battle of Ypres
The first battle at the Belgium town of Ypres in autumn 1914 marked the start of more than three years of stalemate. At the second battle in spring 1915, the Germans tried unsuccessfully to break the deadlock by using poison gas for the first time.

1915

1914
Panama Canal
After 10 years and $300 million, the Panama Canal was completed in 1914. Linking the Atlantic Ocean with the Pacific Ocean, the canal is 77 km (48 miles) in length. The canal was open to traffic from August 1914. Ships no longer had to sail the long Cape Horn route around the southern tip of South America nor the dangerous Strait of Magellan.

A tugboat pulls a ship through the new Panama Canal.

SUFFRAGETTE MOVEMENT

The right for women to be given the vote was fought by political campaigners around the world. New Zealand was the first country to give women the vote in 1893, then Australia in 1902, Finland in 1906, and Norway in 1913. The Suffragette Movement in Britain heated up during the early 20th century with women given the vote in 1918. The USA followed in 1920.

Raising awareness
Women did everything they could to capture the public's attention and the campaigners in Britain were particularly violent. They took part in acts of civil disobedience, smashing windows and chaining themselves to railings in the streets.

Media campaigns
Women made use of the media and produced their own publications to promote their cause around the world. Poster and newspaper campaigns saw the female following grow, for example, this poster is advertising *The Suffragette* newspaper.

World War I

At the turn of the 20th century, the countries of Europe were a complicated network of alliances and rivalries. So, when the heir to the Austrian throne, Franz Ferdinand, was assassinated by a Serbian nationalist in 1914 and Austria declared war on Serbia, other nations were quickly drawn into the crisis. In Europe, the fighting took place on two fronts: the Western Front, stretching from Belgium to Switzerland, and the Eastern Front, from the Baltic to the Black Sea. However the conflict soon spread to European colonies all over the world. The war raged for four years, and more than 20 million people lost their lives.

Trench warfare

On the Western Front, the war was fought from long trenches fortified with barbed wire, machine guns, and heavy artillery. Each side launched offensives, sending the men "over the top" to attack the enemy. The result was usually the mass slaughter of the attackers in the muddy "no man's land" between the two front lines. In the trenches, both sides deployed deadly chlorine gas, but the use of protective masks greatly reduced its effectiveness.

Divided Europe

Europe lay at the centre of the conflict. The opposing sides were the Central Powers (Germany, Austria-Hungary, and the Ottoman Empire) and the Allies (Britain, France, Russia, and later, Italy and the USA). The lines of the Western and Eastern Fronts changed during the war.

- Allies (Entente)
- Central Powers
- Neutral
- Western Front
- Eastern Front

Map labels: Atlantic Ocean, NORWAY, SWEDEN, IRELAND, DENMARK, RUSSIA, ENGLAND, NETHERLANDS, GERMANY, PORTUGAL, FRANCE, AUSTRIA-HUNGARY, ROMANIA, Black Sea, SPAIN, SWITZERLAND, ITALY, BULGARIA, SERBIA, GREECE, OTTOMAN EMPIRE, MOROCCO, ALBANIA, ALGERIA, Mediterranean Sea

> **"Success will come to the side that has the last man standing."**
>
> General Philippe Pétain, French army commander, 1916

Key events

1914

When Archduke Franz Ferdinand was assassinated, war erupted in Europe. By the end of the year, opposing forces in Europe were dug in, facing each other on the Western Front.

1915

The Allied attack at Gallipoli in Turkey failed to knock the Ottoman Empire out of the war, while in the east, the Germans drove back the Russians, capturing Poland.

1916

In France, the German offensive at Verdun lasted almost a year but the town was not captured. More than 700,000 were killed in the Allied offensive at the Somme.

1916

As both sides fought to control shipping routes, there were battles at sea. At Jutland, off Denmark, battle raged between 250 vessels, but ended in stalemate.

New weapons of war
World War I saw new weapons used in battle for the first time. Early zeppelins and planes proved useful for spying, but inflicted only limited damage on the enemy. Tanks were unreliable, but hinted at possibilities for the future.

Zeppelin attacks
The Germans used airships, mainly for spying. They also launched bombing raids on Britain with limited effect.

Airplanes
This was the first war where aircraft were used on a large scale. Small biplanes took part in aerial dogfights, but they had little influence on the conflict's outcome.

Tanks
First used by the British at the Battle of the Somme in France, tanks often got stuck in the muddy battlefields.

I WANT YOU FOR U.S. ARMY
NEAREST RECRUITING STATION

America calling
In May 1915, the British liner *Lusitania* was sunk by a German submarine, killing 1,201 people on board, including 128 Americans. Outrage at the attack was a major factor in the USA joining the war in 1917, alongside the Allies, giving a big boost to manpower and morale. "Uncle Sam" featured on a poster calling on Americans to join the army.

THESE WOMEN ARE DOING THEIR BIT
LEARN TO MAKE MUNITIONS

Women at war
As more and more men were called up to fight, women were hired to fill their places in the workplace, with the largest numbers employed in factories and farms. In Germany, by the end of the war, women made up more than half of the total domestic workforce. The wartime role of women would later help them to win the vote.

Casualties of war
About 65 million men fought in World War I, of whom 8.3 million died. Germany suffered the highest number of casualties.

Country	Military deaths
USA	116,000
Ottoman Empire (Turkey)	325,000
Italy	460,000
Britain and the Commonwealth	1,114,800
Austria-Hungary	1,200,000
France	1,385,000
Russia	1,700,000
Germany	1,808,000
Civilians of all countries	8,000,000
Estimated combatants killed, all nations	8,300,000
Estimated wounded soldiers, all nations	19,536,000

An end to war
The final Allied offensives began on 8 August 1918, and pushed towards the German border. As the Allies advanced, the Central Powers collapsed. Revolution spread throughout a crumbling and weakened Germany. On 11 November, an armistice was agreed, ending the war. Peace treaties redrew the map of Europe, penalizing the defeated nations. Surviving soldiers received a hero's welcome home.

1917
The US entered the war, while the revolution forced the Russians to make peace with Germany. Major Western offensives by the Allies at Ypres failed in their objectives.

1918
The German Spring Offensive pushed the Allies back 65 km (40 miles) in just four days. However, an Allied counter-offensive pushed the Germans back towards Germany.

1918
By November it was clear that neither Germany, nor its allies, could continue the fight and an armistice was signed on 11 November, ending the war.

Remembrance
The poppies that grew on the World War I battlefields have become a symbol of remembrance for the war dead.

1915 ▶ 1920

Soldiers from an Australian artillery unit wait offshore.

Crowds in London celebrate after the signing of the armistice ended World War I.

1918
The 100 Days
Following the failure of the German Spring Offensive, the Allies began to fight back in August, pushing the German troops towards Germany over a 100-day period. An armistice was signed on 11 November 1918, ending the war.

1918
End of the Tsars
Russian Tsar Nicholas II and his family were imprisoned by the communists in the Ural Mountains. They were then assassinated by Bolshevik gunmen.

1916
The Eastern Front
Less stable than the Western Front, the Eastern Front was where the Russians confronted German and Austrian troops. The Russians were victorious when an attack led by their general Brusilov forced the Austrians briefly into retreat. It was the Russians' greatest success of the war.

1915
Gallipoli campaign
During World War I, the Allied forces started their fight against Turkey by targeting Gallipoli, near the Turkish capital of Constantinople. The Turks repelled the invasion, inflicting a quarter of a million Allied casualties, including many ANZACs (Australian and New Zealand Army Corps).

1915

1916
The Western Front
From 1914–1918, British and French troops faced the German army along a line of trenches called the Western Front. In 1916, there were two attempts to break through the front. First, a German attack against the French city of Verdun resulted in 400,000 casualties on both sides. Then Britain launched an equally disastrous offensive at the Somme, in which more than 300,000 Allied and German soldiers were killed.

Poster for the Russian Revolution, showing a worker smashing his chains

German submarine U-10 served during World War I.

1917
Russian Revolution
By 1917, the Russians were losing World War I as German forces pushed them back. Tsar Nicholas II abdicated, leading to revolution. Eventually the Communists, led by Vladimir Lenin, seized power. He signed an armistice with Germany that saw one-third of Russia's pre-war population placed under German control.

1917
America declares war
The USA entered World War I for two reasons: the launch of unrestricted submarine warfare by Germany, which saw the loss of several US ships; and the publication of a telegram showing that Germany was seeking an alliance with Mexico should America join the war. American manpower was a huge boost to the Allies.

Atlantic aviators

In 1919 British aviators John Alcock and Arthur Brown flew nonstop across the Atlantic Ocean in just under 16 hours. The distance was 3,040 km (1,890 miles). This feat helped them claim a £10,000 prize offered by the *Daily Mail* newspaper.

1919

Amritsar massacre

Fearing a nationalist uprising in India, British troops were ordered to fire on an unarmed crowd gathered at the Jallianwala Bagh gardens in Amritsar for a religious festival. Nearly 400 people were killed, and more than 1,000 injured, prompting outrage and fuelling calls for Indian independence from Britain.

1920

1919

Versailles conference

The treaty agreed at the end-of-war conference in Versailles, France, imposed severe peace terms on Germany. The country lost all its colonies as well as European territory in the east and west. It also faced a huge bill for the war, known as reparations, amounting to US $31 billion.

 The Treaty of Versailles in 1919 resulted in economic crisis for Germany during the 1920s, and a sense of injustice that helped pave the way for the rise of Nazism in the run-up to World War II.

1918   SPANISH FLU

The biggest killer of 1918 was not war, but a powerful strain of flu that killed more than 50 million people worldwide. It was called Spanish flu because most of the reports on the disease came from Spain. This was not because the disease had originated there but because Spain had remained neutral in the war so did not have a media blackout like some other countries.

Global epidemic
The flu was one of the worst natural disasters in history, affecting nations across the world. Hospitals struggled to cope with the volume of casualties – it is estimated that about 3 per cent of the world's population was killed.

Emergency hospital tents for flu patients in Massachusetts, USA

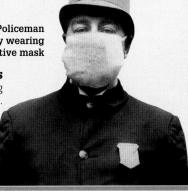

Policeman on duty wearing a protective mask

Taking precautions
People tried to avoid catching the disease by wearing masks. Governments tried to stop its spread by quarantining communities and preventing infected people from moving around – which proved very difficult during a world war.

1920 ▶ 1930

1920
League of Nations
The League of Nations was an international body founded in 1919 to try and solve disputes between countries. It had its first meeting in 1920, but without the USA. Though US President Wilson proposed the original idea, the USA declined to join.

1922   SOVIET UNION ESTABLISHED

From 1917, Russia experienced civil war between the "red" communists and the "white" opposition forces. Victorious communist leader Vladimir Lenin united most of the territory formerly ruled by the Tsar, to form the Soviet Union.

Lenin and Stalin
Vladimir Lenin (left) died in 1924 and, after a brief power struggle, was replaced by Joseph Stalin (right), who consolidated his power as he built his army, assassinating his political rivals. Stalin launched a five-year plan to expand farming and industry, and exerted ruthless control over the state for three decades.

Badge bearing the hammer and sickle – a symbol of communism

> ❝ **Bread, Peace, and Land.** ❞
> Communist slogan, 1917

1922
Mussolini in power
Benito Mussolini was the leader of the Italian Fascist Party, which he formed in 1919. In 1922 he was invited to join the government to deal with a political crisis. By 1925 he had made himself dictator, "Il Duce", with a mission to turn Italy into a major European power.

1920

1920
Prohibition
The sale of alcohol was banned in the USA from 1920 until 1933. During this time, organized crime gangs grew rich selling illegal alcohol and running secret bars, known as "speakeasies".

1922
Irish Civil War
In 1921, Ireland had been divided into Northern Ireland, which remained part of the UK, and the Irish Free State. Many Irish republicans objected to the division, launching a civil war.

Tutankhamun's gold death mask

1923
Turkish settlement
Following its defeat in World War I, much of the Ottoman Empire was divided between Britain and France. However, Turkey fought off the Allies and in 1923 gained their recognition of its modern borders.

Drinkers break the law in an American speakeasy.

Tutankhamun
After years of searching, British archaeologist Howard Carter discovered the tomb of the Egyptian Pharaoh Tutankhamun. Left undisturbed for more than 3,000 years, the tomb was filled with treasures.

1926

Birth of television

Scottish inventor John Logie Baird demonstrated the first flickering television images to a group of 50 scientists in London. Within two years he had sent pictures through a cable across the Atlantic Ocean to the USA.

Early Baird black and white television

Television screen

Walt Disney, with a model of his creation, Mickey Mouse

1928

Mickey Mouse

The famous animated character first appeared in the short cartoon, *Steamboat Willie*. Its creator, Walt Disney, went on to found Walt Disney Productions, creating full-length animated cartoons and opening the theme park Disneyland in the 1950s.

Oscars ceremony

The first Academy Awards celebrating the year's best films were held in a small hotel ceremony in Hollywood in 1929. Each winner received a small gold-plated statue known as an Oscar.

📢 In 1927, *The Jazz Singer*, the first film with spoken words, signalled the beginning of the end for silent films.

1930 ▶▶

1929

Wall Street Crash

The good times of the "roaring twenties" came to a sudden end in October 1929 when panic-selling wiped billions of dollars off the value of businesses on the US stock market and sent the world into the Great Depression.

The Great Depression
See pages 250–251

1928 — DISCOVERY OF PENICILLIN

Scottish scientist Alexander Fleming found that in dishes where *staphylococci* bacteria were being grown, a mould formed that was killing the bacteria. This accidental discovery led to the development of the first antibiotic, penicillin.

Fleming's laboratory

Fleming discovered penicillin and developed it in his laboratory. Then two scientists, Australian Howard Florey and German Ernst Chain, made penicillin a usable drug.

Antibiotics

An antibiotic is a chemical substance derived from a mould that cures infections. By the late 1940s, the antibiotic penicillin was being mass produced and has since saved millions of lives as a treatment for bacterial infection.

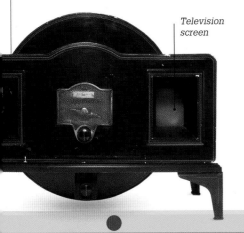

Penicillin mould (green) attacks bacteria (white)

In New York, a man tries to sell his car, having lost all his money in the Wall Street Crash.

247

1930 ▶ 1935

The Chrysler Building is visible (far right) behind a worker constructing the Empire State Building.

1931

Age of the skyscraper
The 319 m- (1,046 ft-) tall Chrysler Building was built in New York, USA, in 1930. A year later, the Empire State Building was constructed nearby. At 443 m (1,454 ft) in height, it was the world's tallest building at the time.

1930

Collectivization of agriculture
In the Soviet Union, dictator Joseph Stalin's attempt to industrialize the countryside by turning small private farms into large state-owned operations was met with widespread resistance. Thousands of those who resisted were sent to forced labour camps known as gulags.

1931

Creation of the Commonwealth
The British parliament passed a law recognizing the British Empire dominions of Australia, New Zealand, Canada, South Africa, the Irish Free State, and Newfoundland as fully equal with Britain. This new arrangement was known as the Commonwealth of Nations.

1932

New Deal
With the Great Depression at its peak and about 13 million Americans out of work, the new US President Franklin D Roosevelt gave a speech on his "New Deal" – a series of plans to try and solve the economic problems. These came into effect a year later.

1930

1930

Salt March
As part of Indian nationalist leader Mohandas Gandhi's campaign of non-violent civil disobedience against British rule, Gandhi led his followers on a march to the sea to collect salt. This activity was banned by the British who had a monopoly on salt.

1931

Japan occupies Manchuria
On the pretence of protecting the South Manchuria Railway from terrorists, the Japanese invaded the Chinese region. They installed the last Chinese emperor, Puyi, who had abdicated in 1912, as a ruler who followed Japanese orders. The occupation lasted until the end of World War II.

1930   **THE AIR INDUSTRY**

The 1930s saw major developments in the airline industry. Airplanes and airships competed to be the main form of passenger transport. The public was also fascinated by the feats of pioneering aviators, such as Amelia Earhart and Amy Johnson.

Lockheed Vega flown by Earhart

Female fliers
During the 1920s, male aviation pioneers had become international celebrities. In the 1930s it was the turn of women, as British amateur pilot Amy Johnson became the first woman to fly solo from England to Australia. She was followed in 1932 by the American Amelia Earhart, who made the first unaccompanied flight across the Atlantic Ocean.

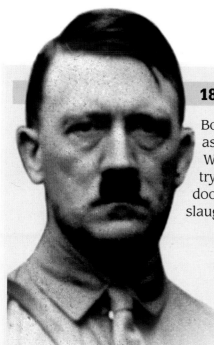

1889–1945 ADOLF HITLER

Born and raised in Austria, Adolf Hitler served as a soldier in a German regiment during World War I. Defeat was his motivation to try building a new German Empire, but his doomed attempt unleashed carnage and slaughter on an unimaginable scale.

Rise of a dictator
Hitler was a gifted public speaker who convinced many people to support the Nazis. But when the Nazis came to power in 1933, they turned Germany into a dictatorship with Hitler as the supreme Führer (ruler).

Nazi origins
After serving in the war, Hitler became the leader of the far-right National Socialist (Nazi) Party. The Nazis blamed Germany's economic problems on the Versailles Treaty and the influence of other races, particularly the Jews, who they considered inferior to the Germans.

Haile Selassie, emperor of Ethiopia

1935

Ethiopia invaded
Having failed to conquer Ethiopia several decades earlier, Italy tried again. Despite determined resistance by the Ethiopians, led by their emperor Haile Selassie, Ethiopia fell the next year.

1935

1933

Famine in Ukraine
According to official Soviet propaganda, the Soviet Union's economy was thriving while the rest of the world suffered in the Great Depression. In reality, the Ukraine was suffering one of the largest famines in history with millions dying of starvation.

The Great Depression
See pages 250–251

1935

Dust Bowl
The Depression in the USA was made even worse by an agricultural disaster. Poor farming techniques and severe storms ripped the top soils from farmland in Oklahoma, Texas, and several other states, creating a "Dust Bowl" that forced thousands of farmers to migrate.

Failed flights
In the early 1930s, airships looked like the future of flight. But a series of disasters caused people to lose faith in the industry. The British *R101* crashed in 1930, but the final blow came when the German *Hindenburg* exploded in flames (above) in 1937 while docking in New Jersey, USA, killing more than 30 people.

A truck drives away from a giant dust cloud in Colorado, USA.

Wall Street Crash
In the 1920s boom time, people over-invested in stocks, sending prices soaring. But in 1929, stock prices plummeted, plunging the USA into economic turmoil. Here, a panicked crowd surrounds the New York Stock Exchange on Wall Street.

The Great Depression

On Monday 28 October 1929 the New York Stock Exchange crashed. Known as Black Monday, it caused thousands of companies to go bankrupt, and widespread unemployment and poverty ensued. The effects soon spread around the world, causing a global Depression. The election of President Franklin D Roosevelt in 1932 and the introduction of his "New Deal" policies would turn the country around, with aid for the unemployed and big building projects to create jobs.

Who's who

Herbert Hoover
Elected US President in 1928, Hoover is often blamed for not realizing the scale of the problem. He thought the economy would fix itself. He was voted out of office in 1932.

Franklin D Roosevelt
Hoover's successor, "FDR", introduced a policy – the New Deal – to solve the problems. This involved spending government money on public construction projects to employ people.

> **"Any lack of confidence in the economic future of the United States is foolish."**
>
> President Herbert Hoover in a speech after the stock market crash, 1929

Housing crisis
During the Depression, about 20,000 companies and 1,600 banks went bust, and hundreds of thousands of farms were sold. Many people ended up homeless, and were forced to live in hastily-built shanty towns, known as "Hoovervilles", after President Hoover.

Key events

1929
The US economy was plunged into crisis as stock prices suddenly crashed.

1930
More than three million people were unemployed in the US, but President Hoover continued to believe that prosperity would return.

1931
As the Depression spread around the world, many banks collapsed, taking the life savings of thousands of people.

1932
Franklin D Roosevelt was elected President in a landslide victory. He was committed to solving the country's economic problems.

1933
Adolf Hitler came to power in Germany, promising to solve the problems of the Depression with his extremist policies.

Desperate for work

Unemployment figures soared during the Great Depression. By 1932, more than 12 million Americans were out of work as banks closed, firms went out of business, and factories laid off staff. People took to the streets of New York, wearing banners stating their professions and skills. They were prepared to work for only a dollar a week. Without money, families grew desperate for food, and were forced to queue for free soup at public kitchens.

Two men advertise their need to find work during the Great Depression.

Escapist entertainment

The Depression also coincided with the arrival of "Talkies", new films that became one of the most popular forms of entertainment for the masses. The cinema was a cheap way for many people to escape the harsh reality of daily life.

Technicolor camera used to shoot early colour films

Industrial unemployment

Unemployment rose and trade declined in all the main industrialized countries during the Depression. Germany was the hardest-hit nation of all, and the public's dissatisfaction became a contributing factor in Hitler's rise to power.

Country	Millions unemployed	Percentage of population
Germany	5 million	30.1%
UK	3 million	22.1%
France	1 million	15.4%
USA	13 million	26.3%

Mass protest

Protests against the Depression took place across the world. In 1936, one of the most famous protests involved 200 unemployed shipbuilders who marched nearly 500 km (300 miles) from Jarrow in northeast England to London to appeal to the government for help.

Wartime recovery

Although the economy improved in the late 1930s, the Depression did not properly end in the USA until it entered World War II. Factories supplying vehicles and weapons to the war effort created thousands of jobs.

Poster to advertise war-related work in factories

UNITED WE WIN

1933
Roosevelt launched the "New Deal" for America, a set of policies designed to bring the USA out of economic gloom.

1933
President Roosevelt began his "fireside chats" – weekly radio broadcasts to the nation.

Men queue for work

1935
The "Dust Bowl" forced the migration of thousands of farmers in the US Midwest. The Great Depression deepened.

1936
Roosevelt introduced the "Second New Deal", including pensions and schemes for sickness benefit and unemployment benefit.

1941
The USA's economic recovery was back on track, following the country's entry into World War II.

251

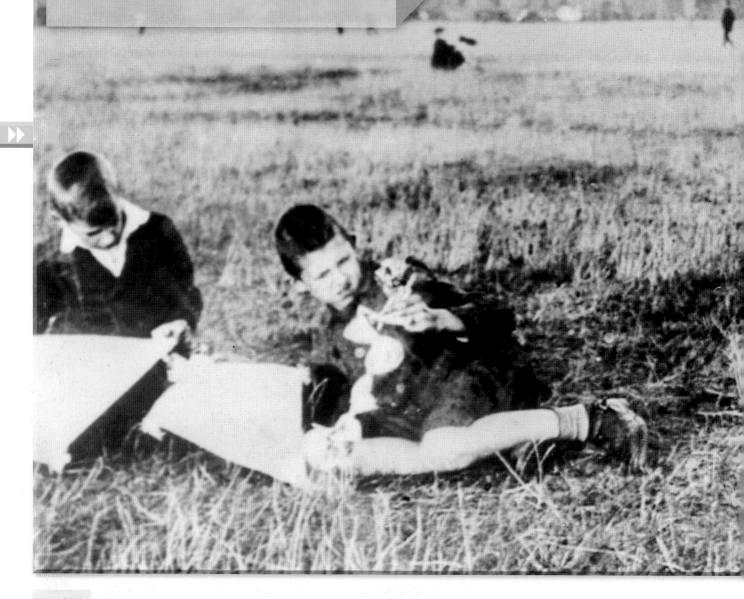

Worthless money

After World War I, Germany was faced with huge war debts and also reparations – money demanded by the Allies to compensate for the damage of the war. In an attempt to deal with the financial crisis, the government printed money. This only made it worthless and sent prices soaring, a situation called hyperinflation. A loaf of bread that cost 163 marks in 1922 cost 1.5 million by September 1923, and 200 billion by November 1923. Germans used wads of notes as fuel, to paper their walls, and let children play with it.

> "The chief value of money lies in the fact that one lives in a world in which it is overestimated."
>
> Henry Louis Mencken, American journalist

Children playing with kites made of Germany's worthless banknotes

1935 ▶ 1940

Jesse Owens
Hitler used the Berlin Olympic Games of 1936, the first games to be televised, to showcase Nazi Germany to the world. But his theories of racial superiority were blown away when the African American Jesse Owens won four gold medals.

Jesse Owens competing in 1936

1936–1939   SPANISH CIVIL WAR

In 1931, Spain's king abdicated and the country became a republic. However, in 1936, the Nationalist Party, led by General Francisco Franco, wanted to return to the old ways and revolted against the new Republican government.

Franco in power
Thousands were killed during three years of fighting. General Franco emerged victorious against the Republicans and went on to rule Spain as a dictator for the next 36 years.

Republican poster

1937
Second Sino-Japanese War
Already in control of Manchuria in northeast China, Japan launched an all-out war on China, taking several cities, including the capital Nanjing. The war continued until Japan's defeat by US forces at the end of World War II.

1938
Kristallnacht
"The Night of the Broken Glass" saw the Nazis' antisemitic (anti-Jewish) policies put into deadly effect as Jewish businesses and synagogues across Germany were destroyed. About 30,000 Jewish people were arrested and taken to concentration camps.

1936
Edward VIII's abdication
Less than a year after becoming king of Britain, Edward VIII gave up the throne so he could marry the American divorcee Wallis Simpson – the rules of the time did not allow the British monarch to have a wife who had already been divorced. His brother George VI took over the throne.

Edward and Mrs Simpson on their wedding day in 1937

German troops in Vienna, Austria

1938
Union of Germany and Austria
The next stage in Hitler's plan for a Greater German Reich (empire) was to create an *Anschluss* (union) of Germany and Austria, the country of the dictator's birth. In March, Hitler's troops marched unopposed into Austria.

1938
Munich Conference
At the Munich Conference, Germany, Italy, France, and Britain signed the Munich Agreement, which tried to limit German expansion. Only part of Czechoslovakia (the Sudetenland) was given to Germany. Hitler broke the Munich Agreement by taking all of Czechoslovakia.

British Prime Minister Neville Chamberlain after signing the Munich Agreement

Child star Shirley Temple presents the Oscar to Walt Disney.

1939

Award-winning cartoon
It took three years to make and cost more than $1 million, but the first feature-length cartoon *Snow White and the Seven Dwarfs* proved a huge hit when it was released in 1938. Its producer, Walt Disney, was presented with an Oscar for the film in 1939.

1940

1940

France surrenders
German forces quickly overran Belgium, the Netherlands, Denmark, and Norway. France was hit with such ferocity that it surrendered within weeks. The Germans then ruled the north while the French "Vichy" government ruled the south. In 1942, the Germans took over the whole of France.

1939

World War II begins
Germany invaded Poland on 1 September. Shortly after, Britain and France declared war on Germany, while the USA announced its neutrality, as did Italy before entering the war on Germany's side in 1940.

War in Europe
See pages 256–257

1940   BATTLE OF BRITAIN

After the defeat of France, Germany turned its attention to Britain, which had started the war badly with much of its army forced to evacuate France at Dunkirk. In the summer and autumn of 1940, the British Royal Air Force (RAF) and the German Luftwaffe engaged in intense combat in the skies above Britain.

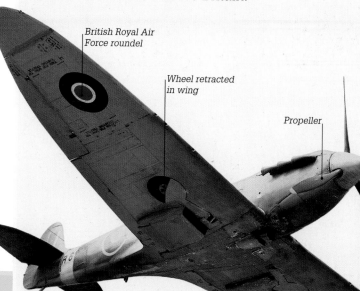

British Royal Air Force roundel

Wheel retracted in wing

Propeller

British spitfires took to the skies to repel German attacks, engaging in hundreds of aerial "dogfights".

Rivals in the skies
Hitler's plan was to destroy Britain's air defences to prepare for a full-scale invasion. From July onwards, squadrons of German Messerschmitts and Stukas targeted British airfields and aircraft factories. In September, the Germans changed tactics, launching devastating bombing raids on London. When Britain did not surrender, the Germans called off the attacks on 31 October to prepare for their imminent invasion of the Soviet Union.

Cockpit

Nazi swastika

The Messerschmitt, the main German battle aircraft

1935 was a year for music legends, with both American rock n'roll star Elvis Presley and Italian opera singer Luciano Pavarotti being born.

War in Europe

In 1939, the army of Nazi Germany invaded Poland. This was the first step in the plan of the German dictator, Adolf Hitler, to conquer Europe. Two days later, Britain and France declared war on Germany, but his invasion of Europe continued and by 1940 France, Holland, Belgium, Denmark, and Norway had all fallen. The Allied forces of Britain, Australia, New Zealand, Canada, and the exiled French and Poles, were joined in 1941 by the Soviet Union and the USA. Their enemies were the Axis powers of Germany and Italy and from 1941, Japan, as the war expanded across the world.

Lightning war
Germany achieved a number of swift victories in World War II using the speed and surprise of joint tank and aircraft attacks to catch the Allied forces unawares. This tactic became known as "blitzkrieg" (lightning war).

Allies
Allies controlled or allied
Neutral
Axis
Axis controlled or allied
Front lines, 1942

ICELAND
Atlantic Ocean
FINLAND
NORWAY
SWEDEN
SOVIET UNION
NETHERLANDS
IRELAND
DENMARK
UNITED KINGDOM
GERMANY
DENMARK
UKRAINE
SWITZERLAND
PORTUGAL
FRANCE
HUNGARY
ROMANIA
ITALY
Black Sea
SPAIN
BULGARIA
GREECE
TURKEY
SYRIA
MOROCCO
Mediterranean Sea
JORDAN
IRAQ
ALGERIA
LIBYA
EGYPT

German expansion
By 1942 German troops had overrun much of Europe and North Africa. In many of the lands they occupied, such as France, Russia, Yugoslavia, and Greece, there was resistance from the non-military population.

Battle of the Atlantic
The conflict was fought at sea as well as on land. In the Atlantic, German bombers and U-boats (submarines) off France and Norway tried to sink ships carrying supplies of food and weapons from the USA. Allied battleships and aircraft carriers fought back.

A US ship destroys a German U-boat.

Key events

1939
Germany invaded Poland, causing Britain and France to declare war on the Nazis.

Little ship of Dunkirk

1940
France surrendered. British troops were forced to make an emergency evacuation from the French port of Dunkirk using a mix of naval vessels and private "little ships".

1941
Germany turned on its former ally, the Soviet Union, in 1941. From August 1942 to March 1943, German troops tried and failed to take the city of Stalingrad.

1942
The Battles of El Alamein in northern Africa saw the British forces attack and defeat the German Afrika Korps.

1943
Germany surrendered at Stalingrad. Germans and Italians were expelled from North Africa. Mussolini was forced to resign.

Code breakers

Both the Allies and the Axis powers disguised their communications using codes. One breakthrough of the war was the success of British code breakers in deciphering German messages encoded by the Enigma machine. As a result, valuable military information fell into Allied hands, giving them a great advantage over their enemies in the war.

German Enigma machine

Who's who

Winston Churchill

One of the few politicians to warn against Hitler during the 1930s, Winston Churchill led Britain through the war as prime minister.

Dwight Eisenhower

A general in the US Army, Eisenhower commanded the Allied Forces in Western Europe, and directed D-Day. He later became president.

Adolf Hitler

It was the ambitions of Germany's leader, Hitler, that drove the country to war and led to its defeat. At the end of the conflict, Hitler took his own life.

Joseph Stalin

Soviet leader Joseph Stalin led the retaliation after Germany's attack in 1941, but ended up taking over many of the countries "freed" from German control.

African advance

The war reached north Africa by 1940. Italian forces invaded Egypt, but the defending British troops drove them back. The conflict continued until the British victory at El Alamein, Egypt, in 1942. British and American forces arrived in Algeria and Morocco, leaving the Axis armies caught between the Allies. The Axis armies surrendered in 1943.

British soldiers advance at the Battle of El Alamein in 1942.

Russian military hat

Turning point

During intense conflict on Europe's Eastern Front, the Russians beat the Germans at Stalingrad in 1942, and then pushed them steadily westward, capturing Warsaw in January 1945 and then encircling Berlin in April. Meanwhile, Allied troops pushed into Germany from the West. On May 7, Germany finally surrendered as Berlin lay in ruins. Hitler had killed himself in his bunker. On May 8, a formal announcement came that the war in Europe was over.

1944

The Allies invaded France on June 6— D-Day. Thousands of British, American, Canadian, and French troops landed to push the Germans back.

1944

The Italian government signed an armistice in 1943, but the Germans remained in control of much of Italy until 1944, when US forces captured Rome.

1944

Hitler used new weapons, the V-1 (an unmanned jet-propelled flying bomb) and the V-2 (a supersonic rocket bomb), but with limited success.

V-2

1944

Allied troops continued to push through France, capturing Paris. At the Battle of the Bulge, the Germans carried out their final counteroffensive until they were forced back.

1945

By 1945, Germany was losing the war. The Allies attacked Germany from east and west to capture Hitler's capital of Berlin. On May 7, Germany surrendered.

War in the Pacific

Japan, which had been allied to Germany since 1940, wanted to create an empire across Asia and the Pacific. However, Japan feared American interests in the area might prevent its ambitions. So in 1941, the Japanese launched an attack on the US fleet at Pearl Harbor, Hawaii. The idea was to inflict so much damage that the US would be unable to wage war. The battle for control of the Pacific Ocean turned the war into a global conflict. With its Allies, the US fought back against Japan, finally claiming victory when it dropped devastating atomic bombs on Hiroshima and Nagasaki.

Who's who

Franklin D. Roosevelt
The US president described Pearl Harbor as "a date which will live in infamy." He led his country to the edge of victory, but died before the war ended. He was succeeded by Harry S. Truman.

Emperor Hirohito
Japan's ruler was not prosecuted for war crimes, and remained in power until the 1980s, overseeing an economic boom in his country.

Japan against the Allies

Japan started the war at a furious pace, declaring war on both the US and Britain. After Pearl Harbor, it took control of the Philippines, Indonesia, Hong Kong, Malaya, and Burma, as well as many Pacific islands. But from mid-1942 onward, it was mainly in retreat as the Allies went on the offensive.

- Allies
- Axis
- Axis control
- Neutral
- Extent of Japanese control, 1942
- * Atom bombs

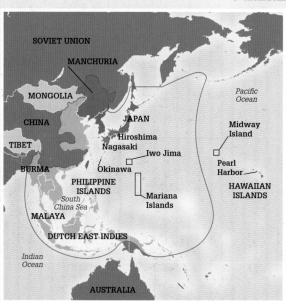

Key events

1941
In December, Japan attacked the US naval base at Pearl Harbor, Hawaii. The United States declared war the next day.

1942
Japan stepped up its Asian campaign, conquering territories across Southeast Asia and the Pacific.

1942
By the middle of the year, the US had begun to push the Japanese back, preventing their attempt to take the US naval base at Midway Island.

1943
The US defeated Japanese forces at the Battle of Tarawa, the bloodiest yet in the Pacific. More than 1,000 American and 4,000 Japanese soldiers perished.

1944
The Japanese attacked the British in northeast India. The British regrouped and, with the Burmese army, drove the Japanese out of Burma in 1945.

Pearl Harbor memorial in Hawaii today

Japanese fliers

At the start of the war, the Japanese Mitsubishi Zero fighter aircraft (left) was much faster and more agile than anything the Allies could produce. However, Allied technology caught up, and the Japanese began to lose more battles, forcing them to adopt more desperate tactics.

Japanese Rising Sun emblem

Kamikaze bombers

In the latter stages of the war, with the conflict going badly, the Japanese came up with a new military strategy: kamikaze, meaning "divine wind." It involved pilots launching suicide attacks against US vessels in planes loaded with explosives. About 50 Allied vessels were destroyed in this way with at least 4,000 kamikaze pilots sacrificing themselves.

Kamikaze pilots

Pearl Harbor

In December 1941, Japan's surprise attack caused huge devastation. More than 2,000 people were killed, 188 aircraft were destroyed, and many warships were damaged. But it was not a knock-out blow. The US was able to replace its losses and lead the attack on Japan in 1942.

Nuclear warfare

Developed by American and British scientists, the two nuclear bombs dropped on Japan caused massive devastation. The impact of the bombs was like nothing the world had ever seen before. In the city of Hiroshima, more than 90,000 people were killed, and 70 percent of the buildings were destroyed, while in Nagasaki, at least 60,000 perished. After the second blast, Japan surrendered. World War II was over.

Cloud of debris over the city of Nagasaki

Cities under attack

Between March 10 and June 15, 1945, six major Japanese cities were decimated by heavy US bombing raids.

Japanese cities	Number of raids	Percentage of city destroyed
Tokyo	5	50%
Nagoya	4	31%
Kobe	2	56%
Osaka	4	26%
Yokohama	2	44%
Kawasaki	1	33%

Replica of the nuclear bomb dropped on Hiroshima

"I realize the tragic significance of the atom bomb... We thank God it has come to us instead of our enemies."

President Harry S. Truman, August 9, 1945

1944
The Battle of the Philippine Sea ended in defeat for Japan at the Mariana Islands.

1944
In the war's largest naval battle, and the first to feature kamikaze bombers, the US defeated the Japanese fleet near the Philippine island of Leyte.

1945
Fighting for the tiny but strategically important island of Iwo Jima was fierce. The US lost more than 6,000 troops, and the Japanese at least 20,000.

1945
The US spent two months conquering the heavily defended island of Okinawa. It lost 12,000 soldiers, while the Japanese lost more than 100,000 men.

1945
The US finally ended hostilities by dropping two nuclear bombs on the Japanese cities of Hiroshima and Nagasaki. Japan surrendered.

1940 ▸ 1945

War in Europe
See pages 256–257

1940

The Blitz

Germany tried to break Britain's resolve to continue fighting by bombing 16 major cities. German Luftwaffe carried out aerial attacks on London on 57 consecutive nights. About 40,000 people died before the raids were called off in 1941.

St. Thomas's Hospital in London was wrecked by bombing in the Blitz.

1942

Battle of El Alamein

In north Africa, an Allied offensive at El Alamein, Egypt, forced the Germans into retreat. The following year, the German army in north Africa had surrendered to the Allies.

1942

Battle of Stalingrad

Germany's failed attempt to capture the Soviet city of Stalingrad (now Volgograd) was one of the major turning points of the war. The Soviets held out for more than six months, eventually destroying the Nazi forces.

The ruins of Stalingrad in 1942

1944

Siege of Leningrad ends

The longest and deadliest siege of the war was Leningrad. Started in 1941, it finally came to an end when the Soviets reopened the communication lines to the city and forced the Germans out. The conflict resulted in more than one million Soviet casualties.

1944

Battle of the Bulge

In December, the Germans launched their last major offensive against the Allies. The attack initially created a break, or "bulge," in the Allied lines in France and Belgium, but this was quickly closed up and soon the Germans were retreating back toward Germany.

1940

1941

Operation Barbarossa

In June, Germany launched Operation Barbarossa—an all-out attack on its former ally, the Soviet Union. By the end of the year, German troops were at the gates of Moscow. However, a Soviet counterattack in January 1942 managed to push the Germans back.

1941

US enters the war

Although the United States had declared its support for the Allied cause, public opinion was firmly against the country joining the war. That changed when the Japanese attacked the US naval base at Pearl Harbor, Hawaii, on December 7. The United States Congress declared war the next day.

1944   D-DAY

On June 6 (code-named D-Day), thousands of Allied troops landed on France's Normandy coast for a surprise attack. The Allies faced stiff resistance, but by June 17, more than half a million troops were on French soil and the push toward Berlin, Germany, had begun.

Beach landings
Troops and equipment were gathered in Britain ready for the attack, and then sailed across the English Channel. Soldiers waded ashore on Normandy's beaches under heavy fire, but were eventually able to break through the German defenses.

Parachute drops
The attack began with thousands of paratroopers being dropped behind the German lines. Their task was to capture key targets and destroy German defenses and communication systems before the invasion force marched across France.

1945
Italy defeated
Allied troops invaded Italy and took the city of Rome in 1943. The war continued until May 1945, when German forces in Italy surrendered. Italy's dictator leader, Benito Mussolini, had tried to flee, but was captured and executed.

War rationing
To preserve precious resources, both the UK and Germany rationed what the public could eat during the war. Everyone was issued a ration book. Sweets were limited to 12 ounces per month.

1945
Germany surrenders
With German forces retreating in the East, the Soviets were ordered by their dictator leader, Joseph Stalin, to "race" to Berlin to capture Hitler. But knowing that all was lost, Hitler committed suicide. Berlin was captured and on May 7, Germany surrendered. The next day, May 8, was declared V-E (Victory in Europe) Day, and saw mass celebrations across Europe.

British girls danced with American soldiers to celebrate V-E Day in London.

1945

1945
Japan's surrender
Japan continued to fight for a few months after the defeat of Germany. It finally surrendered in August after the US dropped two nuclear bombs, destroying the cities of Hiroshima and Nagasaki.

American boxer Muhammad Ali was born Cassius Clay in 1942. He was the first person to win the heavyweight championship three times.

1933–1945 THE HOLOCAUST

The Nazis' antisemitic (anti-Jewish) and racist policies led to the slaughter of more than six million Jews, gypsies, homosexuals, and disabled people. This systematic killing was known as the Holocaust, meaning a burned offering or sacrifice.

Anne Frank's diary
In 1942, a Jewish girl named Anne Frank and her family went into hiding in a secret apartment in the Netherlands. The diary she kept reveals the fear of a life in hiding. In 1944, they were discovered and Anne died in a concentration camp.

Yellow star worn to identify Jews

Concentration camps
Jewish people were rounded up and sent to concentration camps, where they were imprisoned and forced to do hard labor. Later, the Nazis established "extermination" camps such as Auschwitz (above), where millions of people were murdered.

Jewish label
In Nazi Germany, Jewish people were forced to sew yellow stars onto their clothing to identify them to the rest of the population and the authorities. The stars were marked with the word *Jude*, German for "Jew."

Saying goodbye
These Kindertransport children are saying their final goodbyes to their parents at the train station in Vienna, Austria.

> **We all leant out of the carriage window and my parents waved white handkerchiefs. I didn't know that would be the last time I would see any of them alive.**
>
> Vera Schaufeld, Czechoslovakian girl, who left on the *Kindertransport* at age 9

A safe haven
Children stand outside their rooms at a British holiday camp in Harwich. Many Kindertransport children were housed here while foster accommodation was arranged.

Fleeing the Nazis

In November 1938, as the Nazi persecution of Germany's Jews grew worse, Jewish leaders appealed to Britain for help. This led to the development of the *Kindertransport* (German for "transportation of children"), a rescue operation set up by British Jews to help Jewish children in Nazi-occupied countries. As a result, thousands of Jewish children were sent to Britain for their own safety. It was meant to be a temporary measure until the situation improved, but once war broke out, the children were forced to stay.

The lucky few
The plan's organizers chose the most vulnerable children to be rescued: orphans, those with poor parents, or those with parents in a concentration camp. About 10,000 children from Germany, Austria, Poland, and Czechoslovakia made the journey before war broke out.

Traveling light
The children were allowed to bring just one small suitcase each and no more than 10 German marks in money. They were issued a simple ID card, which was often pinned to their clothing. Then, leaving their parents behind, they faced the long journey to Britain by train and boat.

Life in Britain
About half of all the *Kindertransport* children ended up in foster homes. The rest lived in hostels, group homes, and farms. Some of the older children went to work, mainly on farms, as servants in houses, or as nurses. Once they turned 18, many *Kindertransport* refugees joined the military and fought with the Allies against the Nazis.

After the war
Some children were reunited with their parents after the war, but many learned that their parents had died in concentration camps. Despite their misfortunes, most went on to lead happy lives in their new country. Two Nobel Prize winners were former *Kindertransport* children: German-born American Arno Penzias won the Prize for Physics in 1978, while Austrian-American Walter Kohn won the Prize for Chemistry in 1998.

> **I was one of the lucky ones in that I saw my parents again. The majority of children, in fact, didn't.**
>
> Marion Marston, German *Kindertransport* child, at age 14

Parting gifts
This stuffed dog was the last thing Evelyn Kaye's father gave her as she left Vienna at age 9.

New arrival
Recently arrived in Britain, a young German girl holds her doll and her bag as she waits to be placed in temporary accommodation in Harwich.

❝At the time I thought it was quite an exciting adventure. I said 'goodbye' to my mother, 'see you soon.' Who could tell what was going to happen?❞

Inga Joseph, an Austrian *Kindertransport* child who left Vienna at age 9

1945–2018
Fast forward

After World War II, two superpowers emerged and a 40-year standoff
began, with the United States and its capitalist allies on one side and the
Soviet Union and its Communist allies on the other. The period also saw
the disintegration of European overseas empires, and the formation
of the European Union. Meanwhile, technology was leaping forward,
putting men on the Moon and personal computers in most homes,
and linking people all around the globe through the World Wide Web.

1945 ▶ 1950

1947   INDIAN INDEPENDENCE

Calls by Indian nationalists for their country to be freed from British rule had been growing throughout the 20th century. With Britain economically exhausted after World War II, India was finally released from the British Empire in 1947 and partitioned (divided) into mainly Hindu India and mainly Muslim Pakistan.

Gandhi
The Indian independence movement was led by Mohandas Gandhi (above), who preached a policy of *satyagraha*, or nonviolent protest, against the British Empire. He was assassinated in 1948 by an Indian Hindu.

Mass migration
Independence led to instant turmoil as millions of Muslims in India, and Hindus and Sikhs in Pakistan, were forced to leave their countries. It was the largest mass migration in history, leading to religious riots and many deaths.

New countries
Indian independence eventually resulted in the creation of three new countries. India and Pakistan were founded in 1947. In 1971, a region of Pakistan broke away to form Bangladesh. These are the three nations' flags today.

Pakistani flag

Indian flag

Bangladeshi flag

**" Victory attained by violence is...
a defeat, for it is momentary. "**

Mohandas Gandhi

1945

Nuremberg trials
In the German city of Nuremberg, 20 surviving Nazi leaders were charged with crimes against humanity and genocide for their part in World War II. While 12 of them were sentenced to death by hanging, the others were sent to prison, including Rudolph Hess, Hitler's deputy until the early 1940s.

Rudolph Hess (second from left) on trial

1945 ▶   **1946 ▶**

Singles were also known as "45s" because they were played at 45 rpm (revolutions per minute).

1946

United Nations
The United Nations (UN) was established after World War II as a global organization where nations could meet to discuss their disagreements without resorting to violence. From its original 51 members, the UN has expanded to represent 193 countries. Its logo (above) shows the world framed by olive branches— a symbol of peace.

German pro–Marshall Plan poster

1948
Birth of Israel
After World War II, the United Nations proposed dividing the Middle Eastern region of Palestine into a Jewish state and an Arab state. The Jews agreed, but the Arabs did not. The subsequent war was won by the Jews, and the new Jewish State of Israel, which included parts of the proposed Arab state, was proclaimed in May 1948.

LEBANON

Mediterranean Sea

SYRIA

Gaza Strip was taken over by Egypt in 1948.

West Bank was taken over by Jordan in 1950.

ISRAEL

JORDAN

EGYPT

☐ Israel after 1948
☐ What remained of proposed Arab state after 1948

1947
Marshall Plan
US secretary of state George Marshall persuaded his government to provide $13 billion in aid to help the recovery of Europe's war-ravaged economies. The US government also believed the aid would help prevent the spread of Communism, then taking hold across Eastern Europe.

1949
USSR develops atomic weapons
To catch up with the military power of its great rival, the United States, the Soviet Union became the second nation to develop nuclear weapons. Its program, code-named "First Lightning," relied heavily on secrets stolen from the US by Soviet spies.

1949
People's Republic of China
After a truce in World War II, China's ruling Nationalist Party reentered a civil war with the Communist Party. In 1949, the leader of the victorious Communists, Mao Zedong, became the head of the new People's Republic of China. The Nationalist leader, Chiang Kai-Shek, fled to Taiwan to form the Republic of China.

Chinese pro-Communist propaganda

1947 ▶ **1948** ▶ **1949** ▶ **1950** ▶ ▶▶

📢 **The Korean War is not over as no peace deal was ever signed.**

First 7-inch single
Introduced in March 1949, the new, smaller, 7-inch vinyl record format revolutionized the music industry and helped fuel the rock-and-roll explosion of the 1950s.

1950–1953   THE KOREAN WAR

Previously controlled by Japan, Korea was split into two states after World War II: Communist North Korea and democratic South Korea. In 1950, the North invaded the South, prompting three years of intense fighting and the first major conflict of the Cold War.

US bombers attack North Korea.

International war
Communist North Korea, led by Kim Il Sung (above), was backed by the Soviet Union and China. South Korea was supported by the US and the UN. What began as a local dispute threatened to escalate into a world war.

Stalemate
After early gains, North Korea was driven back with the help of US tanks, soldiers, and bombers (above). The North was only saved from collapse by China. The result was a stalemate with no eventual change to the borders of the two countries.

The Cold War

After World War II, the capitalist United States and the Communist Soviet Union (USSR) emerged as rival world "superpowers." However, since both were armed with enough nuclear weapons to destroy the other several times over, they couldn't risk an outright war. Instead, they engaged in a "Cold War" that lasted more than 40 years, conducting their conflict by other means: by forming alliances, backing rival opponents in conflicts, developing new technologies, and spying.

Cold War alliances

Both superpowers maintained a tight network of alliances with other countries throughout the Cold War. In 1949, the United States brought together 13 countries to form a military union called the North Atlantic Treaty Organization (NATO). The Soviet Union responded by establishing the Warsaw Pact in 1955. Both sides also regularly backed opposing allies in other conflicts, as happened in the Korean War, the Vietnam War, and the Afghanistan War.

- ◼ NATO countries
- ◼ Warsaw Pact countries
- ◼ Other US allies
- ◼ Other USSR allies

Cold War leaders

Joseph Stalin
The USSR's leader did more than anyone else to set the Cold War in motion by bringing Eastern Europe under Soviet control.

John F. Kennedy
The US president confronted the Soviets in 1962, demanding that the USSR remove their nuclear weapons from Communist ally Cuba.

Leonid Brezhnev
A slight thaw in the war came when this Soviet leader met US president Nixon to discuss the reduction of their nuclear arsenals.

Children in Berlin celebrate as an Allied plane drops off essential supplies.

Berlin airlift
After World War II, the German capital of Berlin was divided into different zones, controlled by the USSR and the Allies. In 1948, the Soviets tried to force the Allies out by cutting off road and rail links to starve the city into submission. However, a massive, almost year-long Allied airlift of supplies foiled the plan.

Map labels: CANADA, UNITED STATES, MEXICO, GUATEMALA, CUBA, DOMINICAN REPUBLIC, PUERTO

Key events

1946
British ex-Prime Minister Winston Churchill (right) described the division between Western and Eastern Europe as an "Iron Curtain."

1949
The Berlin blockade ended, NATO was established, and the Soviets developed atomic weapons.

1949
Capitalist West Germany and Communist East Germany were founded. China became Communist and an ally of the USSR.

1950
The superpowers backed opposing sides in the Korean War, the first major conflict of the Cold War.

1955
The Warsaw Pact was established, making allies of the USSR and seven Eastern European Communist states.

Cold War flashpoints

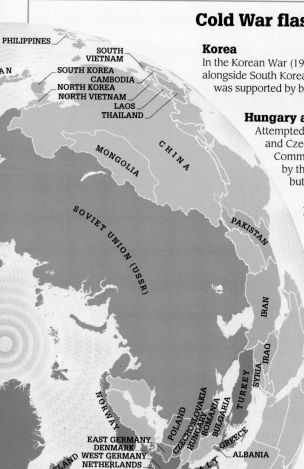

Korea
In the Korean War (1950–1953), the US and UN fought alongside South Korea, while the Communist North was supported by both the Soviets and China.

Hungary and Czechoslovakia
Attempted uprisings in Hungary (1956) and Czechoslovakia (1968) against Communism were violently quashed by the USSR. The West was appalled, but chose not to intervene.

Berlin Wall
Facing increasing numbers of people fleeing Soviet-controlled East Berlin for West Berlin, the Communist government of East Germany built a huge security wall in 1961 to divide the city in two.

Cuba
The Cold War heated up during a tense standoff between the United States and the USSR over the Soviet Union's stationing of nuclear missiles in Cuba in 1962. The USSR eventually backed down after a US blockade.

Vietnam
American troops fought alongside South Vietnam, while the Soviets provided aid and military equipment to Communist North Vietnam in a 20-year war that began in 1955. It ended in victory for the Communists.

Afghanistan
The Soviets invaded Afghanistan in 1979, but faced fierce resistance from the Afghan Mujahideen fighters, who had been secretly trained and armed by the US. The USSR finally withdrew in 1989.

Arms race
During the Cold War, the United States and the Soviet Union took part in an arms race, producing vast reserves of nuclear weapons and other military equipment, such as cruise missiles (above). But they also invested in smaller technology, particularly spy gadgets, such as secret cameras and bugs, which they used to try to discover each other's military and political secrets.

The handshake that ended the Cold War

Peaceful conclusion
The conflict came to a peaceful end in the late 1980s, when both sides agreed to reduce their store of weapons. In 1989, US president George Bush met the Soviet leader Mikhail Gorbachev in Malta (above) to declare the Cold War over. The USSR was weakening, and dissolved less than two years later.

A Soviet missile

1962 The United States and the USSR went head-to-head over the Cuban missile crisis. The Soviets backed down.

1972 The signing of an Anti-Ballistic Missile Treaty was the first attempt by the two Cold War powers to limit their nuclear arsenals.

1987 US president Ronald Reagan and Soviet leader Mikhail Gorbachev signed a treaty reducing their nuclear arsenals.

1989 The leaders of the United States and the Soviet Union met in Malta to declare an official end to the Cold War.

1991 The Soviet Union collapsed and the Warsaw Pact was dissolved.

Across the divide
A young boy in East Berlin gazes through the barbed wire that divided the city just before the wall was erected.

> **I'm tired of everyone in the West thinking we're unhappy here. I'm not saying I love it here all the time. Sometimes I do want to leave, look around. But I *can't*. And even if I could, this is my home; and I would return here if I left.**
>
> 12-year-old boy from East Berlin

CHILDREN IN HISTORY

Divided Berlin

After World War II, Germany and its capital, Berlin, were divided into zones by the Allies. The East was controlled by the Communist Soviet Union; the West by the United States, France, and Britain. By 1961, hundreds of families a week were fleeing the poverty of East Berlin for the promise of opportunity in the West. Fearful of damage to the economy, the East German authorities built a wall between East and West Berlin. It stopped migration, but at a terrible cost to the families who were split up by the wall.

In the shadow of the wall
West German children play beside the wall that divided the city from 1961 to 1989.

Building the wall
On August 13, 1961, East Berlin closed its border with the West, sealing off roads, cutting train lines, and putting up barricades and barbed wire. The dreams of thousands were over. Construction began on a huge concrete wall manned by armed guards told to "shoot to kill."

Divided families
The barrier tore families apart. It went up overnight, so people couldn't leave either side. Parents were separated from children, and children from their siblings. As time passed, split families knew less and less about how their relatives were living their lives.

Side by side
West Germany was more prosperous than the East. Families shopped for luxuries, such as sweets and toys, and traveled freely. They could visit shops, restaurants, and museums. Life in East Berlin was much more regulated. Families lived in fear of the secret police, the *Stasi*. If parents were suspected of trying to escape, their children could be taken away. Two-thirds of children belonged to Communist youth movements, which taught them not to question the system or try to leave the country.

Escaping the East
The Berlin Wall made escape to the West almost impossible, yet many tried. Some dug under it, while others flew over it in homemade balloons or hid in cars. More than 130 people died trying to cross it. The city and its people would remain divided until the wall came down in 1989.

> **❝I heard people... yelling, screaming, and crying... a wall had gone up overnight. Friends and relatives who had been visiting in East Berlin were now stuck and would not be allowed to return. ❞**
>
> Marion Cordon-Poole,
> American child who was staying with her German mother's family in 1961

> **❝The whole village was like a prison. Wherever you went, you had to see the Wall. ❞**
>
> Gitta Heinrich, from East Germany

Failed escape
East German troops arrest a man trying to escape to the West through the sewer system.

Separated families
Parents in West Berlin hold their babies up so their grandparents on the other side of the wall can see them, shortly after the border closed in 1961.

1950 ▶ 1960

The highest mountain on Earth, Mount Everest, was scaled for the first time by Edmund Hillary of New Zealand and Tenzing Norgay of Nepal in 1953.

Testing of the hydrogen bomb in the Pacific

1952

Mau Mau uprising
In Kenya, an anticolonial group called the Mau Mau led an uprising against British rule. It was brutally put down, with 13,000 Kenyans killed as the British fought to hold on to the country. Seven years later, Kenya achieved independence.

1952

A deadly weapon
Seven years after the first atomic bomb was dropped, the United States revealed a deadlier weapon: the hydrogen—or thermonuclear—bomb. The first test of the device completely destroyed a Pacific island.

1952

Queen Elizabeth II
After the death of King George VI, his daughter Elizabeth became Queen of the United Kingdom and Head of the Commonwealth. She was crowned the next year in a lavish ceremony at London's Westminster Abbey.

1950 • **1952** • **1954**

1950

Apartheid in South Africa
In 1948, South Africa's National Party launched a policy of racial segregation known as apartheid, aimed at controlling the majority black population. From 1950, the African National Congress party (ANC) began to attack the apartheid laws with acts of defiance that sometimes led to violent clashes.

The black population of South Africa was banned from voting, living in white areas, and denied access to Whites-only areas.

Crick (standing) and Watson demonstrate the structure of DNA.

1953

The structure of DNA
Scientists James Watson and Francis Crick mapped out the structure of DNA—the molecule found in every cell that contains the instruction, or gene, that builds and runs the cell. Its shape, like a twisted ladder, is known as a double helix.

1954

French leave southeast Asia
Following years of intense fighting, French-ruled Laos and Cambodia became independent while Vietnam was divided in two. North Vietnam had a Communist government, and the South declared itself to be a democratic republic.

Elvis's first record
Elvis Presley, also known as the "King of Rock and Roll," released his first single in 1954 called "Jailhouse Rock." He would go on to sell more than 100 million records before his death in 1977.

1955
Bus boycott
In Montgomery, Alabama, a black woman named Rosa Parks refused to give up her bus seat to a white person as the law of the time required. She was jailed, leading to a boycott of the bus system by the black population, and eventually an end to segregation on Montgomery's buses.

1955
Warsaw Pact
In response to the formation in 1949 of NATO, a military alliance of Western powers led by the United States, the Communist countries of Eastern Europe formed their own alliance—called the Warsaw Pact—led by the Soviet Union.

Soviet Union stamp commemorating *Sputnik 2* and Laika

1957
Sputnik 1
The Soviet Union took an early lead in the Space Race, launching the first artificial satellite, *Sputnik 1*, into Earth's orbit in October. A month later, *Sputnik 2* carried the first living creature, a dog named Laika, into space.

1959
Castro's Cuba
After a six-year campaign, Cuban revolutionaries led by Fidel Castro overthrew the US-backed Cuban dictator Fulgencio Batista. Castro established Cuba as a Communist state, which he led until 2008, despite numerous US attempts to assassinate him.

Cuban revolutionary
Fidel Castro

1956 | **1958** | **1960**

1956
Hungarian revolution
When Hungary attempted to form a liberal government and withdraw from the Warsaw Pact, Soviet tanks came rolling in (below). After a week of heavy fighting, the Soviet Union reasserted its control.

1957
Treaty of Rome
After the bitter conflicts of the 1940s, the countries of Europe began to establish better relations in the 1950s. The Treaty of Rome set up the European Economic Community (EEC), a trading union between six nations: West Germany, France, Italy, the Netherlands, Belgium, and Luxembourg.

1957
Independence for Ghana
Ghana, formerly known as the Gold Coast, gained independence from the British Empire.

1958
China's Great Leap Forward
China's leader, Mao Zedong, devised a program of reform, called the Great Leap Forward, to change the country from a rural economy to an industrial one. It forced people to produce steel rather than food. The policy was a disaster, resulting in famine and the death of 35 million people.

高举毛泽东思想伟大红旗 把我军真正办成毛泽东思想的

Chinese propaganda poster

1960 ▸ 1965

Soviet cosmonaut Yuri Gagarin

1962

Algerian independence

Since 1954, the French army and Algerian protestors—who wanted their country freed from French rule—had fought a bloody war. French wartime leader Charles de Gaulle was brought back as president in 1958 and was expected to lead France to victory. However, he granted Algeria its independence in 1962.

1962

Cuban missile crisis

US spy planes discovered that the Soviet Union was installing nuclear weapons on Communist-controlled Cuba, just off the American coast. President Kennedy demanded that Soviet leader Nikita Khrushchev remove the weapons or face retaliation. For several days, the world stood on the brink of nuclear war before the Soviets backed down.

Algerian crowds celebrate their independence, waving the country's new flag.

1961

First man in space

Soviet pilot Yuri Gagarin captured the world's attention when he became the first man to travel into space. Aboard his rocket, *Vostok 1*, he took just under two hours to orbit Earth before returning to the ground an instant international celebrity.

1960

1961

Berlin Wall erected

By 1961, thousands of people were leaving Communist East Berlin for democratic West Berlin, seriously weakening the East's economy. Immigration was halt ed when the East Germans built a heavily guarded wall, splitting the city in two.

Divided Berlin
See pages 270–271

1962

Beatles release first single

Having spent years playing small clubs, a pop group called the Beatles, from Liverpool, England, finally got a record deal and released their first single, "Love Me Do." The group went on to become the most popular musicians in the world during the 1960s.

The Beatles in concert

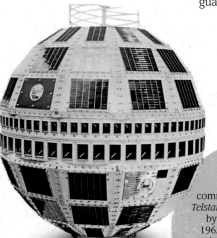

Telstar 1

The first communications satellite, *Telstar 1*, was sent into orbit by the United States in 1962. It relayed television, telephone, telegraph, and other signals to Earth, but technical faults caused it to fail after less than a year.

1963
Women's Liberation
Triggered by the release of American writer Betty Friedan's book *The Feminine Mystique*, the Women's Liberation Movement campaigned for women to have the right to do the same jobs and earn the same pay as men. They also demanded equal status for women in society.

Betty Friedan

The "hotline," a direct communication line between the US and the USSR, was set up after the Cuban missile crisis.

1963
March on Washington
At an American civil rights rally in Washington, DC, Martin Luther King, Jr., gave a famous speech, stating "I have a dream that one day this nation will rise up and live out the true meaning of its creed... that all men are created equal."

1964
Nelson Mandela jailed
In the early 1960s, Nelson Mandela was one of the leaders of the African National Congress (ANC), which fought for the rights of black South Africans. He campaigned for the overthrow of the apartheid regime of racial segregation but was arrested and sent to jail—where he spent the next 26 years.

Nelson Mandela

1963
Organization of African Unity
In the two decades since World War II, a number of African countries had become independent from their former European colonial masters. In 1963, 32 African states set up the Organization of African Unity to promote their economic, political, and cultural interests.

1965

1963   PRESIDENT KENNEDY ASSASSINATED

The world was shocked by the assassination of US president John F. Kennedy in November. According to the official report, a lone gunman killed Kennedy as the president was riding in an open-top car through the streets of Dallas on an official visit. His killer was identified as Communist sympathizer Lee Harvey Oswald.

Death in Dallas
As Kennedy's car drove slowly through the Dallas crowds, it is alleged that Oswald fired three shots from the sixth floor of a nearby building, killing the president.

Lee Harvey Oswald
Oswald (left) was arrested, but was killed while being transferred to jail before standing trial. This led some to believe that there had been a cover-up and that the true killer of the president was someone else.

Civil Rights

During the mid-20th century, most Southern states in the US enforced policies of racial segregation. These forced white and black people to live in different areas, go to different schools, and use different public services. The services provided for the black population were nearly always worse than those provided for white people. In the 1950s and 1960s, there was a series of protests against this discrimination, known collectively as the Civil Rights Movement, which triggered major changes in the law.

Rosa Parks rides on a bus after the Supreme Court ruling.

Parks's protest
A protest against racial segregation on buses by Rosa Parks, a seamstress from Montgomery, Alabama, became one of the most important events in the Civil Rights Movement. Martin Luther King led a year-long boycott of the bus company by Montgomery's black residents. In 1956, the Supreme Court ruled that segregated bus seating had to end.

Movement leaders

Martin Luther King, Jr.
The leader of the Civil Rights Movement, Dr. King organized numerous strikes, protests, and marches against segregation, but always preached a policy of nonviolent civil disobedience.

Robert Kennedy
As US attorney general, and brother of President John F. Kennedy, Robert Kennedy oversaw the passing of several of the most important civil rights laws.

Malcolm X
A passionate protestor for civil rights, Malcolm X believed that African Americans should be prepared to use violence, if necessary, to achieve their goals. He was assassinated in 1965.

Key events

1954
The Supreme Court ruled that states had to provide an integrated education, teaching white and black children in the same schools.

1955
Rosa Parks's refusal to give up her seat to a white passenger led to a year-long bus boycott and a change to the segregation laws on public transportation.

A Montgomery bus

1957
President Eisenhower was forced to send troops to protect a group of black students—known as the "Little Rock Nine"—attending an all-white high school in Little Rock, Arkansas.

1960
Activists protested against segregation, staging "sit-ins" at the whites-only sections of restaurants, "wade-ins" at segregated swimming pools, and "kneel-ins" at segregated churches.

> **"Now is the time to make justice a reality for all of God's children."**
>
> Martin Luther King, Jr., 1963

On the march

After the success of the Washington protest, King organized another march in 1965, from Selma to Montgomery. This was a protest against restrictions placed on black voters. In Alabama, black people often had to pass a literacy test or pay a tax in order to vote. The Voting Rights Act, passed the same year, banned these practices.

Martin Luther King and his wife, Coretta Scott King, lead the march.

March on Washington

In 1963, Martin Luther King led the largest march of the Civil Rights Movement. About 250,000 people arrived in Washington, DC, to call on the government to do more to end racial discrimination. With the crowd gathered in front of the Lincoln Memorial, King delivered his famous "I have a dream" speech. The march is widely credited for spurring the government to pass the Civil Rights Act the next year.

New legislation

As a result of the Civil Rights Movement, several important pieces of legislation were passed by the federal government:

★ **1964 Civil Rights Act**
This banned employers from hiring employees on the basis of their "color, religion, or national origin."

★ **1965 Voting Rights Act**
This made it illegal for states to have extra voting requirements designed to stop black people from voting.

★ **1968 Fair Housing Act**
Ensured equality when selling or renting out property.

Civil rights progress

In 1968, King was assassinated by James Earl Ray, who opposed the Civil Rights Movement. By that time, segregation had legally ended. The extent of the country's progress in race relations over the next few decades became clear in 2008 when the United States elected its first black president, Barack Obama. He was sworn in for his second term in 2013 on King's own copy of the Bible (right).

1963

Martin Luther King electrified a nation with his famous "I have a dream" speech in Washington, DC, at the largest rally of the civil rights era.

1964

Following years of protests and the mass rally in Washington, DC, the government passed the Civil Rights Act, outlawing discrimination on the basis of race, religion, or gender.

1965

The government passed laws to protect the voting rights of African Americans in the South, where they often faced harassment at the voting booths.

1968

The year witnessed both the triumph of the Fair Housing Act, which banned discrimination in the housing market, and the tragedy of the assassinations of both Dr. King and Robert Kennedy.

THE SPACE RACE

From the mid-1950s to the mid-1970s, the United States and the USSR were locked in a competition to lead the exploration of space. But the "Space Race" was also a battle for international prestige and military advantage between the two superpowers.

This Soviet postage stamp depicts Leonov's space walk.

The USSR takes the lead
Most of the early victories went to the Soviets, who launched the first satellite, *Sputnik*, in 1957 and the first manned spaceflight four years later. Then, in 1965, Soviet cosmonaut Alexei Leonov became the first man to step outside a spacecraft on a "space walk."

The US catches up
The US pulled ahead of the Soviets in the late 1960s with their Apollo space program. In 1967, the Americans successfully launched the *Saturn V* rocket (right). Two years later, a *Saturn V* put the first man on the Moon.

Apollo-Soyuz mission patch

Cooperation in space
In 1975, the Apollo-Soyuz Test Project marked the end of the Space Race, when US Apollo and Soviet Soyuz crafts docked in space.

1965–1975   VIETNAM WAR

In the late 1950s, Communist North Vietnam attacked South Vietnam. The United States entered the conflict in 1965 in support of South Vietnam, to try to prevent Communism from spreading to other countries in the region—a theory called the "Domino Effect." Despite its superior firepower, the US was unable to defeat the North and signed a cease-fire in 1973. In 1975, North Vietnam finally defeated the South.

Viet Cong
Much of the North's fighting was carried out by the Viet Cong (left), a group of South Vietnamese Communist rebels who undertook guerilla raids and acts of sabotage against South Vietnam's government.

1965

1966

Cultural revolution in China
China was plunged into anarchy when leader Mao Zedong unveiled the Cultural Revolution. Its aim was to remove capitalist sympathizers from positions of power across society. Hundreds of thousands were murdered before Mao declared the revolution over in 1969.

 The first flight of the supersonic airliner Concorde took place in 1969.

Chinese children read from the Little Red Book, a collection of Chairman Mao's quotations.

US pulls out

By 1969, thousands of US troops had been killed, and North Vietnam's resistance was as strong as ever. President Nixon began withdrawing troops, while the US national security advisor, Henry Kissinger, negotiated a cease-fire in 1973.

President Nixon (left) with Henry Kissinger

Peace protests

The war in Vietnam was the first where day-to-day conflict could be followed on television. Protest grew as people were shocked by the violence against both US troops and innocent civilians.

Woodstock

This three-day American music festival in 1969 featured some of the biggest bands of the time and was a high point of the "hippie" youth movement dedicated to peace and love.

1968

Assassinations

Two of the leading figures of the Civil Rights Movement fell to lone gunmen. On April 4, Martin Luther King was shot while in Memphis supporting a strike by local black workers. His death triggered race riots across the country. In June, Robert Kennedy was assassinated while campaigning for president. His Palestinian killer, Sirhan Sirhan, had objected to Kennedy's support of Israel in the Six-Day War the previous year.

1969

Gaddafi comes to power

The young army officer Muammar al-Gaddafi seized power in Libya while the king was out of the country on vacation. He led the country for the next 42 years, until he too was overthrown in 2011.

1970 ▶▶

1967

Che Guevara killed

A leading figure in the Cuban Revolution, Ernesto "Che" Guevara left Cuba in 1965 to start Communist uprisings in other countries. However, he was hunted down by US troops in Bolivia and killed.

Images of Che Guevara became a popular symbol of protest and revolution.

1968

Strikes in France

Students in Paris rioted over the government's education policy. Soon, a revolutionary mood had swept the country, with more than 11 million workers putting down their tools to demand higher wages. The protests stopped only after the government stepped down and new elections were called.

1968

Czechoslovakia invaded

In January, the new leader of Communist Czechoslovakia, Alexander Dubcek, began a program of reform known as the "Prague Spring," designed to give the people more freedom. Alarmed at the changes, the Soviet Union invaded in August and stopped the reforms.

A student protests during the May 1968 Paris riots.

❝I ask every citizen to reject the blind violence that has struck Dr. King, who lived by nonviolence. ❞

President Lyndon B. Johnson, 1968

Man on the Moon

In July 1969, millions of people around the world tuned in to see if the *Apollo 11* mission to the Moon would be successful. American astronauts Neil Armstrong and "Buzz" Aldrin landed their craft and made their way down to the featureless, gray surface, becoming the first humans to set foot on a world other than Earth. Ten other people have repeated their feat since.

"That's one small step for [a] man, one giant leap for mankind."

Neil Armstrong, on becoming the first human to walk on the Moon

This boot print, left by Aldrin, is still on the Moon since there is no wind to erode it.

1970 ▶ 1975

A soldier clashes with a protestor during Bloody Sunday.

1970
Palestinian plane hijackings
Palestinian terrorists hijacked three large passenger aircraft and flew them to a remote airfield in the Jordanian desert. There, 40 passengers were taken hostage and the planes were blown up. The passengers were later freed in return for seven Palestinian prisoners being released from Western jails.

1972
Bloody Sunday
In Northern Ireland, conflicts between the Nationalists, who wanted the region to become part of the Republic of Ireland, and the Unionists, who wanted it to stay in the UK, became known as "The Troubles." In one of the most notorious incidents, known as Bloody Sunday, 13 unarmed Nationalist protestors were shot dead by the British army during a march.

 1970

1970
East Pakistan cyclone
The deadliest cyclone in recorded history hit East Pakistan, leaving more than half a million dead. The limited help from West Pakistan provoked resentment and calls for independence. In 1972, the region broke free from West Pakistan's rule, forming the new country of Bangladesh.

1971
Idi Amin seizes power
The commander of the Ugandan Army, Idi Amin, overthrew the president in January. He proved to be a brutal ruler, and was responsible for the death of more than 100,000 Ugandans.

A Black September terrorist

1972
Munich Olympic killings
Eleven members of the Israeli Olympic team were taken hostage in Munich by members of the Palestinian terrorist group, Black September. After a botched rescue attempt by the German authorities, all of the hostages—and most of the terrorists—were killed.

1972
Nixon meets Mao
Since 1949, the US had refused to recognize China's Communist regime. However, relations improved when Richard Nixon became the first US president to visit China, meeting its leader, Mao Zedong. In 1978, the US finally recognized China.

Survivors dig through the debris caused by the East Pakistan cyclone.

1973

Yom Kippur War

Egyptian and Syrian forces launched a surprise attack against Israel on the holiest day of the Jewish year. But Israel fought back successfully. In retaliation for assisting Israel, Arab nations cut oil supplies to the West, triggering a recession.

 Microsoft, the computer company Bill Gates founded in 1975, made him the wealthiest man in the world by 1995.

1973

Coup in Chile

From 1970 to 1973, Salvador Allende led one of the few democracies in South America. That changed when the head of the army, General Augusto Pinochet, launched a coup that sucessfully toppled Allende. Pinochet ruled as dictator until 1990.

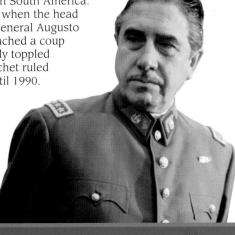

Chile's dictator, General Pinochet

Sears Tower
Upon its completion in 1973, this 1,451-ft- (442-m-) high Chicago skyscraper, now called the Willis Tower, was the world's tallest building. In 2004, construction started on Dubai's Burj Khalifa, which currently holds this record, standing at 2,716½ ft (828 m).

1975 ▶▶

1974

Turkey invades Cyprus

Turkey invaded the Mediterranean island of Cyprus, fearing it would become part of Greece. The northern part declared independence as the Turkish Republic of Northern Cyprus, but only Turkey has recognized this.

1974

Lucy discovered

Scientists digging in an Ethiopian valley found the fossil remains of one of humankind's oldest ancestors—an apelike female who lived about 3.2 million years ago and walked on two legs. She was given the species name *Australopithecus afarensis*, but the research team called her "Lucy."

1974

Watergate

In 1973, seven men were jailed for bugging the Democratic Party's headquarters in the Watergate building in Washington, DC. An investigation by the *Washington Post* newspaper proved that President Nixon had been involved in the scheme, forcing him to resign from office.

President Nixon just before leaving the White House for the last time

Arab-Israeli conflict

The establishment of the State of Israel in 1948 was intended to signal a more peaceful era for the world, giving the Jewish people a safe homeland after the horrors of World War II. Instead, it led to decades of conflict with the people who had been displaced—the Palestinians—as well as with neighboring Arab countries.

Israel founded

In 1948, Jewish people living in the Middle Eastern region of Palestine declared the creation of a new country, Israel, with a new flag (left). However, the Palestinians living there objected. War soon followed.

Yom Kippur War and the oil crisis

Egypt and Syria launched an attack on Israel on the Jewish holiday of Yom Kippur in 1973. Once again, Israel managed to reverse the attack and push into both Egypt and Syria, before a cease-fire. During the conflict, Arab countries cut oil supplies to nations, such as the United States, that were supporting Israel. The ban stayed in place until March 1974, leading to worldwide fuel shortages, lines at gas stations, and a global recession.

Six-Day War

In June 1967, Syrian, Egyptian, and Jordanian military forces began massing on Israel's borders. Israel decided to strike before they invaded, and, in six days, claimed the Golan Heights from Syria, the West Bank from Jordan, and the Gaza Strip and the Sinai Peninsula from Egypt.

Wars

★ **1948 Arab-Israeli War**: When Israel was created, its Arab neighbors launched an immediate attack. Israel managed to repel the attack and eventually claim more land.

★ **1967 Six-Day War**: Israel launched a swift assault, taking the Gaza Strip from Egypt and the West Bank from Jordan.

★ **1973 Yom Kippur War**: Egypt and Syria launched their own surprise attack on Israel's holiest day. They enjoyed some initial success, but were pushed back again.

★ **1987–1993 First Intifada**: Palestinians in Gaza and the West Bank launch a six-year-long mass uprising, the Intifada against Israel, in which hundreds of Israelis and thousands of Palestinians die.

★ **2008 Gaza Invasion**: The Israeli army invades Gaza in retaliation for Hamas rocket attacks on Israel. Over 1,000 Palestinians die. Israel launches another ground invasion of Gaza in 2014.

Jordanian tanks roll into battle in the Six-Day War.

Key events

c. 1200 BCE

The Jewish people emerged in the Middle Eastern region of Palestine and went on to form the Kingdom of Israel.

c. 133 CE

The Jews were expelled from Palestine following their revolt against the Romans.

638

Now part of the Byzantine Empire—the Eastern Roman Empire—Palestine was conquered by Arab Muslims.

1897

A Zionist (pro-Jewish) conference called for the establishment of a Jewish homeland in Palestine to curb European antisemitism.

1922

Control of Palestine passed to Britain after the collapse of the Ottoman Empire, and Jews began to immigrate to the region en masse.

The Peace Process

★ **1978–1979 Camp David Accords**: The 1970s ended with an agreement between Egypt and Israel, committing the two sides to a peaceful future and limited self-government for the Palestinians.

★ **1993 Oslo Accords**: Under the terms of the deal arranged in Oslo, Norway, the Palestinians recognized Israel's right to exist, while Israel allowed a Palestinian government, the Palestinian Authority, to be established in the West Bank and Gaza.

★ **1998 Land for peace**: In another deal negotiated by the US, Israel agreed to withdraw from Palestinian territories in return for an end to the Palestinian campaigns of violence.

★ **2002 Road Map**: US president George W. Bush's "Road Map" called for an end to Palestinian violence and Israeli settlement building in Palestinian territory. A short-lived peace was followed by a return to violence.

★ **2012 UN Resolution**: The United Nations General Assembly voted for Palestine to be given non-Member Observer State status, meaning they can take part in UN meetings but not vote on any decisions.

Palestinians throw rocks during the First Intifada.

Palestinian opposition

In the early years, opposition to Israel was provided mainly by Arab nations in the region. But gradually the Palestinian people found their voice, with the formation of the Palestinian Liberation Organization (PLO) in 1964. In 1987, Palestinians launched the First Intifada, or uprising, against Israeli presence in the West Bank and Gaza Strip.

West Bank barrier

Continued Israeli settlement building in Palestinian areas triggered a Second Intifada in 2000. Israel responded by constructing a giant concrete barrier around parts of the West Bank (below). Designed to prevent terrorist attacks, it was internationally criticized for also preventing law-abiding Palestinians from traveling freely.

Hope for peace

In recent times, Israel has indicated that it requires the Palestinians to accept its right to exist, and that it will do the same for Palestine if there is an end to violence on Israeli territory. The Palestinians seek an end to the Israeli occupation of the West Bank and Gaza, and a full recognition of their statehood.

The flag of the Palestinian people

1948
The State of Israel was proclaimed against Palestinian objections, leading to the Arab-Israeli War.

1964
The PLO, the main political voice of the Palestinian people, was founded. Yasser Arafat became its leader in 1969.

Yasser Arafat

1967
Israel captured the West Bank and the Gaza Strip during the Six-Day War. In time, these became the Palestinian territories.

2006
The two main parties in the Palestinian Authority split, with Fatah ruling the West Bank and Hamas ruling the Gaza Strip.

2017
Despite Palestinian protests, US president Donald Trump announces US recognition of Jerusalem as the capital of Israel and moves the US embassy there.

1975 ▶ 1980

Northern troops seize the presidential palace in the South.

1976
Death of Mao
The leader of Communist China since the revolution of 1949, Mao Zedong died at age 82. His disastrous policies, particularly the Great Leap Forward and the Cultural Revolution, led to the deaths of many millions.

1975
End of the Vietnam War
US troops pulled out of Vietnam in 1973, but fighting between the North and South continued. In 1975, Northern troops overran the South, which surrendered soon after.

Johnny Rotten, lead singer of the Sex Pistols

1976
Punk rockers
Pop music was shaken up when the "punk" movement began. Punk songs were fast and loud, with shouted lyrics often about politics or social problems. Bands such as the Sex Pistols caused outrage with their spiky hair, ripped clothing, and aggressive attitude.

1975

1975
The Khmer Rouge
Pol Pot, the leader of the Khmer Rouge, Cambodia's Communist party, overthrew the Cambodian government. He tried to turn the country back into a simple, rural society, forcibly emptying cities and ruthlessly massacring anyone who opposed him. An estimated 1.7 million people died before Vietnam invaded, toppling Pot's brutal regime.

1979   INVASION OF AFGHANISTAN

The Communist party of Afghanistan seized power in a 1978 coup, renaming the country the Democratic Republic of Afghanistan (DRA). However, after a rebellion by Islamic militants, the Mujahideen, the Soviet Union sent in troops to help secure the country for the Communists.

Mujahideen
Throughout the 1980s, the Mujahideen (below) successfully repelled the Soviets. They were backed by a number of countries, including Pakistan, Saudi Arabia, and, most importantly, the US, who supplied them with weapons.

1975
Lebanese Civil War
In Lebanon, tensions had been rising between the Christians, who controlled the government, and Palestinian refugees led by the Palestine Liberation Organization (PLO). An attack on a bus full of Palestinians in Beirut by armed Christians triggered a brutal 15-year civil war.

Wreckage of the bus

286

1979   IRANIAN REVOLUTION

The king, or shah, of Iran, Mohammad Pahlavi, was a close ally of the United States. This made him very unpopular, and, in 1979, he was overthrown by Muslim rebels. The country became an Islamic Republic headed by the cleric Ayatollah Khomeini.

Iran-Iraq War
In 1980, Iraq tried to take advantage of the situation in Iran by launching a surprise invasion. However, Iran fought back and the conflict soon became a stalemate. The 1988 cease-fire returned both countries to their prewar borders.

Support for Khomeini
Although he had been exiled since 1964 for calling the Shah "a puppet" of the West, Ayatollah Khomeini still had a lot of support within Iran. Big demonstrations, such as the one shown here, eventually led to the shah fleeing, and Khomeini returning.

Members of *Solidarnosc* (Solidarity) hold a union banner.

1980

Solidarity
Cracks began to appear in the Soviet Union's authority when striking ship workers in Poland founded the first independent trade union in Soviet-controlled territory. Known as Solidarity, it was banned two years later and its leader, Lech Walesa, was imprisoned, but the government was later forced to negotiate with the union.

1980 ▶▶

1979

Sandinista policies
After overthrowing Nicaraguan president Anastasio Somoza Debayle, the left wing Sandinista party introduced a series of liberal policies. In the 1980s, they faced regular attacks by the US-backed right-wing militia group, the Contras.

President Robert Mugabe

1980

Zimbabwe elections
In response to international pressure and internal rebellions, the Rhodesian government finally ended white-minority rule. After free elections, Robert Mugabe became the first black president of the country now known as Zimbabwe.

Soviet withdrawal
Despite years of bloody fighting, the Soviet Union couldn't stop the uprising and withdrew its troops in 1989 (above). The Mujahideen finally overthrew the DRA government in 1992, but then began fighting among themselves. One faction, the Taliban, would eventually emerge victorious.

First Walkman
The introduction of the Walkman, a small portable cassette player with lightweight headphones, revolutionized the experience of listening to music, allowing people to enjoy recorded music on the move.

1980 ▸ 1985

1982
Falklands War
Argentina had long disputed Britain's ownership of the Falkland Islands in the South Pacific. In April, its army invaded the islands, prompting Britain to send troops (above) to take them back. After two months of fighting, Argentina surrendered.

Columbia prepares for launch

1981
Space shuttle
In April, the US launched the first reusable space vehicle, the space shuttle *Columbia*. Five space shuttles were built in total, two of which exploded during missions. Shuttles flew on 135 missions before the program was retired in 2011.

1982
Invasion of Lebanon
In June, Israeli troops entered Lebanon to attack the Palestine Liberation Organization (PLO) forces based there. A cease-fire was called two months later, and the PLO leadership moved to Tunisia, in North Africa.

Infected white blood cell

1980

1981
Assassin attacks
In separate attacks, gunmen attempted to kill both US president Ronald Reagan and Pope John Paul II. After his attack, the Pope began traveling in a bulletproof vehicle known as the "popemobile." In Egypt, President Sadat was assassinated by a solider angry at the recent peace deal between Egypt and Israel.

1983   ETHIOPIAN FAMINE

In the 1980s, Ethiopia received the lowest rainfall since records began, resulting in a devastating famine and more than 400,000 deaths. Television images of the starving population shocked the world and provoked musicians to record charity singles and stage Live Aid, a day of concerts in the UK and US, to raise money for famine relief.

Pope John Paul II after being shot at by a Turkish gunman

Refugee camps
Thousands of people left their homes to seek help, with many people ending up in refugee camps (left). The suffering in Ethiopia was made worse by the policies of the government, which spent more than half its national budget on the military.

Coal miners on strike

1983
Sri Lankan Civil War
Tensions in Sri Lanka between the majority Sinhalese people and the minority Tamils, who wanted to establish their own separate state, erupted in 1983 into a 26-year long civil war. An estimated 700,000 people died in the fighting, which eventually ended when government forces defeated the main rebel group, the Tamil Tigers.

Microscopic image of a white blood cell infected with HIV virus

1983
AIDS identified
In the early 1980s, a mystery disease began killing people. It was eventually identified as Acquired Immune Deficiency Syndrome (AIDS), which is caused by the HIV virus, which attacks the patient's immune system. Since then, AIDS has killed more than 20 million people. Medicines have been developed that can lessen its effects, but not cure it.

HIV virus

1984
Miners' strike
In Britain, coal miners went on strike for more than a year in protest over pay and planned mine closures. However, the conservative government of Prime Minister Margaret Thatcher refused to give in to their demands. Eventually the miners, facing destitution, were forced back to work.

1985

1984
Indira Gandhi assassinated
In June, Indian Prime Minister Indira Gandhi (below) ordered troops to attack Sikh rebels in Amritsar's Golden Temple, resulting in hundreds of deaths. Four months later, two of her Sikh bodyguards took revenge, assassinating her.

1985
Democracy in Brazil
After 21 years of military dictatorship, Brazil became a democracy again. However, its first president, Tancredo Neves, died before he could take office and was immediately succeeded by his deputy José Sarney.

Live Aid
After seeing television pictures of dying Ethiopian families, Irish pop singer Bob Geldof gathered musicians to record a charity single called *Do they know it's Christmas?* In 1985, he organized the Live Aid concerts, which raised more than £50 million for the cause.

Thriller
The sixth album by the American pop star Michael Jackson, *Thriller*, became a global phenomenon and the biggest-selling record of all time, with sales of more than 60 million.

Decolonization

Before World War II, Europe's major powers controlled large overseas empires, as did Japan. Italy and Japan lost their empires at the end of the conflict. The victorious European nations held on to theirs for slightly longer, but with their economies shattered by the war – and nationalist sentiments stirring worldwide – the once-mighty European empires gradually melted away to almost nothing. By the early 1980s, the process was largely complete.

- United Kingdom and colonies
- France and colonies
- Denmark and colonies
- Spain and colonies
- Portugal and colonies
- Netherlands and colonies
- Norway and colonies
- Belgium and colonies
- Italy and colonies
- Australia and colonies
- United States and colonies
- Japan and colonies

1973
1981
1962

Wind of change
At its peak, the British Empire was the largest in history, but it began to break apart after World War II. In 1960, British Prime Minister Harold Macmillan gave a speech to the South African parliament (above), where he predicted that a "wind of change" – meaning independence – would sweep through Africa. Over the next two decades, most of Britain's colonies declared independence.

Indonesia
In 1945, nationalist rebels in Indonesia declared the country free of the Dutch, who had ruled since 1800. The Dutch disagreed. Three years of fighting ensued before the Dutch withdrew, and Indonesia became independent in 1949 under President Sukarno (above).

End of empires
This map shows the world's majo empires in 1938 on the eve of Wo War II. The colours show the diffe empires, and the dates are when colonies finally became indepen Some territories are still colonies

Egypt
Egypt had officially become independent in 1922, but Britain continued to occupy the country and exert control over its ruler, King Farouk. British influence was finally ended by the 1952 Egyptian Revolution led by Colonel Nasser (left), who went on to become president.

Ghana
The British colony of the Gold Coast began campaigning for independence after the war. Britain initially resisted but eventually gave in, and in 1957 the newly independent, and newly named, country of Ghana was born. Shown here are Ghanaians holding a parade to celebrate their independence.

Key events

1947
Countries that became independent: India and Pakistan (from Britain).

1948
Countries that became independent: Burma and Sri Lanka (from Britain).

Sri Lankan flag

1956
Countries that became independent: Morocco and Tunisia (from France); and the next year Malaysia and Ghana (from Britain).

1960
Seventeen African countries became independent. These included Cameroon and the Ivory Coast (from France).

1962
Countries that became independent: Rwanda (from Belgium); Algeria (from France); Jamaica, Trinidad and Tobago, and Uganda (from Britain).

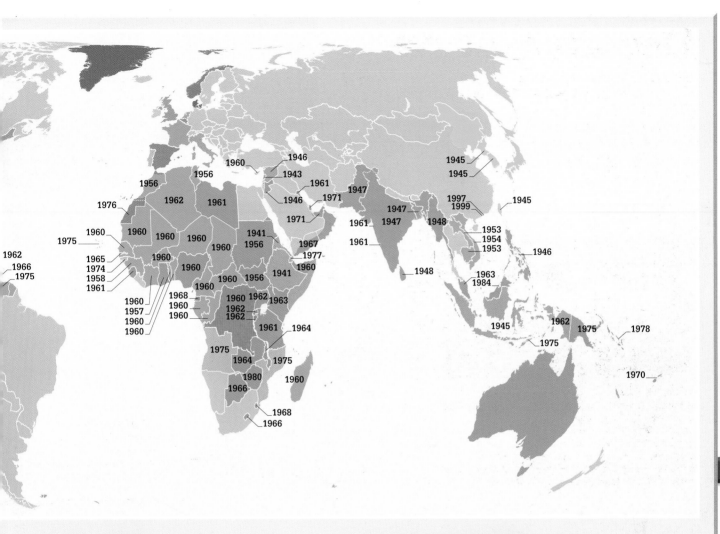

1960 1946
1956 1943
1956 1961
1976 1962 1961 1946 1971 1947
1971
1960 1960 1960 1941
1975 1960 1956
1962 1947 1945
1947 1945
1997
1999 1945
1947
1948
1961 1945

1962
1966
1975
1965
1974
1958
1961 1960
1960

1960
1960 1961 1953
1954
1953
1946

1948
1963
1984

1960
1957
1960
1960 1968
1960
1960 1960 1960 1962
1962
1962 1963 1961 1964
1975 1945 1962 1975 1978
1975
1975 1964 1975
1980 1960
1966 1970
1968
1966

Jamaica

In the late 1950s, Britain brought together several Caribbean islands, including Jamaica, as the Federation of the West Indies. However, the federation broke up, and in 1962 Jamaica became independent. Shown here is Princess Margaret, sister of the British Queen, attending Jamaica's independence celebrations.

Angola

Angolan nationalists began fighting the Portuguese dictatorship that ruled their country in 1961. The conflict ended only when the dictatorship was overthrown by a coup in Portugal in 1974. Agostinho Neto (left) became Angola's first president, but the country was soon drawn into a 26-year-long civil war.

1964

Countries that became independent: Malawi, Zambia, and Malta (from Britain).

1966

Countries that became independent: Guyana, Botswana, Lesotho, and Barbados (from Britain).

1968

Countries that became independent: Mauritius and Swaziland (from Britain); Equatorial Guinea (from Spain).

1975

Countries that became independent: Angola, Mozambique, Cape Verde, Sao Tome and Principe (from Portugal).

1981

Countries that became independent: Antigua and Barbuda, and Belize (from Britain).

1985 ▸ 1990

1986

Challenger disaster

Until 1986, the American space shuttle program had been an enormous success, with 24 missions completed safely. But disaster struck in January when a faulty seal caused the *Challenger* shuttle to explode shortly after take off, killing all seven crew members.

Debris and smoke from the exploded *Challenger*

1986

Chernobyl explosion

The worst nuclear disaster in history took place when a reactor at the Chernobyl plant in Soviet-controlled Ukraine exploded. It sent a cloud of harmful radiation out over Europe, forcing thousands of people to evacuate the area.

 1985

1987

First Intifada

The Palestinians launched an Intifada, or uprising, against Israel's continued occupation of Gaza and the West Bank. It resulted in the deaths of more than 150 Israelis and 2,000 Palestinians over the next six years.

Arab-Israeli conflict
See pages 284–285

1987 BLACK MONDAY

On Monday, 19 October, 1987, stock markets around the world suffered the biggest crash since 1929. However, unlike the earlier crash, it didn't lead to a global economic depression – just a slowdown.

Computer trouble
A trader at the US Stock Exchange feels the impact as the crash takes hold on 19 October. The crash was partly caused by computers that had recently been installed in stock exchanges, as they could sell stocks much quicker and in greater volumes than ever before.

October slump
This graph, showing the value of the top 100 companies trading in the UK between July 1987 and January 1988, shows a sharp decline for October, when 26 per cent was wiped off their value. The crash started in Hong Kong, but affected every market in the western world.

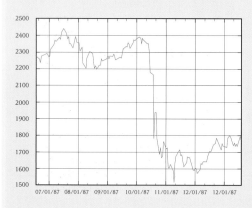

Crowds celebrate a united Germany outside the *Reichstag* (parliament).

1990
Gulf War
Iraqi leader Saddam Hussein ordered his troops to invade Kuwait and seize its oil reserves. In retaliation, the USA launched an international operation that forced the Iraqis out, but did not topple Hussein from power.

A US marine watches an oil fire in Kuwait.

1989
The Berlin Wall falls
Berliners in both the East and West of the city tore down the Berlin Wall, after a series of events that also led to the fall of the government in the East. In 1990, East and West Germany were reunited.

Fall of communism
See pages 294–295

1990

1988
Lockerbie bombing
In December, Libyan terrorists planted a bomb on a transatlantic flight from London, England, to New York, USA. It exploded, killing all 259 people on board. The wreckage crashed onto the Scottish town of Lockerbie, where another 11 people on the ground lost their lives.

1989
Tiananmen Square
The Chinese authorities initially allowed pro-democracy protests by students in Beijing's Tiananmen Square to go ahead. However, tanks were eventually sent in to stop the demonstration, resulting in hundreds of deaths.

1989
Exxon Valdez oil spill
Loaded with oil and heading for California, USA, the *Exxon Valdez* oil tanker ran aground off Alaska. A rupture in its hull spilled more than 750,000 barrels of oil, seriously damaging the environment and killing wildlife. The Exxon shipping company was forced to pay nearly $1 billion in compensation.

1990
Nelson Mandela released
After 26 years of international pressure, the anti-apartheid campaigner Nelson Mandela was finally released from prison in South Africa. He immediately returned to politics, becoming head of the African National Congress and negotiating an end to apartheid with South African President F W de Klerk.

Looking at the Universe
Built in America, the Hubble Space Telescope was sent into orbit around Earth in 1990. It has taken some of the most detailed and far-reaching images of the Universe ever produced.

Fall of communism

Throughout the Cold War, the Soviet Union had seemed a powerful force. But behind the scenes, the USSR was struggling. By the mid 1980s, it could no longer match the US militarily, and its citizens were demanding more control over their lives. The new Soviet leader, Mikhail Gorbachev, decided to try and rejuvenate the USSR by granting the people greater freedom. Ultimately, this precipitated the fall of communism, as people across the USSR and its allies used the opportunity to break away from Soviet control.

Fall of the Berlin Wall

The Berlin Wall, the most iconic symbol of the Cold War, had divided the city since 1961. As communist regimes fell across Europe in 1989, pressure grew on the East German government to open the border. In November, it announced that the barrier would open. Thousands of people rushed to the wall to tear it down.

Key events

1989

In January, the USSR, the Warsaw Pact countries, and Yugoslavia had communist regimes.

1989

In July, Gorbachev gave the countries of the Warsaw Pact the chance to choose their own governments.

1989

Poland voted out its communist regime in favour of the Solidarity Party in August.

A Solidarity Party banner

1989

The Velvet Revolution in November saw Czechoslovakia peacefully move away from communism.

1989

The Berlin Wall, which had divided the city for nearly 30 years, fell on November 9.

A copy of Gorbachev's book on *perestroika*

New policies
Until the mid 1980s, Soviet society was strictly controlled. But Gorbachev broke with the past with his new policies of *glasnost* (openness) and *perestroika* (restructuring). These gave people more personal and economic freedom, but once these were gained, they wanted political freedom and rejected communism.

Yeltsin delivers a speech from a tank used in the failed military coup

Key figures

Mikhail Gorbachev
The last Soviet leader unleashed changes he probably didn't foresee. Though he received the Nobel Peace Prize, he lost his political power as the Soviet Union collapsed.

Boris Yeltsin
Yeltsin became the leading politician of the post-Soviet Russian world. He served two terms as president, ensuring the country's transfer to democracy.

Nikolai Ceausescu
Head of communist Romania, Ceausescu was a brutal leader, living a life of luxury while his people starved. In 1989, he was overthrown, put on trial, and executed.

End of the Communist Bloc
In 1989, Gorbachev allowed the Warsaw Pact countries to hold free elections, resulting in the toppling of communist governments across Central and Eastern Europe. In the Soviet Union, communists opposed to the changes staged a military coup against Gorbachev. But it was defeated by democrat Boris Yeltsin (above) and the USSR disintegrated.

"Why not?"
Mikhail Gorbachev in May 1989, when asked by a reporter if the Berlin Wall should be dismantled

The Warsaw Pact
Eight countries signed the Warsaw Pact, a treaty that promised military aid in the case of foreign threat:

Albania	Hungary
Bulgaria	Poland
Czechoslovakia	Romania
East Germany	USSR

Russian Federation
Following its dissolution in December 1991, the USSR split into 15 separate countries. Shown here is the flag of the Russian Federation, the largest and most powerful state to emerge from the former Soviet Union. Boris Yeltsin became its first president.

1989
Romania's communist regime was overturned in a bloody uprising in December.

1990
In March, free elections were held in East Germany, and voters chose to reject communism.

An election ballot box

1990
In October, West and East Germany were reunified for the first time since World War II.

1990
Communism was rejected in the six republics making up Yugoslavia, but they soon began fighting among themselves.

1991
Gorbachev resigned in December and the Soviet Union officially ceased to exist.

1990 ▶ 1995

European Union

1992

Maastricht Treaty

The gradual coming-together of Western European nations, which had begun at the end of World War II, culminated in the Maastricht Treaty. This created the European Union, with member countries agreeing common foreign and defence policies. Some also committed to adopt a single currency, the Euro, in the future.

1993

Oslo Accords

Israel's leader Yitzhak Rabin and Palestine Liberation Organization (PLO) leader Yasser Arafat shake hands on a peace deal, looked on by US President Bill Clinton. This followed secret talks in Oslo, Norway, in which Israel had agreed to withdraw from some Palestinian territory, while the PLO had agreed to end violence and recognize Israel's right to exist.

1991

End of the Soviet Union

After more than 40 years as one of the world's two superpowers, the Soviet Union suddenly disintegrated following popular protests in the Soviet republics. The Soviet Union divided into 15 separate countries.

1992

LA riots

In 1991, police officers were filmed viciously beating a black suspect, Rodney King. Charged with using excessive force, they were acquitted at their trial the next year, prompting a 6-day race riot in which 53 people died.

1990

1993

The Waco siege

In Waco, Texas, USA, the US Bureau of Alcohol, Tobacco, and Firearms stormed the headquarters of the Branch Davidians, a secretive Christian sect, using tanks and tear gas. The raid was a disaster and the compound caught fire, killing about 70 people, including several children and the sect's leader, David Koresh.

1991–1996   WAR IN YUGOSLAVIA

The break up of Yugoslavia after the fall of communism was a bloody affair. As four of its states – Slovenia, Croatia, Macedonia, and Bosnia and Herzegovina – tried to become independent countries, Serbia waged war to try to hold on to power and create a "Greater Serbia".

Siege of Sarajevo

A ferocious four-year Serbian siege of the Bosnian city of Sarajevo was ended by NATO air strikes in 1995. Soon after, a peace deal was signed, but more than 11,000 civilians had died or gone missing.

Ethnic cleansing

In 1992, Bosnia and Herzegovina declared itself independent. This was rejected by the Bosnian Serbs. Supported by the Serbian president, Slobodan Milosevic (right), they began to violently remove all non-Serbs from Serb-dominated areas – a policy known as "ethnic cleansing".

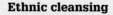

1994

Rwandan massacre
Some 800,000 people – 20 per cent of the population – were killed in Rwanda when the Hutu ethnic group attacked their long-term rivals, the Tutsis. Extremist Hutu leaders used the recent assassination of the Hutu President Juvénal Habyarimana as justification.

In 1991, two German tourists found a mummified Copper-Age man frozen deep in a glacier in the Alps.

1994

US invades Haiti
Haiti's first elected president, Jean-Bertrand Aristide, was overthrown in 1991 in a military coup. Three years later, the US led a military mission that put Aristide back in power – although he was overthrown again a decade later in a second coup.

1995

Barings bank
The UK's oldest merchant bank, Barings Bank, was ruined by the activities of a single "rogue trader". Nick Leeson gambled huge sums in unauthorized, risky investments, racking up losses of £800 million – almost the bank's entire assets.

1918–2013   NELSON MANDELA

Nelson Mandela spent his whole life fighting prejudice. As a young man, he helped lead the African National Congress (ANC) protests against South Africa's apartheid regime. Later, he became the country's president and was awarded the Nobel Peace Prize in 1993.

1995

1994

First Chechen War
The Chechnyan region's attempt to break away from Russia was fiercely resisted by the Russian army. Chechen forces fought back, and a ceasefire in 1996 gave Chechnya its independence. However, Russia regained control of the region after the Second Chechen War (1999–2000).

1995

Oklahoma bombing
In protest against the government's handling of the Waco siege, ex-soldier Timothy McVeigh planted a huge bomb next to a government building in Oklahoma City. It exploded, killing 168 people. McVeigh was arrested and executed in 2001.

International hero
Imprisoned in 1964 for trying to overthrow South Africa's government, Mandela became an international hero during his time in jail. In the 1980s, concerts were staged and records were recorded calling for his release – which eventually came in 1990.

Prison life
Life in prison was hard. Mandela slept in a tiny cell (right), was allowed to receive just one visitor a year, and had to do hard labour. After his release, Mandela sought to heal the divisions between blacks and whites.

Brazil win FIFA World Cup
The South American nation became the first country to win the football World Cup four times in 1994. They defeated Italy on penalties in the final, held in California, USA.

New flag
South Africa adopted a new flag in 1994. It combines the green, white, and gold of the ANC with the red, white, and blue of the Netherlands and the UK, South Africa's old colonial rulers.

Living under apartheid

Apartheid (meaning "separateness") was introduced in South Africa in 1948 by the ruling white Afrikaner National Party to give the government control over the majority black population. During apartheid, families lived very different lives, depending on the colour of their skin – one privileged, the other impoverished. Black and white children were not allowed to play together.

Kept out
Black children stand behind a fence watching white children play on a "whites only" beach. Everything in apartheid South Africa was segregated (separated along racial lines), including the taxis.

Racial divide

Under apartheid, black people were told where to live and were only allowed to take menial jobs. When they were sick, black children were taken to hospital in "black only" ambulances. Black children only glimpsed the privileged lives of white South Africans if they went to work with their parents as servants in white homes.

Living apart

Black familes were forcibly moved to townships – poor areas with few facilities and overcrowded schools. Black people could only enter white areas to work, and had to carry an identity document known as a passbook wherever they went. In some places, a six o'clock siren signalled a curfew. Any black person out after this time could be arrested, so children waited nervously for their parents to hurry home each day.

> **"At all the schools I attended from pre-school right up to university, the only black people I met were cleaners or people serving tea or looking after the gardens."**
>
> Gerrit Cooetzee, a white teacher, describing growing up in apartheid South Africa

Protesting against the regime

Children in the townships lived in the shadow of violence. Any protest was violently put down, such as the march of young people in Soweto in 1976. Opposition to apartheid was headed by black rights groups, such as the African National Congress (ANC). One of the figureheads of the ANC was Nelson Mandela, who was imprisoned for 26 years.

The end of apartheid

As international awareness of apartheid increased, pressure grew on South Africa to change. In 1989 President F W de Klerk lifted the ban on protest marches and ended the segregation of public facilities. In 1994, Nelson Mandela was elected president. He urged people to heal the old divisions and for black and white South Africans to unite.

Student uprising
In 1976, students in the Soweto township marched against apartheid. The police opened fire, killing 600 people.

> **"If you met a policeman on the road, the first thing they'd say was 'where is your passbook?' and if you didn't have it you knew where you'd spend the evening – in prison."**
>
> John Biyase, teacher, describing life in the Soweto township

Together at last
These children are waiting for a visit from Nelson Mandela, the country's first black president. Their faces are painted with the new South African flag, adopted in 1994.

Back to school
A child sits in class in a "black only" school during the apartheid era. As protest gathered pace in the 1980s, education in townships was interrupted by class boycotts.

"The school I went to was overcrowded. We'd have 70–80 children in one class."

Obed Bapela, member of parliament, describing schooling for black children in the Alexandra township

299

1995 ▸ 2000

Rise of the Taliban
The Taliban (left) overthrew the Afghan government, which had been in power since 1992. They established the Islamic Emirate of Afghanistan, an extremist Muslim state.

Hong Kong
In 1898, China granted Britain a 99-year lease for the island of Hong Kong, which became a major financial centre. It was handed back to China in 1997, but has been allowed to continue operating semi-independently with its own currency and local laws.

Skyscrapers in Hong Kong

Flowers laid by mourners outside Diana's home at Kensington Palace

Princess Diana's death
The ex-wife of Prince Charles of the United Kingdom and mother to princes William and Harry died in a car crash in Paris. The nation was stunned, and millions watched the funeral service at Westminster Abbey on television.

Dayton peace accords
A peace agreement signed in Dayton, USA, ruled that Bosnia would be split into the Bosnian Serb Republic and the Muslim-Croat Federation, both forming part of the country Bosnia–Herzegovina. The treaty ended the Bosnian War, the most devastating war in Europe since World War II.

▸▸ 1995

1995   GROWTH OF THE WORLD WIDE WEB

The first networks of computers were created in the 1960s, but were complicated to use. In 1990, a British computer researcher called Tim Berners-Lee (left) came up with a simple way of distributing information, using hyperlinks to connect between documents. He called his invention the World Wide Web.

A slow start
Berners-Lee's innovation was used by only a handful of people during the first few years, but, with the introduction of Internet browsers in 1993, it soon became very popular. By 1995, the web was on its way to becoming a global phenomenon.

A world online
This computer is the first Internet server, and it hosted the first webpage when it was set up by Berners-Lee in 1990. He scrawled a notice on the side to remind people not to turn it off.

Harry Potter
The first of J K Rowling's Harry Potter books, *Harry Potter and the Philosopher's Stone*, was released in 1997, and became an instant smash hit. The seven Harry Potter books have sold more than 500 million copies worldwide.

Flag of East Timor

1999
East Timor is born
In 1999, East Timor voted to become independent of Indonesia. This triggered a violent revolt by a minority who wanted to remain part of Indonesia. UN troops restored order, and in 2002 East Timor became the first new country of the millennium.

Dolly the sheep
In 1996, scientists managed to successfully clone an adult mammal for the first time. Known as Dolly, she was an exact copy of her parent sheep.

1999
Coup in Pakistan
After being defeated by India in a border conflict, the elected Pakistani government of Prime Minister Nawaz Sharif was overthrown in a bloodless military coup. The coup leader, General Pervez Musharraf, became the country's dictator.

1998
The Kosovo War
The Serbian President Slobodan Milosevic sent Serbian troops to prevent Kosovo – a region in Serbia – from becoming independent. The Serbs were driven back by NATO air strikes, and Kosovo finally declared independence in 2008.

2000

1998
Peace in Ireland
A major breakthrough in the Northern Ireland peace process was made when Nationalist and Unionist political parties agreed to serve in a power-sharing government. The treaty was supported in both Northern Ireland and the Republic of Ireland.

Irish Prime Minister Bertie Ahern, US Senator George Mitchell, and British Prime Minister Tony Blair after signing the agreement.

2000
New millennium
Billions of people welcomed the new millennium with celebrations around the world. In the run up to the new year, there were concerns that a so-called "millennium bug" might cause a global computer meltdown. Ultimately, these fears proved unfounded.

Revellers celebrate the millennium in 2000.

The Harry Potter books have been translated into 80 languages.

1998
Nuclear weapons for India and Pakistan
Since independence, India and Pakistan had become fierce enemies, clashing several times over the disputed border area of Kashmir. In an attempt to prove its military superiority, India tested a nuclear device in May. This was followed shortly after by Pakistan's own nuclear test.

2000 ▶ 2005

The clean-up operation begins after the devastating earthquake in Gujarat.

Refugees from the Angolan Civil War carry grain past a land-mine field.

2002
End of Angolan Civil War
The Civil War in Angola finally ended after 26 years. Meanwhile, the African Union was launched, the successor to the Organization of African Unity.

2001
Gujarat earthquake
A giant earthquake, measuring 7.9 on the Richter scale, rocked the state of Gujarat in northwest India. It resulted in the deaths of more than 20,000 people and the destruction of at least 400,000 homes. About 600,000 people were left homeless.

2002
Milosevic on trial
Former Yugoslav president Slobodan Milosevic stood trial at the International Court of Justice in The Hague, Netherlands, for war crimes during the Bosnian War. However, he died in prison before the trial ended.

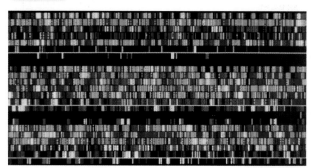

Sequence of human DNA

2001
Al-Qaeda attacks
Members of Al-Qaeda flew planes into New York's World Trade Center on 11 September in the worst terrorist attack in US history. America responded by launching attacks on Afghanistan where Osama bin Laden, head of Al-Qaeda, was hiding.

2001
Human Genome Project
Begun in 1990, the Human Genome Project employed scientists around the world to map and identify the role of more than 20,000 genes that make up human DNA – the blueprint for life. By 2001, the project had published its first draft of the genome.

War on Terror
See pages 304–305

2001
Enron collapses
Considered to be one of the most profitable energy companies in the world, Enron suddenly collapsed when it was found to have created false accounts that made it look like it was making more money than it actually was.

2002
The Euro
On 1 January, 17 countries in the European Union gave up their old currencies and adopted the Euro as their new joint-currency. Euro notes and coins are now used every day by more than 330 million people.

Euro bank notes

2004   BOXING DAY TSUNAMI

In the early hours of 26 December 2004, an enormous earthquake occurred under the Indian Ocean. It created a tsunami (a series of huge waves) more than 30 m (100 ft) in height, which raced across the ocean, pummelling the surrounding coastlines with devastating force.

Disorder and devastation
The huge tsunami struck 14 countries, destroying homes and property, and killing more than 230,000 people. As there were no warning signals, the waves took most of the victims by surprise.

Cars stack up after the tsunami

The aftermath
These images show Banda Aceh, Indonesia, before (top) and after (bottom) the tsunami. The waves flattened most buildings, leaving a bare landscape.

iPod launched
In 2001, Apple came out with a revolutionary new product – the iPod – a small portable device that could store and play thousands of songs.

Playlists
Favorites   >
Monday Morning   >
Party Mix   >
Road Trip   >
Top 5 Break-Up Songs >
Workout Tunes   >

2005 ▶▶

2003
Sudanese conflict
The Darfur region of Sudan rebelled against the government, claiming they were being oppressed. As many as 300,000 lives were lost before a peace accord in 2010. Another civil war (1983–2005) resulted in South Sudan becoming an independent country in 2011. However, civil war broke out again in 2013. Since then more than 2 million refugees have fled South Sudan.

Sudanese rebels

2003
War in Iraq
As part of the "War on Terror", the US invaded Iraq to over-throw its leader, Saddam Hussein. Hussein's regime quickly crumbled, and US troops left in 2011. However, the rise of the Islamic State led to instability in the country, and in 2014 US troops returned to help put down the terrorist group.

2004
Beslan hostage crisis
Chechen separatists protested against Russian rule by taking 1,000 people hostage in a school in the town of Beslan. A rescue attempt by Russian troops ended disastrously with the deaths of 186 children.

Submerged homes in New Orleans

2005
Hurricane Katrina
The US city of New Orleans was devastated by hurricane Katrina. The levees (embankments) that were meant to protect the city from flooding broke under the extreme pressure of the storm surge, leaving much of the city underwater and thousands homeless. It caused billions of dollars worth of damage.

War on Terror

In the 1980s, the militant Islamist terrorist organization Al-Qaeda was formed with the aim of establishing a worldwide Muslim nation. It carried out a series of attacks, culminating in the destruction of New York's World Trade Center in 2001. This prompted the USA to launch a "War on Terror" against the group's worldwide network.

❝Today, our fellow citizens, our way of life, our very freedom came under attack.❞

US President George W Bush speaking to the nation on 11 September 2001

Under attack
On 11 September 2001, 19 members of Al-Qaeda hijacked four US planes. Two were flown into the Twin Towers of New York's World Trade Center, one hit the Pentagon in Washington DC, while the final flight crashed into a field in Pennsylvania. Almost 3,000 people were killed.

Osama bin Laden
A member of a wealthy Saudi family, Osama bin Laden fought with the Mujahideen against the Soviets in Afghanistan during the 1980s. He later founded Al-Qaeda (meaning "the base" in Arabic) to wage a worldwide *jihad* (holy war) against what he saw as the corrupt Western world.

Invasion of Afghanistan
The Taliban rulers of Afghanistan harboured bases of bin Laden's Al-Qaeda movement. In 2001, US President George Bush ordered an attack on the country. Initially, the war went well for the USA and the Taliban was quickly overthrown. But the Taliban fought back, and the war continued for more than a decade. Bin Laden slipped out of the country.

Key events

1988
Following the end of the Afghanistan War, Osama bin Laden founded Al-Qaeda.

1991
Bin Laden set up terrorist training camps in Sudan, but was later asked to leave the country.

1996
Bin Laden returned to Afghanistan and called on his followers to launch a holy war against the USA.

1998
Al-Qaeda killed more than 200 people by planting bombs at US embassies in Kenya and Tanzania.

Bombed embassy

1998
The USA retaliated against the embassy bombings with air strikes on Al-Qaeda training camps in Afghanistan.

Iraq war

In 2003, the USA turned its attention to Iraq. They believed its ruler, Saddam Hussein, was hiding Weapons of Mass Destruction (WMD) that could potentially be used against the West, and invaded the country to destroy them. Hussein was quickly forced from power. But no WMD were ever found and the new US-backed Iraqi government faced years of fighting against rebel groups.

A statue of Saddam Hussein is toppled by the Iraqi people, with help from US forces.

Al-Qaeda attacks

In the 2000s, Al-Qaeda and its associated organizations continued to launch terrorist attacks targeting the West as protests against the wars in Afghanistan and Iraq.

★ **December 2001**
British terrorist Richard Reid was arrested trying to detonate a bomb in his shoe on a plane from Paris, France, to Miami, USA.

★ **October 2002**
Two bombs set off in a nightclub in Bali, Indonesia killed more than 200 people.

★ **March 2004**
Bombs on trains in Madrid, Spain, killed more than 190 and injured at least 1,800.

★ **July 2005**
Bombs on underground trains and a bus in London, UK, killed 52 people and injured more than 700.

★ **April and December 2007**
Bomb attacks in Algiers, Algeria, kill more than 70 people, including 17 United Nations staff.

Bin Laden's compound

Bin Laden's death

For a decade, the USA's most wanted man – Osama bin Laden – evaded capture. He continued to organize terrorist attacks and released regular public messages, urging his supporters to continue the fight against the West. But, in 2011, he was tracked down to a specially built compound in Abbottabad, Pakistan. US soldiers helicoptered in, stormed the compound, and shot bin Laden dead.

2001

The terrorist attacks on the US triggered the "War on Terror".

2001

On October 7, the USA launched the war in Afghanistan with the aim of finding Al-Qaeda's terrorist bases.

2003

The Iraq War was launched in the face of much international opposition.

Protest banners

2006

Following his capture in 2003, Saddam Hussein was put on trial for "crimes against humanity", found guilty, and executed.

2011

Osama bin Laden was finally tracked down in Pakistan and assassinated by American troops.

2005 ▶ 2010

CLIMATE CHANGE

Earth's average temperature has risen over recent decades. Contributing factors include the burning of fossil fuels, which releases greenhouse gases. Global warming causes ice sheets to melt, rising sea levels, and an increase in extreme weather events, such as tsunamis and heatwaves.

Kyoto protocol
In 1997, world leaders met in Kyoto, Japan, to agree on action to stop global warming. The big industrialized nations promised to cut the production of greenhouse gases. However, developing countries, such as India and China, were not subject to this agreement.

Paris climate agreement
In 2015, the leaders of 195 nations met in Paris, France, where they agreed on further action to tackle global warming. Developing countries promised to cut their emissions and developed nations pledged to fund renewable energy initiatives.

School strike
In 2018, Greta Thunberg, a 16-year-old Swedish schoolgirl, staged a protest demanding government action on climate change. Refusing to go to school, she stood outside the Swedish Parliament, holding a banner saying 'School Strike for Climate.' Thunberg inspired schoolchildren around the world to stage their own school strikes.

2006
Twitter
In the USA, Twitter, a new social networking service was launched. It allowed users to post short messages, called "tweets", online. Twitter increasingly replaced conventional media, such as television, as a way of following breaking news stories. It became a popular channel to show reactions to current events.

The social networking site Facebook was founded in 2004. Its popularity grew and, by 2012, more than a billion people had signed up.

2006
Terror in Mumbai
More than 200 people were killed in India when seven bombs went off on trains on Mumbai's railway network. Terror shook the city again two years later when more than 150 people died in shooting and bomb attacks that shocked the nation. In 2011 three bombs killed 26 and left 130 injured. All of the attacks were blamed on Islamic extremists.

2005

2007
Economic crisis
In late 2007, the world was plunged into the biggest economic crisis since the Great Depression. It started in the USA where many people had taken out bank loans they could not afford to buy houses. Bank failures followed and the crisis soon spread around the world, as many financial institutions either went bankrupt or needed to be rescued by governments. In Greece, government workers' pay was cut, leading to riots on the streets.

Riots break out in Greece

2008

Large Hadron Collider

A huge scientific machine began operating beneath the French-Swiss border. It was built to recreate the conditions just after the Big Bang, giving scientists a better idea of how the Universe first formed.

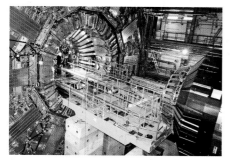

Large Hadron Collider

President Obama

Clouds of volcanic ash pour out of Eyjafjallajökull volcano.

2008

Obama elected

History was made as the USA elected its first African American President, Barack Obama. Representing the Democratic Party, the former lawyer went on to win a second term in office in 2013.

2010

Icelandic volcano

The eruption of Iceland's Eyjafjallajökull volcano sent up a massive ash cloud, which spread across the North Atlantic Ocean and northern Europe. Over the next five days, 95,000 plane flights had to be cancelled.

2010

Deepwater Horizon

A major ecological disaster took place off the US coast when an oil rig, Deepwater Horizon, exploded and sank. Marine life was devastated, as 3.19 million barrels of oil poured into the sea.

2010

2007

iPhone launched

US technology company Apple launched the iPhone, a "smartphone" as powerful as earlier home computers. People could now access the Internet using only a small handheld device with a touch-sensitive screen. The iPhone X, released in 2017, would have facial recognition security.

2008

Usain Bolt

At the Beijing Summer Olympics, the Jamaican athlete Usain Bolt became the fastest man on earth. He set a new world record by running the 100 m race in just 9.69 seconds.

Usain Bolt celebrates at the 2008 Olympics

2010

Chilean miners freed

When a roof collapsed in a gold and copper mine in Chile, 33 miners were trapped. They remained underground for 69 days before a rescue mission brought them all back to the surface safely.

2010

Haiti earthquake

The Haiti earthquake measured only 7 on the Richter scale, but the weak standard of buildings in Haiti – one of the world's poorest countries – meant it caused widespread devastation and more than 230,000 deaths.

Haiti's presidential palace lies in ruins

2011
Arab Spring
A wave of protests and rebellions, known as the Arab Spring, swept across the Arab world, with people calling for democracy and greater human rights. Uprisings started in Tunisia and spread to other countries, toppling several long-standing dictators, but also bringing war and disruption to the region.

2011
Syrian war
When protestors throughout Syria demanded democratic government, President Assad responded with a brutal military crack-down. The conflict escalated into a many-sided civil war that tore the country apart, cost tens of thousands of lives, and caused a major refugee crisis.

2011
Japanese tsunami
An earthquake just off Japan's northeast coast caused a huge tsunami. Giant waves crashed onto the mainland, destroying thousands of buildings and killing over 16,000 people.

2012
Curiosity
A NASA spacecraft delivered the research vehicle Curiosity to Mars after an eight-month journey. The carlike rover, equipped with cameras and scientific instruments, was designed for a long-term exploration of Mars' surface. Its key mission is to determine whether the planet has ever supported life.

2010

2013
Meteor strike
A 20-m (66-ft) wide meteor, travelling at 20 km (12 miles) per second, burst apart above the Russian city of Chelyabinsk. The shockwaves shattered windows and blew people off their feet. Many were injured by debris.

1997–
MALALA YOUSAFZAI

In 2012, Malala Yousafzai was just 15 when she was almost killed in an assassination attempt because of her campaigning for the right of girls in Pakistan to be educated. After recovery in Britain, Malala became a world-famous ambassador for youth, and the youngest-ever Nobel Peace Prize winner.

> **"Let us pick up our books and our pens. They are our most powerful weapons."**

United Nations speech, 12 July 2013

Champion for education
Malala speaks to and for women around the world, campaigning for their right to an education. Here, she is speaking to girls in a refugee centre based in Kenya, in 2016.

In 2010, the first-ever image – of a dog – was posted on the photo-sharing app Instagram. The social networking site now has 500 million users.

2014   ISLAMIC STATE (IS)

Decades of regional unrest led to the emergence of a new rebel force in Iraq in 2014, with the rise of a militant Islamist group calling itself the Islamic State (IS). War raged as IS fighting forces expanded into Syria, taking key cities. By 2018, IS held just a tiny proportion of its former territory.

Fight-back
By 2014, IS had occupied Mosul (above) in Iraq and Raqqa in Syria, established them as strongholds, and declared a state based around them. The Iraqis and Syrian Kurds struck back, with US military assistance. By 2017, they had retaken both cities, but fierce resistance by IS left them largely in ruins, and millions of their former inhabitants had become refugees.

Palmyra in ruins
From 2015 to 2017, IS occupied Palmyra in Syria, one of the world's best-preserved archaeological sites. Its fighters destroyed much of the ancient city, as part of their campaign to eradicate buildings sacred to previous eras and other faiths, including many revered by other sects of Islam.

2015

Paris attacks
On a single evening in November, in Paris, France, a series of shootings and suicide bombings at sports and concert venues and restaurants killed 130 people and injured more than 350 others. IS claimed responsibility for the attacks.

2018 ▶▶

2016

Trump triumphs in US
Many forecasters were surprised in November when Republican businessman Donald Trump defeated Democrat politician Hillary Clinton to become the 45th President of the United States.

2016

Brexit
In a referendum called by British Prime Minister David Cameron, the UK voted to leave the European Union after 43 years, starting a series of events and negotiations, known as "Brexit" (a combination of "British" and "exit").

2018

Korean leaders meet
During peace talks, North and South Korean leaders crossed the border between their countries for the first time since the end of the Korean War in 1953 and shook hands.

2017

Women's March
Around 200,000 people marched in a demonstration for equality in Washington, D.C., the day after Trump's inauguration. Millions of people around the country and the world participated in local marches.

Star Wars
In 2015, after more than 30 years, the film *The Force Awakens* finally picked up the Star Wars story where the original trilogy left off in 1983 with *Return of the Jedi*. New characters included the rolling robot BB-8.

President of the United States of America Donald Trump

The history of Britain and Ireland

The British Isles were once attached to the continent of Europe. Around 6500 BCE, the ice sheets melted, sea levels rose, and the land bridge between England and France flooded, creating the English Channel. A succession of peoples arrived by boat from Europe to settle, including the Celts, who came to dominate the British Isles until the Romans moved in. After the fall of the Roman Empire, Germanic tribes invaded and occupied much of what would become England, while the future countries of Wales, Scotland, and Ireland continued largely separately.

The history of England

In the 5th century CE, Germanic tribes gave England its name and the English language. These "Anglo-Saxons" settled and set up rival kingdoms. The land was to be invaded again, first by Vikings from Scandinavia and then by Normans under William the Conquerer, who founded the first of one of many royal families, or dynasties, who have ruled the country. Through war and exploration, England took over other lands, including nearby neighbours and faraway colonies. By the mid-19th century, England was an industrial nation at the centre of a vast empire.

4000 BCE British people first adopt farming; they build huge stone monuments, called megaliths.

3000–2500 BCE Farming people build Stonehenge, a great ceremonial centre used for midwinter rituals.

2500 BCE Arrival of the Beaker people from Europe, who introduce copper knives and a new way of burying the dead under individual mounds, with grave goods.

2200 BCE Bronze-making spreads to Britain, beginning a new period, the Bronze Age.

c 600 BCE People speaking Celtic languages and making iron tools and weapons begin to settle Britain.

55–54 BCE Julius Caesar leads two Roman expeditions to Britain.

43 CE The Roman army begins the conquest of Britain; the Romans build a network of roads and dozens of towns, including London and York.

425–500 Following the collapse of Roman rule, Angles, Saxons, and Jutes, from northern Germany and Denmark, conquer large areas of Britain.

597 St Augustine brings Christianity to Kent.

784–96 King Offa of Mercia builds a defensive dyke between England and Wales.

c 790 Scandinavian Vikings attack Portland (in Dorset) and in 793 Lindisfarne (north-east England) in the first of many Viking raids on England.

865–76 A Viking army, from Denmark, invades and conquers the kingdoms of East Anglia and Northumbria and half of Mercia.

871–99 Reign of King Alfred the Great of Wessex; he defeats the Vikings at Edington; following a peace treaty, the Vikings keep their conquests in the east and north, a region that came to be called the Danelaw.

927 Athelstan becomes the first king of all England.

1014–1015 King Sweyn Forkbeard of Denmark conquers England.

1016–35 Sweyn's son, King Canute, rules England as part of a great North Sea empire, including Norway and Denmark.

1042 King Edward the Confessor, who has grown up in exile, in Normandy, restores English rule.

1066 The Normans, under William the Conqueror, invade England, defeating the last Anglo-Saxon king, Harold, at the Battle of Hastings.

1086 William completes the Domesday Book survey of England.

1189–99 Rule of King Richard I, who spends much of his reign on a crusade to the Holy Land.

1215 Following a successful rebellion, the barons force Richard's unpopular brother, King John, to sign the Magna Carta, an agreement to protect the legal rights of English people.

1265 Simon de Montfort, leader of the barons, summons the first English Parliament.

1272–1307 Rule of Edward I, who conquers Wales and defeats the Scots, becoming overlord of Scotland.

1337–1453 Hundred Years War between England and France.

1348–49 A plague called the Black Death kills more than a third of the population.

1381 An unpopular poll tax results in a Peasants' Revolt, which begins in East Anglia and Kent.

1453–85 Wars of the Roses between two branches of the Plantagenet dynasty, the Houses of York and Lancaster.

1485 The Yorkist, Richard III, is killed in battle by the Lancastrian Henry Tudor, who founds the new Tudor dynasty.

1534 The second Tudor king, Henry VIII, breaks with the Catholic Church and becomes head of the Church of England.

1536–9 Henry VIII has the monasteries closed down, seizing their lands and wealth.

1547–53 Under Edward VI, England becomes a Protestant nation.

1553–8 Edward's sister, Queen Mary, attempts to restore Catholicism, burning around 300 Protestants at the stake.

1558–1603 Reign of Queen Elizabeth I, who restores the Protestant religion.

1588 The English navy defeats the Spanish Armada, an invasion force sent by King Philip II of Spain.

1603 On Elizabeth's death, her cousin, King James VI of Scotland becomes ruler, as James I of England, the first of the Stuart dynasty.

1605 The Gunpowder Plot, a Catholic plan to blow up Parliament and kill the king, is foiled.

1642–51 Civil War between King Charles I and the forces of Parliament.

1649 The defeated Charles is beheaded; England becomes a republic, called the Commonwealth, with Oliver Cromwell ruling as "Lord Protector" from 1653.

Stonehenge is one of the most famous prehistoric monuments in the world

1660 The monarchy is restored under Charles's son, King Charles II.

1665–6 A Great Plague sweeps through London, killing 100,000 people.

1666 Great Fire of London destroys most of the medieval city.

1685 King James II, a Catholic, comes to the throne.

1688 James is overthrown by his Protestant son-in-law, William of Orange.

1689 Bill of Rights is passed, limiting the powers of the monarch, and calling for regular elections to Parliament.

1707 Act of Union is passed, uniting the kingdoms of England and Scotland, and abolishing the Scottish Parliament.

1712 Robert Newcomen builds the first practical steam engine, used to pump water out of mines.

1714 The first king of the Hanoverian dynasty, George I, a German, comes to the throne.

1715 The first Jacobite rebellion, aimed at restoring James Stuart, son of James II, to the throne, is easily defeated.

1721 Robert Walpole becomes the first British Prime Minister.

1745 Bonnie Prince Charlie, son of James Stuart, leads a second unsuccessful Jacobite rebellion.

1763 Following victory over France in the Seven Years' War, Britain gains control of French colonies in North America.

1775–83 War between British forces and American colonists; the British are defeated and recognize American independence.

1801 Richard Trevithick, a Cornish inventor, demonstrates the first steam locomotive.

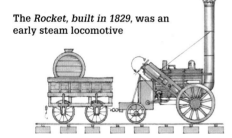

The *Rocket, built in 1829,* was an early steam locomotive

1803–15 The Napoleonic Wars are waged between Britain and her allies and Napoleon Bonaparte of France, who is finally defeated in 1815 at Waterloo.

1821 English scientist Michael Faraday builds the first electric motor.

1825 The first passenger railway opens between Stockton and Darlington.

1829 Robert Peel founds the Metropolitan Police Force in London.

1832 Great Reform Bill extends the vote to half a million more people.

1835 Henry Fox Talbot takes the first photographs, around the same time as Louis Daguerre in France.

ROYAL DYNASTIES

1066–1154	Norman
1154–1399	Plantagenet
1399–1461	Lancaster
1461–1485	York
1485–1603	Tudor
1603–1714	Stuart
1714–1901	Hanover
1901–1917	Saxe-Coberg Gotha
1917–	Windsor

1837–1901 During the reign of Queen Victoria, the population of Britain rises from 16 to 37 million people.

1840 The Penny Post begins, with the first postage stamp, the "Penny Black".

1844 Factory Act limits the working day for children under 13 to six and a half hours.

1854–6 The Crimean War fought by Britain and France against Russia.

1870 Education Act sets up boards to provide elementary schooling for children aged five to ten.

1911 The Parliament Act curbs the power of the House of Lords, making the Commons the sovereign power.

1914–18 World War I, between Britain and her allies and Germany and Austria-Hungary.

1928 The vote is extended to women aged 21 and over.

1936 Following his plan to marry a divorced woman, King Edward VIII is forced to give up the throne.

1939–45 World War II between Britain and her allies and the Axis Powers of Germany, Italy, and Japan.

1948 National Health Service establishes free medical treatment for all in Britain; the *Empire Windrush*, sailing from Jamaica, brings the first West Indian immigrants to the United Kingdom.

1965 The Murder Act suspends capital punishment; it is formally abolished in 1969.

1972 After the Ugandan dictator expels his country's Asian community, around 30,000 Asians settle in the United Kingdom.

1973 Britain joins the European Economic Community.

1979 Margaret Thatcher becomes the first woman Prime Minister.

2003 Britain joins the US-led coalition in the invasion of Iraq.

2012 London hosts the Olympic Games.

2016 United Kingdom votes to leave the European Union.

BRITISH PRIME MINISTERS

1721–42	Sir Robert Walpole
1742–43	Spencer Compton, Earl of Wilmington
1743–54	Henry Pelham
1754–56	Duke of Newcastle
1756–57	Duke of Devonshire
1757–62	Duke of Newcastle
1762–63	Earl of Bute
1763–65	George Grenville
1765–66	Marquis of Rockingham
1766–68	William Pitt the Elder
1768–70	Duke of Grafton
1770–82	Lord North
1782–83	Earl of Shelburne
1783	Duke of Portland
1783–1801	William Pitt the Younger
1801–04	Henry Addington
1804–06	William Pitt the Younger
1806–07	Lord Grenville
1807–09	Duke of Portland
1809–12	Spencer Perceval
1812–27	Earl of Liverpool
1827	George Canning
1827–28	Viscount Goderich
1828–30	Duke of Wellington
1830–34	Earl Grey
1834	Viscount Melbourne
1834–35	Sir Robert Peel
1835–41	Viscount Melbourne
1841–46	Sir Robert Peel
1846–52	Lord John Russell
1852	Earl of Derby
1852–55	Earl of Aberdeen
1855–58	Viscount Palmerston
1858–59	Earl of Derby
1859–65	Viscount Palmerston
1865–66	Earl Russell
1866–68	Earl of Derby
1868	Benjamin Disraeli
1868–74	William Gladstone
1874–80	Benjamin Disraeli
1880–85	William Gladstone
1885–86	Marquess of Salisbury
1886	William Gladstone
1886–92	Marquess of Salisbury
1892–94	William Gladstone
1894–95	Earl of Rosebery
1895–1902	Marquess of Salisbury
1902–05	Arthur James Balfour
1905–08	Sir H. Campbell-Bannerman
1908–16	Herbert Henry Asquith
1916–22	David Lloyd-George
1922–23	Andrew Bonar Law
1923–24	Stanley Baldwin
1924	James Ramsay Macdonald
1924–29	Stanley Baldwin
1929–35	James Ramsay Macdonald
1935–37	Stanley Baldwin
1937–40	Neville Chamberlain
1940–45	Winston Churchill
1945–51	Clement Attlee
1951–55	Winston Churchill
1955–57	Anthony Eden
1957–63	Harold Macmillan
1963–64	Sir Alec Douglas-Home
1964–70	Harold Wilson
1970–74	Edward Heath
1974–76	Harold Wilson
1976–79	James Callaghan
1979–90	Margaret Thatcher
1990–97	John Major
1997–2007	Tony Blair
2007–2010	Gordon Brown
2010–2016	David Cameron
2016–	Theresa May

The history of Scotland

The Romans reached as far as central Scotland, but after frequent battles with local tribes, they were forced to retreat south. By the 9th century, Scotland was home to four different peoples: the Picts of the northeast, the Angles of the southeast, the Britons of the southwest, and the Scots of the west. All were attacked by Vikings from Scandinavia, but the Scots emerged as the dominant power, and by 1019 Scottish kings ruled the whole country. Centuries of conflict followed with Scotland's powerful southern neighbour, England. Although both countries were united under a single ruler in 1603, Anglo-Scottish rivalry would continue for centuries.

3500–2500 BCE Farming people in Orkney build villages of stone houses, large stone tombs, and ritual circles of standing stones.

700 BCE Start of the Iron Age; Celtic people build hillforts, and houses on artificial islands, called crannogs, on Scottish lochs and rivers.

100 BCE–100 CE Iron Age people build stone tower houses called brochs.

73 CE The Romans invade Scotland, winning a great victory over the Caledonians (Scottish tribes) at the battle of Mons Graupius (83 CE); unable to control the territory, the Romans soon retreat south.

122 Roman Emperor Hadrian builds a wall across Britain to separate the Roman province from the unconquered northern tribes.

A statue of Robert the Bruce commmemorates the Scottish victory at Bannockburn

c 400 St Ninian, a British missionary, founds the first Christian church in Scotland, Whithorn, and preaches the faith to the Picts.

c 500 Gaelic-speaking invaders, called Scotti (Scots), cross from Ulster in Ireland to settle in the west of Scotland, establishing the kingdom of Dalriada.

849 Kenneth MacAlpin, king of Dalriada, becomes king of the Picts, whose own kingdom had been devastated by Vikings.

c 870 Vikings from Norway conquer Shetland, Orkney, and the Hebrides.

1018–34 Reign of King Malcolm II, who conquers the southern kingdom of Strathclyde and extends Scottish rule over the Angles of Northumbria.

1072 William the Conqueror invades Scotland, forcing King Malcolm III to recognize him as his overlord.

1138 King David I invades England but is defeated at the Battle of the Standard.

1174 King William the Lion invades England; he is captured by the English; to win his freedom, he is forced to swear loyalty to Henry II of England and pay a huge ransom.

1263 King Alexander III defeats a Viking invasion at the Battle of Largs. As a result, the Hebrides come under Scottish rule.

1296 After the Scots make an alliance with England's enemy, France, King Edward I of England invades Scotland, and deposes Scottish king John Balliol; Edward claims to be king of Scotland.

1297 Scots rise against English rule and, under William Wallace, defeat Edward at Stirling Bridge.

1305 Wallace is captured and executed by Edward.

1306 Robert the Bruce is crowned Robert I at Scone in defiance of Edward.

1314 Robert I wins a great victory against Edward II's English forces at Bannockburn.

1320 In the Declaration of Arbroath, the nobles and churchmen of Scotland swear to support Robert and insist that he is their king.

1328 Treaty of Edinburgh-Northhampton in which the English formally recognize Robert the Bruce as King of Scotland.

1472 King James III makes an alliance with King Christian I of Denmark and Norway, who surrenders Orkney and Shetland to him.

1503 King James IV marries Margaret, daughter of Henry VII of England; as a result, their great grandson, James VI, will inherit the English throne.

1507 Andrew Myllar sets up Scotland's first printing press.

1511 Launch of the *Great Michael* in Edinburgh, then the largest ship in the world.

1513 Disastrous defeat of the Scots by the English at the Battle of Flodden; James IV and most of his nobles are killed on the field.

1542 War between James V of Scotland and his uncle, Henry VIII of England; the Scots are again defeated by the English, at the Battle of Solway Moss.

1560 Reformation Parliament establishes Protestantism, championed by John Knox, as Scotland's national religion.

1567 The Catholic Mary Queen of Scots is forced to abdicate in favour of her one-year-old son, James VI; she flees to England, where she is imprisoned and, in 1587, beheaded.

1603 On the death of Queen Elizabeth I, King James VI of Scotland inherits the English throne, ruling as James I of England.

1637 James's son, Charles I, tries to force the Scots to use a new Prayer Book, leading to a riot in Edinburgh.

1638 The National Covenant, in which male Scots (Covenanters) pledge to defend their Protestant religion against Charles.

1639–40 Charles invades Scotland, but is defeated.

1642–9 Civil War in England; the conflict spreads to Scotland, where there is fighting between Covenanters and Royalists.

1649 Following the execution of Charles I, a Commonwealth is established in England, under Oliver Cromwell; in Scotland, the executed king's son is proclaimed King Charles II.

1650 A Scottish Army, fighting for Charles II, is decisively defeated by Oliver Cromwell at the Battle of Dunbar.

1660 Charles II returns from exile to rule Scotland, England, and Ireland.

1689 The Dutch Protestant William of Orange overthrows his Catholic father-in-law, James II, as king of England and Scotland.

1692 Massacre of Glencoe: thirty-eight members of the Macdonald clan, slow to take the oath of allegiance to William, are killed by government troops.

1698–1700 Many Scottish nobles are bankrupted after investing in a disastrous attempt to found a Scottish trading colony at Darien in Panama.

1707 Following the Act of Union, the Scottish Parliament votes to dissolve itself; Scottish MPs get seats in the English Parliament.

1762–1800 Highland Clearances: thousands of Scottish tenant farmers are driven off their lands, when sheep farming is introduced by landlords.

1776 Scottish inventor James Watt produces the first commercial steam engine.

1802 The world's first steam-driven ship, the *Charlotte Dundas*, is built in Scotland.

1843 A split in the Church of Scotland leads to a group breaking away to form the new Free Church of Scotland.

1934 Foundation of Scottish National Party (SNP) campaigning for Scottish independence.

1945 SNP sends its first MP to Houses of Parliament in Westminster.

1970s Following the discovery of a rich source of oil in the North Sea, the SNP campaigns using the slogan, "It's Scotland's Oil".

1999 A new Scottish Parliament is established in Edinburgh.

2007 The SNP becomes the largest party in the Scottish Parliament.

2011 The SNP increases its number of seats in parliament from 47 to 69.

2014 Referendum on national independence results in a vote to remain part of the UK.

The history of Ireland

Ireland was untouched by Roman invasion, and in its early history it was divided into five provinces: Leinster, Ulster, Munster, Connacht, and Meath. In the 12th century, the Normans from England invaded, and King Henry II declared himself Lord of Ireland. This was the beginning of a bitter Anglo-Irish struggle that was to last 750 years. Although the Republic of Ireland gained independence in the 20th century, the country was divided, with six northern counties remaining under British control.

3200 BCE At Newgrange, farming people build a stone passage grave, 76 m (249 ft) across and 12 m (39 ft) high.

c 500 BCE During the Iron Age, the Irish adopt Celtic languages and styles of art.

432–61 CE St Patrick, a British missionary, brings Christianity to Ireland.

550–800 Golden Age of Irish monasticism, when Irish monks create beautiful books and works of art.

795 Vikings begin to raid Ireland.

841–50 Vikings found a series of towns including Dublin, Cork, and Waterford.

1002 Brian Boru of Munster makes himself "ard ri" (high king) of all Ireland.

1014 Brian Boru defeats the Vikings of Dublin at Clontarf, but is killed.

1167 Anglo-Normans from England invade Ireland, followed, in 1171, by King Henry II who declares himself Lord of Ireland.

1297 First Irish Parliament meets in Dublin.

1366 Statute of Kilkenny prevents Anglo-Norman settlers in Ireland using Irish language, customs, or laws.

1541 Henry VIII declares himself king of Ireland.

1594–1603 Rebellion of Hugh O'Neill, Ulster earl of Tyrone, and other Ulster chieftains against English rule.

1606 Many Protestant Scots settle in Ulster, in lands confiscated from the defeated chieftains.

1649–50 Oliver Cromwell's campaigns in Ireland confiscate land from Irish Catholics.

1689–91 Campaign in Ireland between forces of exiled James II and William III of England; James is defeated at the Battle of the Boyne (1690).

1691 Catholics are excluded from the Irish Parliament.

1798 Rising of United Irishmen against Britain fails, and some leaders are executed.

1800 Act of Union between Britain and Ireland; the Irish Parliament is abolished.

1828 Daniel O'Connell, leader of Irish Catholics, is elected as an MP, despite a ban on Catholics standing for Parliament.

1829 Roman Catholic Relief Act allows Catholics to stand for Parliament.

1845–47 Potato blight leads to terrible famine; more than one million die.

1870 Irish Home Rule movement launched.

1914 Home Rule bill passed, but is suspended due to outbreak of World War I.

1916 Easter Rising in Dublin against British government.

1918 Great majority of Irish seats won by republican candidates in post-war general election; members found their own Parliament in Dublin.

1919–21 War between Irish republicans and Britain.

1921 Anglo-Irish Treaty establishes the Irish Free State in 1922, with six northern counties remaining in the UK.

1922–3 Civil war in the Free State between pro- and anti-treaty forces.

1949 Republic of Ireland is formally declared and it leaves the British Commonwealth.

1968 Violence erupts between Catholics and Protestants in Northern Ireland.

1969 British troops sent to restore order in Northern Ireland.

1971–94 Campaign against the British Army in Northern Ireland by the Provisional IRA.

1972 Northern Ireland Parliament suspended and direct rule by Britain introduced.

1973 Republic of Ireland joins the European Economic Community.

1985 Anglo-Irish Agreement gives the Republic of Ireland a consultative role in the government of Northern Ireland.

1994 The IRA declares a cease-fire.

2002 Republic of Ireland adopts the Euro.

2007 Direct rule in Northern Ireland ends, and power returns to the Northern Ireland Assembly. However the Assembly was suspended in January 2017.

The history of Wales

When the Romans left Britain and the Anglo-Saxons took over, Celts from the south fled to Wales to join their kin. The land was split into princedoms until the late 9th century, when Rhodri Mawr united much of Wales. The Welsh lost their independence in 1282 after King Edward I of England conquered the country. Wales has remained united with England, but the 20th century saw a revival of Welsh language and culture, and the establishment of a Welsh Assembly.

Harlech Castle was built by Edward I

844–78 Reign of Rhodri the Great, ruler of Gwynedd, who wins three great victories against invading Vikings.

916–49 Hywel Dda (the Good), king of Deheubarth, produces a code of Welsh Laws.

1068 Normans begin to invade South Wales, building castles.

1195–1240 Llywelyn Fawr (the Great) rules over most of Wales for 40 years.

1218 King Henry III of England confirms Llywelyn as Prince of all Wales.

1277–83 King Edward I of England conquers Wales, giving the title of Prince of Wales to his son, a custom continued by later English monarchs.

1401–15 Owain Glyndwr campaigns for Welsh independence, making an alliance with France.

1404 Glyndwr sets up Welsh Parliament at Machynlleth.

1535, 1542 Two Parliamentary Acts abolish the Welsh legal system, and prevent Welsh speakers from holding public office.

1588 Translation of the Bible into Welsh helps to save the Welsh language.

1639 First Welsh chapel founded after breakaway from the Church of England.

1893 University of Wales founded at Aberystwyth.

1966 First Plaid Cymru (Welsh National Party) candidate wins a seat at Westminster.

1999 Welsh Assembly set up in Cardiff.

Glossary

abolition
The act of doing away with something completely.

abdication
To formally hand over power or responsibility to another.

ally
A person or country who unites with another person or country against a common enemy.

apartheid
In South Africa, a government policy of racial *segregation*.

apprentice
A person who works for an agreed period of time, in exchange for being taught a trade or craft.

armistice
An agreement between warring parties to end a conflict.

assassination
The murder of a key figure by surprise attack, carried out for political or religious reasons.

barbarian
The name given by the Romans to tribes outside the Roman Empire.

blockade
The isolation of an area so as to prevent supplies from entering or leaving.

Byzantine Empire
The mainly Greek-speaking Christian continuation of the eastern Roman Empire, which lasted for 1,000 years.

caliph
The title of the religious and political leader of Islam (the Islamic world).

Calvinism
A strict form of Protestantism named after 16th-century religious reformer John Calvin.

capitalism
An economic system based on the private ownership of property and free competitive conditions for business.

city-state
A self-governing, independent state consisting of a city and its surrounding area.

civil war
A war between opposing groups of people in the same country.

classical
Relating to the ancient Greek or ancient Roman world.

Cold War
The period of hostility between the West and the *communist* countries dominated by the *USSR*. It lasted from shortly after World War II until 1989.

colonization
The act of sending settlers to establish a *colony* in another country, sometimes involving taking political control over the people already living there.

colony
An area under the political control of another state; or the group of people who have settled there.

communism
The political belief in a society in which ownership of property and wealth is shared.

conquistador
One of the Spanish conquerors of American Indian civilizations.

Counter-Reformation
The period of change in the Catholic church after the Protestant *Reformation*, which included internal reform and opposition to *Protestantism*.

coup
The sudden violent or illegal seizure of power by a small group.

Cro-Magnon man
The first modern humans to settle in Europe, around 40,000 years ago.

crusader
A Christian knight who went on one of the Crusades – military expeditions of the 11th, 12th, and 13th centuries to seize back Jerusalem from the Muslims.

daimyo
A Japanese lord.

democracy
A form of government based on rule by the people, usually through elected representatives.

depression
In history, a period of drastic decline in economic activity, marked by widespread unemployment and hardship.

dictator
A leader who rules a country alone with no restrictions on the extent of their power.

domestication
The taming of wild animals to make them useful to humans.

dynasty
A royal family ruling a country for successive generations.

emir
A Muslim prince or military commander. The territory he rules over is known as an emirate.

empire
A group of lands or peoples brought under the rule of one government or person (emperor).

Enlightenment, the
The period of European history, in the 1700s, when radical thinkers tried to reach a new understanding of society, government, and humanity, and then to reform them.

exile
Forced absence from a person's home or country.

fascism
An ideology stressing *dictatorship* and *nationalism*, and which places the strength of the state above individual citizens' welfare.

feudalism
A political system in Europe from the 700s onwards, under which lords granted land to other nobles in return for loyalty, military assistance, and services.

genocide
The systematic murder of an entire people.

glasnost
The Russian word for "openness". Used by Mikhail Gorbachev of his policies in the *USSR* in the late 1980s.

guerrilla warfare
A type of warfare in which small groups of fighters make surprise attacks.

guild
Organization in 11th–14th-century Europe formed by skilled workers or merchants of the same craft or trade to protect its members and control business.

heresy
Beliefs, held by a member of a religious group, that are considered to be in conflict with that group's established beliefs.

Holy Roman Empire
An *empire* set up in Western Europe in 800 CE, centred on modern-day Germany. The emperor received his title from the pope and was the senior monarch in the Catholic world.

hominin
A member of the biological group that includes humans and their extinct ancestors and relatives.

jihad
Arabic word meaning "holy war".

Khmer Rouge
The *communist* organization that carried out *guerrilla warfare* in Cambodia in the 1960s and 70s, seizing power in 1975.

Lutheran
Someone who follows the ideas of German theologian Martin Luther, a key figure of the *Reformation*.

Mesoamerica
"Middle America", the name for the region stretching from central Mexico in the north, to Guatemala in the south.

Mesopotamia
The region of modern-day Iraq lying between the Tigris and Euphrates rivers, where many of the earliest civilizations began.

missionary
A religious person who seeks to persuade others, often living in foreign lands, to adopt his or her religion.

Mughal
A member of the Muslim *dynasty* that ruled much of India between the 16th and 19th centuries.

Mujahideen
Muslim fighters who carry out *jihad*.

nationalism
The strong support for the interests of one's nation.

Neanderthal
An extinct species of early human closely related to our own species.

Neolithic
The later Stone Age, during which improved stone tools and weapons were made and the first farming began.

nomad
A person who moves from one place to another to find fresh pastures and water for livestock.

Ottoman Empire
Founded by Turkish tribes in about 1300, the *empire* that dominated eastern Europe and the Middle East for nearly 500 years.

paganism
A term used for the religious beliefs of the ancient Greeks and Romans and other early European peoples before the coming of Christianity.

pandemic
A sudden and widespread outbreak of disease.

peasant
A worker on the land, usually an agricultural labourer.

perestroika
Russian word meaning "reconstruction". Used to refer to radical political and economic change, especially in *communist* countries.

persecute
To oppress or harass a person or group because of their origins or beliefs.

pilgrim
A religious follower who makes a journey to a holy place.

protectorate
A superior power with protection and part-control over a dependent nation or region.

Protestantism
A form of Christianity, resulting from the *Reformation*, in which allegiance is no longer offered to the pope.

Reformation, the
The reform movement of the 16th century, in which many churches broke from the Catholic Church headed by the pope in Rome.

regent
A person acting as head of state on behalf of the ruler, usually because that ruler is too young or unfit to rule, or absent.

Renaissance
A period of European history, beginning in the 14th century, when far-reaching changes occurred in the arts and intellectual life.

republic
A country without a hereditary king, prince, or emperor. Modern republics are usually led by presidents.

revolt
An organized uprising intended to overthrow an authority.

revolution
Sudden and fundamental change in society brought about by an organized group of protestors.

Safavid Empire
Islamic *empire*, based in modern-day Iran, that controlled much of the Middle East from the 16th to the 18th centuries.

samurai
A Japanese warrior knight.

script
The written characters that make up a writing system, such as an alphabet.

segregation
Separation, particularly of one race from another within a racist social system.

shogun
One of the military leaders who ruled Japan in the name of the emperor from the 1100s to the 1800s.

siege
To surround and *blockade* a city or fortress with the intention of capturing it.

slave
A person who is held as the property of another.

sovereign
A ruler or head of state exerting supreme power.

Soviet Union
Another name for the *USSR*.

stockade
A line of stout posts or logs set in the ground to form a defence.

stock exchange
An organization that allows trading in shares of companies and other financial assets.

suffragette
In the early 20th century, a woman who fought for the right to vote, known as suffrage.

superpower
A powerful and influential country considered stronger than its allies.

treaty
An official, written agreement between warring parties to bring hostilities to an end.

tribute
Money or goods paid by one king to another, or by one state to another, as recognition of the other's superior status.

tsar
The title of the male rulers of Russia from the 15th century until 1917; a female ruler or the wife of a tsar was titled tsarina.

USSR
The "Union of Soviet Socialist Republics", the *communist* state that existed from 1922–1991 in the former Russian Empire, with its capital in Moscow.

Zionism
The movement to create and maintain a homeland for the Jewish people in Israel.

Zoroastrianism
A religion of ancient Iran. It was founded by the prophet Zoroaster, who taught belief in one god, Ahura Mazda.

▶▶Index

Credits

Dorling Kindersley would like to thank: John Searcy for Americanization; Jackie Brind and Elizabeth Wise for the index; Hazel Beynon for proofreading; Ann Baggaley, Frances Jones, Andrea Mills, and John Woodward for additional writing; Helen Abramson, Carron Brown, Matilda Gollon, Victoria Pyke, Jenny Sich, and Samira Sood for editorial assistance; Paul Drislane and Mik Gates for design assistance; Merrit Cartographic for maps; Peter Bull and Caroline Church for illustrations. Nityanand Kumar for DTP assistance.

The publisher would like to thank the following for their kind permission to reproduce their photographs:

(Key: a-above; b-below/bottom; c-centre; f-far; l-left; r-right; t-top)